Boxing Babylon

BOXING
BABYLON

by Nigel Collins

A Citadel Press Book
Published by Carol Publishing Group

A Citadel Press Book
Published by Carol Publishing Group

Editorial Offices
600 Madison Avenue
New York, NY 10022

Sales & Distribution Offices
120 Enterprise Avenue
Secaucus, NJ 07094

In Canada: Musson Book Company
A division of General Publishing Co. Limited
Don Mills, Ontario

Manufactured in the United States of America
ISBN 8065-0196-0

10   9   8   7   6   5   4   3   2   1

Library of Congress Cataloging-in-Publication Data

Collins, Niegel.
    Boxing Babylon / by Nigel Collins.
        pm   cm.
        "A Citadel Press book."
        ISBN 0-8065-1183-4 : $18.95
        1. Boxers—Biography.   2. Boxing—Corrupt practices.   Title.
    GV1131.C64   1990
    796.8'8'0922—dc20   90-45320
    [B]   CIP

Carol Publishing Group books are available at special
discounts for bulk purchases, for sales promotions, fund
raising, or educational use. Special editions can also be
created to specifications. For details contact: Special
Sales Department, Carol Publishing Group, 120
Enterprise Avenue, Secaucus, NJ 07094.

"Goodbye, Gypsy Joe" orginally appeared in Boxing
News, March 23, 1990, and is reprinted by permission
from H & D Publications, Ltd., London, England.

To Edgar and Ray Collins, who got me started—
and Shani Collins, who keeps me going.

Contents

Acknowledgments

While God, everyone has been told, helps those who help themselves, this book could not have been written without the earthly assistance of numerous people and publications. I would be greatly amiss if I didn't attempt to acknowledge and thank each and every one of them. If there are any omissions, my apologies; they are quite unintentional.

First, I have to thank my father and grandfather, to whom this book is dedicated, for instilling in me my love of boxing. One of my earliest memories is of Grampy Collins sitting me on his knee and spinning tales of such legendary fighters as "Ruby" Bob Fitzsimmons, "Gentleman" Jim Corbett, and Peter Jackson. In later years, my father and I not only attended numerous fight cards together, we spent more time talking about boxing than any other single subject. It is a bond which has helped us endure even the most trying of times.

Next, I must express my undying gratitude to Jeff Jowett for his astute suggestions and masterful job of proof reading. His ill-paid labor made my editor's task at least semi-bearable.

A special thanks must also go to J. Russell Peltz who helped with the research and allowed me unlimited access to his excellent boxing library. His encouragement and enthusiasm for this project will always be fondly remembered.

Many others provided a wealth of information and countless insights. They are, in no particular order: Jack McKinney, Hal

Conrad, Milt Bailey, Jack "KO-JO" Obermayer, Teddy King, Johnny Tocco, Lou Duva, Tim Leone, Willie O'Neill, Joseph D'O'Brian, Maureen Sacks, Al Braveman, Harry Legge, Harry Mullan, Dale Ogden, Frank Gelb, Brad Jacobs, Bruce Kielty, Stanley Simco, Tex Hennessey, Ben Cognetta, Steve Sneddon, Joe Hand Sr., Lew Eskin, Mike Everett, Lt. Alan August, James Stabile, Jack Rose, Phil Woolever, Carlos Irusta, Betsy Tunis, Steve Farhood, Jessie Reid, and all the kind people at the microfilm and inter-library loan departments of the Philadelphia Free Library.

Two books of indispensable help were *Beyond The Ring* by Jeffrey T. Sammons and *The Manly Art* by Elliot J. Gorn. These scholarly works are highly recommended to all who seek a deeper understanding of boxing's unique place in Western culture. I also leaned heavily on Jack Birtley's revealing biographies, *Freddie Mills* and *The Tragedy of Randolph Turpin*.

Other books which provided significant information were: *The Ring Record Book and Boxing Encyclopedia* (various editors), *Black Dynamite, Gentleman Jim*, and *Fifty Years at Ringside* (all three) by Nat Fleischer, *Give Him to the Angels*, by James R. Fair, *Papa Jack* by Randy Roberts, *King of the Canebreaks* by Jimmy Jones, *Penny a Punch* by Harry Legge, *Brown Bomber* by Barney Nagler, and *I Only Talk Winning* by Angelo Dundee.

The Ring magazine was a constant source of information, as were the following newspapers: *The New York Times*, the *Los Angeles Times*, the *Philadelphia Inquirer*, the *Philadelphia Daily News*, *Reno Gazette-Journal*, *Boxing News* and *The Springfield Leader*.

Photo credits go to G.C. London Publishing Associates Inc., Peltz Boxing Promotions, Tom Casino, Able Abel, The Big Fights Inc., and Harry Mullan of *Boxing News*.

Finally, many thanks to my editor Allan J. Wilson for helping transform a concept into a reality.

Nigel Collins
Maple Shade, NJ
March 1990

Boxing Babylon

Introduction

Intrinsically violent and populated with some of the most outrageous characters to ever walk this planet, boxing has held the public's attention throughout its long and often tumultuous history. While the drama of combat lies at the very foundation of boxing's appeal, it is the men who climb between the ropes who have captivated the imagination of the masses. Their deeds both in and outside the ring have inspired adulation and scorn in almost equal measure. Boxing and boxers have always provided us a mirror in which we can glimpse, not only the reflection of mankind's courage and nobility, but the darker side of the human soul.

From the early bareknuckle days in 18th century England, many of boxing's greatest heroes have risen from humble beginnings to achieve fame and fortune through the power of their fists. More often than not, they squandered their hard-earned rewards on lavish living and eventually sank back into the squalor which spawned them. There have always been exceptions, of course, but the stereotype has ample basis in fact. Boxing history is rife with men who followed this pattern. They seem irrevocably lured to their doom by an unquenchable thirst for hedonistic pleasures, unable, or unwilling, to escape the cycle of debauchery.

One of the earliest victims of this self-destructive behavior was Henry "Hen" Pearce, the 21st heavyweight champion of the bareknuckle era. Known to his fans as the "Game Chicken," Pearce was, according to the jargon of the day, "a noble specimen of valour, hardihood and science." Unfortunately, Pearce also "poured down copious libation at the shrine of Bacchus," and following a meteoric, undefeated career, died a physical wreck in 1809 at age 32. The "Game Chicken" blazed a trail of indulgence now trodden bare by those who stumbled in his footsteps. Though his name does not appear in *The Ring Record Book*, John Barleycorn has KO'd more boxers than any punch. Among the more notable examples was John L. Sullivan. While the legendary John L. was undoubtedly the greatest sporting hero of the 19th century, he was also a hopeless lush. To this day, booze and drugs continue to decimate the ranks of boxing's finest practitioners. The recent decline of Aaron Pryor, ravaged by the horrors of cocaine addiction, is a perfect case in point.

Even boxers who successfully negotiate life's temptations are far from immune to calamity. They kill (and are killed) in relatively small numbers between the ropes, but murder (and are murdered) at a disproportionate rate outside the confines of the ring. It could be argued that this propensity towards violence can be directly traced to the social classes from which boxing recruits its participants. True, convicts, street fighters and other assorted riffraff have always swelled boxing's ranks and populated its rankings, but this is too simplistic a view. Something more than socio-economic factors seem to be at work. There is an aura of tragedy surrounding boxing, a recurring theme of pathos haunting its participants. Bizarre accidents, strange twists of fate, and outright bad luck have invariably shadowed the knights of the squared circle. Their love lives, often involving actresses or other public beauties, have been routinely reduced to tabloid fodder. Not even boxers who led spotless lives are exempt from catastrophe. Rocky Marciano, a relative paragon of virtue, died prematurely when his plane crashed into an Iowa cornfield.

Perhaps the star-crossed character of boxers' lives is just a matter of balance. Great triumphs usually incur great costs somewhere along the line. Nothing is free. But if you must ultimately pay the piper, you may as well enjoy the dance. Boxers, like practically no other breed of men, have practiced this credo to the max. Certainly, they have broken our hearts time and again, but they've also shared their lust for life in a way that can't help but bring a smile to even the sourest puss. After all, who can forget the story of the gloriously drunk Battling Nelson taking a bath in a concessionaire's vat of lemonade on the eve of the Jack Dempsey-Jess Willard bout; or the tale of Battling Siki, Africa's first world champion, strolling through the Montmartre district of Paris with a lion cub on a leash? In more recent times, the noble art was enriched by the dashing genius of Sugar Ray Robinson, a truly regal champion, resplendent with one of boxing's first major league entourages and a marvelously ostentatious pink Cadillac. Of course, no short list of boxing's extroverts would be complete without including the incomparable Muhammad Ali, who took his unique brand of magic beyond the ring to become perhaps the most famous sports personality of his time.

Prize fighters infuse their admirers with a passion that frequently follows a boxer to his grave . . . and beyond. Joe Louis, retired since 1951 and dead since 1981, is almost as beloved today as he was during his reign as heavyweight champion of the world. Sonny Liston, who died mysteriously in 1970 while still technically an active boxer, is still despised in some quarters. Louis, truly a wonderful fighter, is adored as much for who he was as for what he accomplished. Liston, a formidable fighter in his own right, is hated just as much for his disagreeable personality as for his dubious distinction as the only heavyweight champion to abdicate the throne while sitting in his corner. Though Louis and Liston are extreme examples of the phenomenon, the reputations of practically all prominent fighters were greatly influenced by factors outside of the ring. It is this, as much as anything, that makes boxing and boxers such fascinating studies in human nature.

Despite the fact boxing's roots can be traced back to 4000 B.C., to a time when the Egyptian Pharaohs attended fights in which contestants bound their fists in leather straps, scholars still debate the thorny question: What is boxing? To many it is simply a sport. To others it is more: a metaphor, a microcosm of life's triumphs and tragedies. Some even consider boxing a lost religion, the last refuge for the warrior in a society which no longer embraces the fighting man. Critics, who long have strived in vain to eradicate what admirers have lovingly dubbed the "Sweet Science," think of boxing as nothing more than a sinfully vicarious form of entertainment, a brutal spectacle sometimes leading to legalized murder. But both detractors and devotees are forced to agree on one point—boxing makes for great theater.

Is it any wonder boxers lead such remarkable—and often tragic—lives? Considering the nature of their calling, could it be otherwise? Whether driven by economical or emotional needs, boxers are, by temperament, risk takers. They literally place their lives in jeopardy every time they enter the ring. They do so willingly, sacrificing their bodies on the altar of their art. Though apologists for boxing attempt to dilute or camouflage this fundamental reality, it remains, steadfast, the underlying truth which separates boxing from all other so-called "sports." Every boxer, even those who choose to banish this disturbing knowledge to their subconscious, know, deep down, they are wagering the ultimate stake. Whether the inherent danger of their profession encourages boxers to abandon caution outside the ring, or whether those who turn to prize fighting are already predisposed toward recklessness, is an intriguing chicken/egg conundrum. Yet if life is not a problem to be solved but a reality to be experienced, it is also true few of us experience life—or death—as extravagantly as boxers.

1

A Bullet for Breakfast

It was strange going back to the Dickerson farm after all those years. To tell the truth, it would have been fine with him if he never had to see the damn place again. Of course, J.P. Dickerson didn't own it any more. The old son-of-a-bitch had sold it to the Summer family. It was the Summer farm now. Still, the bad memories hadn't gone away. The few days he'd spent there so many years ago had ruined his life, and he couldn't help cursing the irony that brought him back again. He'd needed a job when he got out of prison and was lucky to get one with the gas company reading meters. But wouldn't you just know it. The farm was on his route.

The place looked a little different, but he still recognized it. Christ, how could he ever forget it? The nightmare that began there twenty-four years ago had never ended. Sure he was finally free, but his youth was gone, his health shot. He'd be lucky if he lasted another five years. But at least he'd shown them. He'd shown them he didn't take any crap. Not even from that square-headed bastard, Stanley Ketchel.

As Walter A. Dipley stood there looking around at the old farm, he couldn't help thinking back to that October morning in 1910 when his life turned upside down in a fraction of a second. The memories were as indelible as the tattoo marks on his arms. He'd gotten them (a dragon and bracelet on one forearm, the words "Hong Kong, China" and some flowers on the other) when he was still in the Navy, still a man with a future. In fact, when he thought about it, that was when all his problems really began; back when he deserted from the Navy.

Dipley had enlisted February 26, 1907. It seemed like a good idea at the time, but soon turned sour. Oh sure, he'd seen a bit of the world, but after seventeen months he'd had a belly full. The officers were always on his back about something or other, always trying to push him around. He didn't take any of their crap either. Hadn't he beaten the tar out of that smart-assed lieutenant? Of course, he didn't stick around after that, waiting to be court-martialed. He'd jumped ship in Manila and never looked back. It was lucky he'd run into that Hurtz fellow and talked him into selling his identification papers. Dipley had made it all the way back to Missouri using Hurtz's name, and he kept right on using it until the day they arrested him.

Then there was Goldie. Damn, if he hadn't hooked up with her, they might never have caught up with him. He'd known her back home in Webb City before joining the Navy. She was a good kid. She'd had a tough time of it. Her parents had married her off to some old buzzard when she was just twelve years old. Then he'd up and left her, taken a powder. People looked down on her because she bounced from one man to another. But what the hell was she supposed to do? Starve to death? About the only thing she had going for her was her body. And that sure was sweet enough. Dipley knew what it was like to be on your own, making ends meet the best way you can. That's why he was sort of glad he'd run into her again. In a way, they had a lot in common. And besides, Goldie knew how to keep her mouth shut.

Dipley picked up a dollar where he could, working as a barber and miner. Out-of-the-way locations were preferable for obvious reasons, and just to be on the safe side, he moved around a lot. He was on his way to visit his sister in Chadwick when he ran into Goldie. They renewed acquaintances and he told her all about how he'd deserted from the Navy, how he was using Hurtz's identification. She was sympathetic and Dipley talked her into accompanying him to his sister's house. They decided to travel together, maybe find work on a ranch, maybe even get married; anything to stay one step ahead of their past.

On Wednesday, October 12, 1910, Dipley presented himself at the Springfield office of employment agent S.C. Speers and announced he was looking for work for himself and his wife. He wanted to know if there was anything available on a farm or ranch. Speers had been dubious at first. The man who called himself Hurtz was slightly built, about 140 pounds at best, and didn't look robust enough to handle the heavy chores involved in the sort of job he was looking for. But he insisted he could do the work and said his wife had worked on a ranch before. Speers knew R.P. Dickerson, who owned a ranch near Conway, was desperate for help, so he reluctantly agreed to give the couple a chance. They left for Dickerson's place that same afternoon.

Stanley Ketchel knew he needed a rest. If he kept going the way he had the past eight or nine years, he'd grind himself down to nothing. He'd left his parents home in Grand Rapids when he was fifteen, seeking fame and fortune, but happy just to be on the move. It sure was crazy the way everything had turned out so well. Not that there hadn't been plenty of hard times. He'd cast his lot with the knights of the road, riding the rods, seeing the Rocky Mountains from a crack in a boxcar door. There were nights he went to sleep cold and hungry, wishing he'd never left his crummy five-dollar-a-week job polishing furniture. But he kept drifting westward, working when he could and living by his wits when he couldn't.

Ketchel wanted his slice of the American pie and wasn't about to go running home to his mother. Besides, there were more good times than bad.

Butte, Montana, was a wide-open, freewheeling town, crawling with miners, cowboys, gamblers and prostitutes; the kind of frontier outpost that gave the American West its rowdy reputation. For the teenage Ketchel, it proved both a training ground and launching pad to his legendary boxing career. He got a job at a cafe, waiting on tables, running errands, anything that needed to be done. The job he liked the best was bouncer. Years later, boxing manager "Dumb Dan" Morgan said, "Ketchel had the soul of a bouncer, but a bouncer who loved his work." It was true. Steve, as everyone called him, loved to fight. He didn't quite understand why. All he knew was that once the first punch was thrown, a wonderful feeling swept over him. It was like he was transported to another dimension; the rest of the world would disappear and every ounce of his being would focus on the task at hand. It was almost as good as sex.

Butte teemed with dance halls, saloons and seedy theaters, all intent on relieving the miners and cowboys of their hard-earned pay. After drinking and whoring, the most popular form of entertainment these establishments offered was boxing. Ketchel was always in need of a few extra dollars and naturally gravitated towards these rough-and-tumble bouts. He'd learned how to duck fighting black-jack-toting railroad dicks, but was basically an all-out slugger. People were amazed at his uncanny ability to throw punches non-stop, round after round. There seemed no end to his stamina. As his reputation spread, Ketchel was hired by the Casino Theater for twenty bucks a week to take on all comers. "I hit 'em so hard that they used to fall over the footlights and land in people's laps," he liked to brag.

Not even Ketchel kept count of how many of these semi-professional bouts he fought before his first "official" contest against Kid Tracy in May of 1904. There must have been a couple of hundred of them. But Ketchel never forgot the look on Tracy's face

STANLEY KETCHEL.

Stanley Ketchel strikes a typical fighting pose. The "Michigan Assassin" learned his trade fighting in hobo camps and saloons, but eventually became middleweight champion of the world. (Photo courtesy of Big Fights, Inc.)

as he tore into him at the sound of the opening bell. The poor sap
never knew what hit him. What a great feeling it was to knock
another man senseless. People used to tell him how he would turn
white with anger when he fought, but that was all just talk as far as
Ketchel was concerned. He just did what came naturally, which was
to keep throwing punches as fast as he could until the other guy was
comatose. Ketchel's reputation for viciousness, first established in
hobo jungles across the west and later reinforced in the ring, was
well deserved.

Ketchel became somewhat of a personality in Butte. He cavorted
around town wearing cowboy boots and a "ten gallon" hat, and
considered himself a playboy. Most of his piddling ring earnings
were quickly thrown away in pursuit of pleasure, especially the sort
provided by Butte's substantial population of "painted ladies." By
the end of 1906, he'd racked up a long string of conquests, both in
the bedroom and the prize ring, but was getting nowhere fast.
Ketchel had outgrown Butte, and if he wanted to be world
champion, he'd have to move to California, the center of big-time
boxing. It took him awhile to obtain his first match on the West
Coast, but once he got started, Ketchel rapidly became the
sensation he always knew he would be.

The next two years were absolutely incredible. He won recognition as the world middleweight champion with a twenty-round
knockout over Jack "Twin" Sullivan in May of 1908, and then
embarked on his famous four-bout series with Billy Papke. Ketchel's tear-away style was pure box office and it wasn't long before
the man they called "The Michigan Assassin" was among the
nation's most popular—and best paid—professional athletes. In the
limited sense of America during the first decade of the 20th
century, Ketchel was a star. He once rode down New York City's
Fifth Avenue wearing an outrageous pink dressing gown, tossing
peanuts to the cheering multitudes. During his first East Coast
campaign, Ketchel fought two classic bouts with light heavyweight
champion Philadelphia Jack O'Brien, disposed of several other less
lights, and still found time to romance a Ziegfeld Girl. But he

wanted more. It wasn't enough to be king of the middleweights. Ketchel wanted to be heavyweight champion of the world.

White America had gone into a state of shock when Jack Johnson beat Tommy Burns in 1908 to become the first black man to win the world heavyweight championship. Unlike most of the ponderous "white hopes" jockeying for a chance to restore the title to the caucasian race, Ketchel could fight. Of course, there was the matter of the huge weight discrepancy. Johnson was much taller and at least fifty pounds heavier. Nevertheless, promoter "Sunny Jim" Coffroth knew a healthy gate when he smelled one and matched Johnson and Ketchel, October 16, 1909, at Colma, California.

Coffroth planned to make a motion picture of the bout and didn't want a quick knockout to ruin the movie's box office potential. As a hedge against an early victory for Johnson, he made an "arrangement" with the champion to carry Ketchel for the entire twenty rounds. Ketchel was privy to the plan, but was reportedly so overcome with racial pride and the desire to win, he decided to double-cross Johnson and go for a knockout. For most of the early rounds, things went according to the script: Johnson slapped Ketchel around the ring, humiliating him without ever really trying to inflict any serious damage, apparently satisfied to coast home a points winner. The grinning champion was so nonchalant, he began to neglect his defense and gave Ketchel the opening he was looking for. In the twelfth round, the challenger threw a looping, overhand right that caught Johnson behind the ear, sending him flopping awkwardly to the floor.

Ketchel's moment of glory was short lived. Still smiling but smarting with embarrassment, Johnson jumped to his feet before the referee even had a chance to count. Ketchel charged in determined to apply the finisher and Johnson greeted him with a barrage of punches; among them an exquisite right uppercut. The punch caught Ketchel square in his gaping mouth, jarring loose several teeth. According to the *San Francisco Examiner,* Ketchel fell "as if shot through the heart," landing heavily on the canvas, where he stayed for the full count. Later that night, however, Ketchel had a measure of revenge when he won $700 from Johnson in a craps game.

There are those who say Ketchel was never the same after his loss to Johnson. He traveled East again for a series of bouts in 1910, and though he continued to win, it was obvious the "fast life" was draining the boxer of his vigor. In an effort to avoid big city temptation and regain his strength, Ketchel visited his lifelong friend R.P. Dickerson in Springfield. Ketchel had always wanted to own a farm, and purchased a parcel of land near Dickerson's ranch in Conway. After staying in Springfield a few weeks, Ketchel decided to spend some time on Dickerson's place. It would give him a chance to get used to ranch life and look over his property at the same time. He arrived at the Dickerson ranch Tuesday, October 11. The next day, he met Dipley and Goldie Smith for the first time. They introduced themselves as Mr. and Mrs. William Hurtz.

Ketchel hadn't liked the looks of Hurtz from the beginning. He was a squirrely little fellow with shifty eyes and soft hands. His moon-faced wife looked okay, though. She had a trim figure and Ketchel couldn't help wondering what delights lay hidden beneath her petticoats. Maybe he'd have to see for himself. The ranch hands were busy plowing in preparation for the fall sowing of wheat, and Hurtz was out in the fields as soon as there was enough sunlight to work. There would be ample opportunity to explore her charms should the mood strike him.

It wasn't long before Ketchel's suspicions about Hurtz were confirmed. He was lazy and mean, and if Pete (Dickerson) hadn't been so desperate for help, Ketchel would have run him off the ranch. On Friday evening, Ketchel discovered Hurtz was mistreating the horses and gave him a real tongue lashing. Goldie, of course, was a different story. She cooked a decent breakfast, and Ketchel quickly fell into the routine of eating his first meal of the day with her in the screened porch that served as a summer kitchen. It soon proved to be a fatal habit.

There are many versions of what occurred at the Dickerson ranch the morning of October 15, 1910. But one fact is unchallenged: around 6:30, Walter A. Dipley shot Stanley Ketchel in the back with a .22 caliber Marlin rifle as the pugilist sat at the breakfast table. The only other witness to the shooting was Goldie Smith.

Ranch foreman Charles E. Baily and John Noland, another Dickerson hand, were the first people to encounter Dipley and Smith after the shooting. They were walking away from the house and Dipley was carrying the rifle.

"What's the matter?" asked Baily, noticing the agitated expressions on Dipley's face.

"I shot that goddamn son of a bitch," replied Dipley excitedly. "I'll show him he can't come out here and run over me. He tried to 'glom' that big gun of his and I shot him."

Baily and Noland were joined by George Thompson, another ranch employee, and as they stood around discussing the situation, Dipley headed back towards the house.

"You'd better stay out of there. He's got a revolver," shouted one of the men to Dipley, referring to the pistol Ketchel had worn since arriving at the ranch.

"He'll have to be a mighty good man to get me with a revolver or anything else," Dipley replied with an air of bravado, as he reentered the house.

Fearing the man they knew as Hurtz might shoot one of them next, the trio of unarmed men kept their distance and Dipley soon reappeared. He was armed with both the rifle and the revolver, and was working the lever of the rifle as he walked. When he discovered there were no more cartridges in the rifle, he threw it against the woodshed, cracking the stock. Baily asked why he'd shot Ketchel, and Dipley replied that the fighter had been guilty of misconduct towards his wife. There followed a brief conversation, in which Baily advised Dipley to surrender to authorities. Dipley said he would go to a nearby farm, telephone the police and wait there for the officers to come and get him. After a hurried discussion with

Goldie, Dipley walked away and disappeared over the ridge in the direction of the Ozark River, about a mile away.

Baily and the other men finally recovered their self-possession and rushed to Ketchel's aid. After carrying him into the bedroom and making him as comfortable as they could, telephone messages were sent to Dickerson in Springfield and Dr. O.C. Bennage in Conway, who arrived at the ranch house shortly after seven that morning.

A feeling of nausea swept over Pete Dickerson the moment he received the news of Ketchel's shooting. It was quickly replaced by anger and a trace of guilt. Ketchel had told him of his dislike for Hurtz, but Dickerson was in dire need of workers and couldn't always hire the kind of men he wanted. Dickerson worshipped the ground Ketchel walked on and knew he had to reach him as soon as possible. The regular train wasn't due to leave Springfield until noon, and that wasn't soon enough. Dickerson, a wealthy member of the Missouri State Legislature, immediately contacted the offices of the Frisco Line and arranged for a "special" to take him and surgeons to Conway. Tracker Al Sampey and a pair of bloodhounds readily agreed to join the party. Also aboard were a number of newspaper reporters. Dickerson wired ahead to the county seat in Marshfield for Sheriff C.B. Shields to meet the train en route. Dickerson was in such a tizzy, he ran over the curb on the way from the Metropolitan Hotel to the train station, breaking the axle of his automobile.

After picking up Sheriff Shields and six heavily-armed deputies in Marshfield, the special steamed towards Conway at a mile-per-minute clip. When the party arrived at Dickerson's ranch, they found Ketchel in a bad way. Sheriff Shields and his men took Goldie Smith into custody and then immediately began to pursue Dipley. Meanwhile, Ketchel was gently lifted onto a wagon for transport to the railroad lines. As he was being carried from the house, the stricken fighter pointed to a box of cigars on a table.

"Take these and give them to the boys," he said weakly.

Doctors C.E. Fulton and J.H. Fullbright, along with Dr. Bennage, accompanied Ketchel and Dickerson back to Springfield, where a large crowd had gathered at the station to greet the train. Springfield was no longer just the county seat, it was suddenly the focal point of a sensational story of international interest. Ketchel was taken to Springfield Hospital, where physicians performed an operation to remove blood which had gathered in the pleural cavity. The bullet had entered his back to the right of the spine, just below the shoulder blade, and ranged upwards and forward.

Ketchel seemed to rally briefly following surgery. He regained consciousness and asked, "Where's Pete?" A few minutes later he gasped for breath and Dickerson and the doctors were hastily summoned. At around 7:05 P.M., roughly thirteen hours after he'd been shot, Ketchel expired. Death was officially attributed to loss of blood and exhaustion.

"I hope he isn't arrested alive," raved the grief stricken Dickerson. "I am ready and willing to give $5,000 to the man who kills him. He deserves nothing better than that and I hope he gets nothing better. You men get out there on your horses and hunt for him. Don't be afraid to shoot, for he is armed and won't hesitate to shoot. He showed that when he shot Stanley Ketchel in the back."

Dipley hadn't known what to do after fleeing the Dickerson ranch. His mind raced. Should he surrender or should he try to escape? He wandered aimlessly for hours through the rugged Ozark foothills, trying to organize his thoughts and decide the best course of action. As darkness approached, he sought shelter for the night and soon came upon a farm near Niangua owned by Tom Hoggard.

Dipley hid the revolver in a corncrib and then approached the house and requested food and a place to stay for the night. He told Haggard he was looking for some runaway horses. Hoggard allowed the stranger to stay, but after Dipley retired, he became suspicious. Hesitant to act on his own, Hoggard recruited his brother Joe and neighbor Zeb Murphy to help confront his mysterious guest. They had learned of the Ketchel shooting and knew the fugitive had tattoo marks on his arms. The three men went to Dipley's room and found him awake, but still in bed. After demanding that Dipley roll up his shirt sleeves and seeing his tattoo marks, Hoggard told him, "You can consider yourself under arrest." Dipley made no effort to resist and was taken to Marshfield, where he was handed over to the sheriff.

"Be ye also ready for in such an hour as ye think not, the Son of Man cometh," intoned Dr. J.T. Bacon, pastor of the Cumberland Presbyterian Church, to the capacity crowd gathered at Springfield Elks Lodge for Ketchel's funeral services. "Women wept and strong men bent their heads in sorrow," reported the *Springfield Leader.* Later that afternoon, Ketchel drew his second standing-room-only crowd of the day when his casket was wheeled into the front room of the Paxson funeral parlor, where all who wished could see him. The next day at noon, Ketchel's body was placed aboard a train for transportation back to his family's home in Belmont, Michigan, a suburb of Grand Rapids. Dickerson wanted his friend interred in Missouri, but Ketchel's parents, Thomas and Julia Ketchel, believed "that the soil of Michigan should receive the body of the fighter who brought it a world's middleweight pugilist champion."

Back home, Ketchel was given quite a send-off. A Polish military band and eight flower girls preceded a white hearse bearing his body to St. Adelbert's Polish church. A melodramatic note was added when Ketchel's fiancée, Miss Jewell Bovine, tried to join her betrothed in the afterlife by swallowing carbolic acid on the way back from the cemetery. She was saved by the timely intervention of the ubiquitous Dickerson, who had accompanied Ketchel's remains to Michigan. Dickerson, riding in the same carriage as Miss Bovine, noticed her raise a vial to her lips and quickly knocked it away before she could drink the deadly potion. The grief-crazed Miss Bovine was inconsolable and claimed she heard the voice of her murdered lover murmuring in her ear.

Meanwhile back in Missouri, battle lines were clearly drawn. Dipley admitted his true identity, but insisted he'd shot Ketchel in self-defense. The story he and Smith told was simple: Dipley was angry with Ketchel for making "improper advances" to Smith. He confronted Ketchel at the breakfast table and shot him when the fighter attempted to draw his revolver. The coroner's jury did not believe the story and both were charged with first-degree murder. Without hesitation, the influential Dickerson launched his own private campaign to assure their conviction.

"I intend to give the prosecution of this man Dipley my personal attention," declared Dickerson publicly. "The best legal talent that I can procure will be employed to assist the prosecuting attorney of Webster county in the prosecution of Ketchel's slayer. This self-defense plea of Dipley is absurd. I am still of the opinion that he was a hired assassin of Ketchel's enemies."

Originally, there had been some local sympathy for Dipley based on the "unwritten law" that a man has a right to protect his wife's virtue. But after it was disclosed Dipley and Smith were not legally man and wife, the good citizens of southwestern Missouri also turned against him. It was discovered Goldie was actually still awaiting a divorce from her fourth husband at the time she met Dipley. Nevertheless, Dipley and Smith persisted in referring to one another throughout their trial as "husband" and "wife." Dipley, however, was not totally without support. His family raised approximately $1,500 for his defense, and his brother, Private Amos N. Dipley, stationed at Fort Bliss in El Paso, Texas, told reporters: "That Ketchel was looking for trouble is shown by the fact he came to breakfast with a gun in his pocket."

From the beginning, it was obvious the trial would be hard fought. When judge Charles H. Skinner ordered Sheriff Shields to summon a venire of forty men for jury selection, attorneys for the defense filed an affidavit asking that Shields be disqualified from summoning the jury and an elisor appointed to replace him. They argued that the sheriff was a friend and recent dinner guest of Dickerson's, and likely to select a venire prejudiced in favor of the state. Judge Skinner overruled the motion and ordered Sheriff Shields to proceed.

The trial attracted tremendous interest. Not only was the courtroom packed every day, there was considerable excitement in the streets. The prisoners were compelled to pass through the main square of Marshfield on the way from the jail to court, and were the object of much attention from large crowds of curiosity seekers. Adding to the carnival-like atmosphere were vendors selling postcards featuring photographs of Ketchel, Dipley, Smith and the Dickerson ranch. Among the interested spectators inside the courthouse were Ketchel's mother and his brother Leon. It was undoubtedly the biggest criminal trial in the history of Webster County.

A jury was finally selected and the court began to hear testimony the morning of January 20, 1911. The first witness called was Dickerson's ranch foreman, C.E. Baily, who outlined the events immediately following the shooting. The defense scored a few points when Baily testified Ketchel carried a revolver throughout his stay at the ranch and had practiced daily. But a real bombshell was dropped when defense attorney T.J. Delaney tried to establish that R.P. Dickerson was actually Ketchel's father! When the prosecution objected to this line of questioning, Delaney argued that the question related to the case in that it would show a cause for the persistent "hounding" of the defendants by Dickerson. Judge Skinner sustained the prosecution's objections, ruling that inasmuch as Dickerson had not been placed on the witness stand it was not an admissable feature in the case.

The state's charge of first-degree murder hinged on the contention that the defendants had plotted to kill Ketchel in cold blood. Baily gave some credence to this theory by testifying that the dining table Ketchel was sitting at when he was shot had been moved from its normal position so the fighter's back would be toward the door. But perhaps the most damaging evidence of premeditation was given by Luther Brazeale, another employee at the Dickerson ranch. Brazeale testified Dipley had obtained the rifle early the morning of the slaying on the pretense he wanted to shoot some rats. Brazeale also told the court Dipley has asked him if the rifle "would kill a man."

The second day of testimony was highlighted by Dipley's appearance on the witness stand. He told the court that when he returned from working in the fields on Friday evening, he noticed a marked change in his "wife's" demeanor, and that later than night she had told him Ketchel had made improper advances toward her. He said they decided to leave the ranch the next day, and that his failure to go to work the following morning caused him to quarrel with Ketchel.

"Ketchel was at breakfast when (ranch hand George) Johnson asked if I had fed the horses," said Dipley. "When he (Ketchel) saw me he remarked 'What in the hell are you doing around here this time of the day? Don't you know you ought to be out in the field?' I stated that I had quit and was not going to work. 'Why?' Ketchel asked. I told him he needn't look so innocent about why I was going.

"Then I saw Ketchel place his hands to the bosom of his shirt as if reaching for his revolver. I secured the rifle at the foot of the bed and went past him toward the kitchen door. At this instant I heard my wife call, 'Don't shoot him,' and fearing for my safety I fired."

Dipley then faced the jury and said, "I killed him in self-defense."

The biggest discrepancy between Dipley's version of events and that given by other witnesses revolved around whether or not he picked up the rifle just before the shooting, or had it in his possession when he entered the house, as Brazeale's testimony indicated. The prosectuion maintained it would have been virtually impossible for Dipley to have retrieved the weapon without passing within reaching distance of Ketchel, and that it was therefore highly likely the defendant had entered the house with the rifle already in his hands.

The following day it was Goldie Smith's turn to take the stand. It had been widely reported that she had a "varied career" and led a life of "dissipation." But according to reports in the local newspaper, "If the woman's experiences have been of such a nature, her general appearance does not disclose that fact. She is fairly well dressed and appears to be in good health and spirits."

Smith testified Ketchel had made an "indecent proposal" toward her while Dipley was working in the fields. She claimed that when she rebuffed his advances, he forced her to submit and raped her. On cross-examination by prosecuting attorney Roscoe Patterson, she admitted she told no one of the alleged assault made upon her at first, saying Ketchel had threatened to kill her if she "even breathed a word about it." Smith added that she finally told "her husband" what had happened around midnight and that they had then decided to leave the ranch the next day.

In order to tie Smith to the shooting, the state attempted to show it was her, not Ketchel, who was interested in instigating a romance.

"Now is it not a fact that you were enamored with Ketchel; that you made overtures to him; that he ignored them and that it made you angry?" asked Patterson.

Smith denied this accusation, and also rejected the suggestion she'd "advised and encouraged" Dipley to kill Ketchel.

Another important link in the state's case against Smith was the testimony of ranch employee George Noland, who was among the first to reach Ketchel's side following the shooting. Originally, Noland's evidence was overruled and heard only by Judge Skinner after the jury left the courtroom. But on the last day of testimony, Noland's statement was read into the record, including a quote from the dying fighter that seemed to implicate both Dipley and Smith in his shooting. "I guess they've got me," Ketchel allegedly told Noland.

Following passionate closing arguments by the defense and the prosecution, the case was handed over to the all-male jury for deliberation. While most observers felt Dipley would be found guilty, opinion was divided as to whether the verdict would be of first or second degree. Practically everyone who had followed the case closely believed Smith would be found innocent and set free. How wrong they were. After being out a little over seventeen hours, the jury found both Dipley and Smith guilty of first-degree murder. In fact, several members of the jury had been in favor of giving the defendants the death penalty, but eventually settled on life imprisonment for both. When Smith was asked if she was shocked by her conviction, she replied, "It was just as I expected."

The defense immediately filed a motion for a new trial, citing a laundry list of alleged irregularities. Sheriff Shields, whose prejudice against the defendants had been a bone of contention since the start of the trial, was accused of mistreating the prisoners and allowing Dickerson to abuse Smith while she was under his guard in Springfield. Shields was also accused of withholding a letter to Dipley which may have been beneficial to the defense. An affidavit from the postmaster at Marshfield showed the letter was received the morning of January 20, but was not delivered to Dipley until January 24, after the verdict had been returned. The letter, from a Grand Rapids physician, stated Ketchel had paid $1,500 in hush money to the parents of a girl who'd been "entertained" by Ketchel at his home in Belmont.

Another affidavit from C.L. Trustey, proprietor of the Marshfield motion picture theater, implicated Dickerson in a scheme to sway public opinion. According to Trustey, Dickerson had suggested he exhibit the film of the Johnson-Ketchel bout two days before the start of the trial, and promised to personally make good any loss incurred by lack of patronage. It was another example of Dickerson's extraordinary—and by today's standards, wildly irregular—influence over the procedings. It should also be remembered that practically all of the damaging testimony against the defendants was provided by employees of Dickerson.

Judge Skinner was unmoved by the defense's allegations, and on January 29, 1911, overruled the motion for a new trial and ordered Dipley and Smith to the state penitentiary to begin serving their sentences. Goldie was paroled after twelve years and quickly faded into obscurity. Dipley served twenty-four years before finally being released due to failing health. He stayed in southwestern Missouri for the remainder of his life, visiting the old Dickerson place once a month on his rounds for the gas company. Less than five years after emerging from prison, Dipley fell ill and died.

Except for the fact Dipley shot Ketchel, practically every aspect of the case is open to debate. What was Dipley's motive? The prosecution hinted at both robbery (Ketchel was known to carry large sums of cash) and jealousy, but failed to introduce any evidence to corroborate the former. Considering the fact Ketchel was carrying a gun at the time of his death, Dipley's claim of self-defense cannot be totally dismissed, either. On the other hand, Dickerson's allegation of a plot to terminate Ketchel's boxing career and the prosecution's suggestion that Dickerson was Ketchel's father were both farfetched. A spur-of-the-moment act of bravado is the most probable explanation of Ketchel's abrupt exit. Such rash behavior was certainly in keeping with what we know of Dipley's character.

There is little doubt Ketchel "had his way" with Goldie. Whether the fighter forced his attentions on her or was welcomed with open legs is academic. Either way, Dipley knew his territorial rights had been violated and was not the sort of man to meekly swallow an insult. Rifle probably already in hand, he confronted Ketchel at the breakfast table and simply blew him away. Though Dipley obviously pulled the trigger, Smith's role was ambiguous and the prosecution's attempt to link her to the shooting flimsy at best. It is highly unlikely she would have been even charged under modern judicial criterion.

Due to Ketchel's fabled fighting prowess and violent death at age twenty-four, interest in him has remained high throughout the ensuing decades. For years after the shooting, writers, historians and fans made pilgrimages to the scene of his bloody demise. For a while, the Summer family humored themselves by splashing a little red paint on the floor and showing their wide-eyed visitors "the spot where Ketchel fell." Recent visitors might be disappointed to discover no permanent marker at the site. Today, an above-ground swimming pool occupies the spot where the fighter drank his last cup of coffee.

2

The Corkscrew Kid

When William G. Ross arrived at his place of business the morning of August 13, 1924, he was expecting just another humdrum day at the office. Though his position as president of a Los Angeles lighting fixture company paid well, it wasn't exactly the most exciting job in the world. But the moment he entered the building, Ross immediately realized this was going to be a day he'd never forget.

To reach his office, Ross had to pass through Mors' antique store, which occupied the ground floor. To his absolute astonishment, the first thing he saw after entering the building was two men sitting in the corner of Mors' shop with their shoes and trousers removed. Before the shock of his discovery had a chance to sink in, Ross was confronted by a wild-eyed man, who drew back his coat and revealed a .45 caliber revolver stuck in his belt.

"Got any money?" the disheveled gunman asked. Before Ross could answer, he was punched in the face and quickly relieved of the $45 he was carrying in his wallet.

A forlorn-looking Kid McCoy at Los Angeles' central police station after he was arrested and charged with murdering Mrs. Teresa Mors, August 13, 1924. (Photo courtesy of Big Fights, Inc.)

"Sorry about that," apologized the man with the gun, incongruously, as he helped Ross to his feet. "Now, take your shoes and pants off and get over there with the rest of them."

Though apparently drunk, crazed, or both, the middle-aged desperado seemed relaxed and in complete command of the situation. Three more men soon wandered into the shop and were also quickly robbed and forced to shed their breeches and brogans. When the gunman turned his back to address the shop secretary, Ross made a dash for the door, ignoring his captor's demand to stop. A pistol barked, Ross felt a bullet thud into his leg, but kept running. He was lucky. Though he spent the next three months recuperating in the hospital, Ross lived to tell the tale. Thirty-two-year-old Teresa Mors hadn't been so fortunate. By the time the Kid McCoy went on a rampage at her shop, she was already dead.

The trial of McCoy made sensational headlines in Los Angeles during the winter of 1924. Born Norman Selby, October 13, 1872, in Rush County, Indiana, McCoy was a former idol of the prize ring, a man who had once held the world middleweight championship. Always regarded as an eccentric—if not a complete lunatic—he'd enjoyed a long and successful career in boxing. Following a professional debut in 1891, McCoy traveled extensively and was responsible for helping popularize the sport, not only in the United States, but also in Europe and parts of Africa.

McCoy was considered one of the craftiest boxers of his day, a colorful performer who often relied on trickery to gain an edge. If McCoy's science and punches were not enough to see him through, he generally figured how to cheat his way to victory. One of his favorite stratagems was to feign illness in the hope his opponent would take pity and pull his punches. If his adversary took the bait, McCoy would suddenly spring to life and deliver a devastating volley upon his unsuspecting victim. He used this and other ruses (such as pretending he hadn't trained for a bout) so often, customers were frequently known to ask, "Is this the real McCoy?" Thus, one of the gloved era's earliest con men inspired a figure of speech still in use today, on the whole, by people who have never heard of McCoy.

McCoy is also credited with developing the "corkscrew punch," a blow delivered in a twisting motion that would frequently tear his opponent's skin. Not exactly the most sporting of inventions, but effective, nevertheless. McCoy was identified with the punch to such a degree, he was often referred to as the "Corkscrew Kid," a nickname that could also very well apply to his twisted personality.

After McCoy won the vacant middleweight title with a fifteen-round technical knockout over Dan Creedon in 1898, he didn't even bother to defend it. He wanted to go after the big money, and that meant invading the heavyweight division. McCoy succeeded in beating a number of larger men, including Joe Choynski and Peter Maher, but lost to Tom Sharkey and former heavyweight champion Jim Corbett. The Corbett fight, held before a capacity crowd at New York's original Madison Square Garden in 1900, was branded a blatant fix by the press. It was not the first time McCoy had been involved in such a scandal. He had also conspired with gamblers to "take a flop" against Maher. But New York Senator "Big Tim" Sullivan got wind of the plot and warned McCoy he would chase the boxer out of the Empire State if he went through with the dive. The Kid wisely heeded the powerful politician's admonition and obediently dispatched Maher in five rounds.

Despite his many unorthodox boxing escapades, it was McCoy's bizarre behavior outside the ring which ultimately led to his downfall. A legendary womanizer, he was married ten times to eight different women. At his trial he was described as "a victor of over one hundred prize-ring battles and the breaker of 1,000 hearts." There is no doubt McCoy was a prolific rake. The question is: did he murder Teresa Mors?

Following the conclusion of his ring career, McCoy, who was rapidly approaching his forty-fourth birthday, enjoyed considerable success as an actor. He appeared in a number of movies for famed silent-era director Max Sennett, and D.W. Griffith made a film loosely based on McCoy's life, starring Lionel Barrymore. By the early 1920s, however, his motion picture career was history. Broke and hooked on alcohol, McCoy briefly went to work for the Julian Petroleum Corporation, guarding the company's collection of cars and filling stations. His $300 per month salary was a pitiful sum to a man who had once earned nearly a quarter of a million dollars in the ring. But McCoy was already involved in a romance (many said scheme) he hoped would solve his financial problems once and for all.

McCoy met Teresa Mors, wealthy antique dealer and wife of Albert Mors, and literally swept her off her feet—and out of her marriage. The Mors' divorce settlement was a particularly sticky issue. They shared much community property and the battle to divide the spoils of their seventeen-year marriage raged for several months, easily rivaling some of McCoy's bloodiest ring encounters. Much of their fortune was still up for grabs, when, on the evening of August 12, 1924, Teresa Mors was shot and killed by a single bullet through her head. The shooting took place at the apartment she shared with McCoy, and he was the only other person present at the time.

The ex-fighter was arrested the following morning when the police finally broke up his reign of terror at the Mors' antique shop. It had been quite a spree. Besides William Ross, McCoy had also shot and wounded Ann Schapps and her husband Sam, friends of the Mors family who had made the mistake of siding with Albert Mors when McCoy came between the couple. Apart from the shootings of Mors, Ross and the Schapps, McCoy was charged with robbery and assault in connection with the weird happenings at the antique shop the morning after Mrs. Mors' death.

The prosecution decided the lesser charges could wait until later and put McCoy on trial for first-degree murder. As there were no other eye witnesses to the shooting, the state's case was built around the theory that McCoy had latched onto Teresa Mors as a meal ticket and killed her in a fit of temper when he learned his chance for getting his hands on her money was slipping away. He claimed Teresa Mors committed suicide.

The state's position was strengthened by McCoy's subsequent rampage and the discovery of a safety-deposit box of his containing a valuable collection of objects once belonging to Mrs. Mors. The overall picture painted by the prosecution depicted McCoy as a ruthless "wife-stealer," bent on seeking revenge against anyone who had stood between him and Mrs. Mors' fortune. It was further speculated that McCoy also planned to kill Albert Mors if he had turned up at the antique store the morning after his ex-wife's death. The dozen other people who had been robbed and taken captive at the shop just happened to be in the wrong place at the wrong time. It was the prosecution's contention that McCoy intended to finance his getaway with the money stolen from them and the objects of art and jewelry found in his bank box. One of the men present at what newspapers referred to as McCoy's "wild-west party" was attorney Lewis Jones, who later gave damaging testimony at the pugilist's trial.

"Stick around kid. You'll see more fun here than you ever have in a courtroom," McCoy reportedly told Jones. "Will you be my attorney? I'm going to bump Mors and a lot of people off and I'll need a good lawyer."

While Jones's testimony certainly indicated the premeditated nature of McCoy's actions that morning, chief defense counsel H.L. Giesler was quick to point out that McCoy was on trial for the slaying of Mrs. Mors, not for his violent antics the next day. Superior Court Judge Crail allowed Jones's testimony to remain on official record, but the case really boiled down to what had happened between McCoy and his paramour after they returned to their apartment around 10:30 P.M. the evening of August 12.

McCoy's training as an actor probably saved him from the gallows. His dramatic performance on the witness stand should have been nominated for an acting award. Ramrod straight and elegantly attired in a blue business suit, the fifty-two-year-old former boxer looked more like a bank president than the homicidal gigolo the prosecution had described. After answering questions regarding the items found in his safety deposit box (he claimed they were gifts), McCoy treated the jury and packed courthouse to a theatrical reenactment of the events surrounding Teresa Mors death. The old thespian pulled out all the stops, his voice dramatically rose and fell to suit the portion of the story he was relating, his facial expressions ran the gauntlet from agony to supreme sorrow. He even managed to shed what the prosecution sarcastically referred to as "crocodile tears."

According to McCoy, after he and Mors had returned home together and shared a sandwich and a drink, Mrs. Mors had suddenly become despondent when he suggested it might be better if he left town for a few weeks. A deal she had worked out with Albert Mors to divide their community property was in danger of falling through, and McCoy figured things might go a bit smoother if he was temporarily out of sight. Teresa allegedly rejected his proposal and jumped to her feet, clutching to her breast a bread knife she'd used to cut their sandwich. At this point in his testimony, McCoy leaped to his feet and demonstrated Mors' alleged actions by pressing the bread knife to his own chest.

"I can't take it any more," shrieked McCoy, suddenly switching to the role of his dead sweetheart. "I'm going to end it all."

To demonstrate how he'd valiantly tried to wrestle the knife away from Mors, McCoy enlisted the assistance of his attorney. For several minutes, the pair rolled around the courtroom floor in an extravagant display of histrionics.

"When I jerked the knife from her, the edge of it struck her on the lip and then was when she screamed," said McCoy, his high-pitched voice echoing through the courtroom. "I was trying to get hold of the knife—and I looked around and I saw her have the gun in her hand. I threw the knife over my head and went after the gun. I no sooner got her by the arm than it went off, and I shook my head. I didn't know whether I was shot or she was shot until I felt her relax. And then I knew—it—was—all over."

As he spoke this last, drawn out sentence, McCoy's voice sank from a high pitch to a whisper. Then he shut his eyes and bowed his head. It was beyond a shadow of a doubt his finest performance.

After a dramatic pause, McCoy continued his story. He graphically related how he'd tried to wipe the blood away from Teresa Mors' head, put her in bed and placed a photograph of himself on her chest.

"I laid down beside her to shoot my head off," McCoy stated. "Why I didn't—I don't know."

"Do you remember what occurred after that?" asked defense attorney Giesler.

"I don't remember ever leaving her," his client replied.

McCoy maintained he'd become faint at that juncture and could not remember anything else that happened until after his apprehension the following day. In an attempt to lend credence to this convenient lapse of memory, McCoy played his ace card and introduced a series of dispositions concerning the mental condition of various members of his family. According to these depositions, McCoy's mother, father and sister were all insane.

Apparently, his father, Frank Selby, and his mother, Mary E. Selby (who had died while McCoy was being held in Los Angeles County jail), were both members of a "free love cult" and had frequently indulged in aberrant behavior. Dr. Max A. Bahr's deposition told how Mrs. Selby had been a patient at the Indiana Central Hospital for the Insane during the time he had been the physician in charge. "Mrs. Selby was insane," wrote Dr. Bahr. "She was irrational and greatly confused at times. She was afflicted with suicidal tendencies, numerous hallucinations and marked self-depredation."

William Van Sickel, a farmer and neighbor of the McCoy family back in Milroy, Indiana, stated in his deposition that McCoy's sister, Mabel Selby, who was constantly at her brother's side during his trial, was also insane in 1915. He wrote that on one occasion when she was being taken to the hospital, Mabel had fought, kicked, screamed and spat in the doctor's face. She had also attempted to perform a "flip-flop" out the back of the car, explaining she was doing stunts for a motion picture.

The defense's reason for introducing the depositions was twofold.

Besides attempting to explain McCoy's memory loss, Giesler and his assistants wanted to lay the groundwork for a possible insanity plea. And at the very least, they hoped to confuse the jury by adding another ingredient to a case already overflowing with strange components. Following closing arguments, in which the prosecution asked for the death penalty, the jury of nine women and three men retired to decide McCoy's fate.

For a while it looked like there might be a hung jury. Half the jurors wanted McCoy hanged, the other half favored setting him free. Finally, after seventy-two hours of deliberation, McCoy was found guilty of manslaughter. It was viewed as a compromise verdict, and while McCoy's life had been spared, he was still bitterly disappointed.

"They might as well have convicted me of murder in the first degree," said McCoy as he left the courtroom under armed guard. "I am innocent. A manslaughter verdict makes me appear just as guilty as if I was guilty of first-degree murder."

McCoy was sentenced to spend from one to ten years behind bars and sent to the state penitentiary at San Quentin. Judging by his lifelong pattern of erratic conduct and his family's history of mental illness, it is reasonable to assume McCoy suffered from some form of manic depression. All the classic symptoms are there in abundance. With the help of modern-day anti-depressants, he may have led a fairly normal life. Of course, such medical treatment would also have deprived turn-of-the-century boxing of its most outlandish character.

Upon his release from prison in 1932, McCoy lectured on the evils of strong drink and then went to work as a gardener on the estate of auto mogul Henry Ford. Always one who knew how to make a theatrical exit, McCoy upstaged the Grim Reaper, and on April 18, 1940, took his own life by ingesting an overdose of sleeping pills. According to a suicide note found in his pocket, he was depressed about the global situation, and could no longer "endure this world's madness."

3

Knockout Drops

P robably the last thing Francisco Guilledo saw was the overhead lights in the operating room. Then again, maybe he was too far gone to notice. He was racked with fever, his throat so swollen the attending physician had great difficulty administering the anesthetic. Eventually the drug took hold and Guilledo sank into a profound sleep. Just as Dr. C.E. Hoffman was preparing to operate, his patient's heart stopped beating. Artificial respiration failed to revive him. Francisco Guilledo was dead.

Few who saw his small body lying on the mortician's slab would have guessed Guilledo had been one of the most popular and highly paid athletes of his time. He was just an inch over five feet tall and seldom weighed more than one hundred twelve pounds, but inside his breast had beaten the heart of a champion, the heart of the greatest prize fighter his native land has ever produced. Guilledo traveled a long way to die in a San Francisco hospital on the morning of July 14, 1925. They shipped his body back home to be buried, back to the Philippine Islands where his journey had begun twenty-four years before in the city of Iloino, on the island of Panay, about three hundred forty miles south of Manila.

As the legend goes, Guilledo was discovered sparring with other boys in a public school playground, just another street urchin trying his hand at the sport American soldiers and sailors introduced to the Filipino people during the Spanish American War. A man with the same first name, Francisco Villa, spotted little Guilledo in action and was impressed with the way the youngster handled his fists. Villa, who just happened to be an official of the Olympic Athletic Club in Manila, persuaded the lad to enter a novice tournament. He was a sensation from the very beginning, and Señor Villa took the skinny waif into his home, adopted him and gave him his own last name. One of boxing's more colorful rags-to-riches stories was underway.

At the same time the teenage Villa was tearing his way through the amateur ranks in Manila, Mexican revolutionary Doroteo Arango, better known as Pancho Villa, was making headlines around the world with his own brand of mayhem. Filipino fans made the inevitable connection and from that point on, the boy born Francisco Guilledo was also known as Pancho Villa. It was a name that would take him halfway around the world and to the pinnacle of his profession, a name still spoken in reverential terms whenever boxing enthusiasts discuss the legendary fighters of the past. It is also a name, like so many in boxing, associated with tragedy and premature death.

Not long after his first amateur bout, Villa attracted the attention of motion picture and sports impresario Frank Churchill, who took the budding boxer under his guidance. Turning pro in 1919, Villa quickly established himself with a string of crowd-pleasing victories. His nonstop, perpetual motion style guaranteed an action-packed fight every time he was on the bill—which was at least a couple of times a month. Villa crammed fifty-two fights into his first three years as a pro, mainly against other local kids like himself, eager to claw their way out of poverty by any means available. The exception was Mike Ballerino, an American soldier from Bayonne, New Jersey, stationed in the Philippines. Villa dominated a series of ten bouts against Ballerino (who eventually went on to win recognition as world junior lightweight champion) and convinced Churchill the time was ripe to invade the United States.

Villa began his American campaign in 1922, but lost his first two bouts against Abe Goldstein and future world flyweight champion Frankie Genaro. Despite his disappointing start, Villa scored big with the American sporting public. They were taken with the diminutive dynamo with the whirlwind style and engaging personality. He had the endearing habit of holding the ropes apart, helping his opponent into the ring, and then shaking his hand as if they were the best of friends. It was practically impossible not to love the little guy. These were the days when boxing's smallest divisions still attracted plenty of attention, and Villa, with his trademark shock of jet black hair and friendly grin, rapidly developed into a major draw at the box office. He won the American flyweight title by knocking out Johnny Buff in September of 1922, and before the year was over fought a total of fourteen times in the U.S.

While he lost his American flyweight crown to Genaro, who always seemed to have Pancho's number, the wildly popular Villa was finally matched with Wales' Jimmy Wilde, June 18, 1923, for the world flyweight championship. Wilde, nicknamed the "Mighty Atom," is considered by many experts to be one of, if not the, greatest flyweights in boxing history. A master of the classic, stand-up British style, Wilde was said to be a "ghost with a hammer in his hands" because of his uncanny ability to score with punishing blows and escape without being hit in return. But by the time he crossed the Atlantic to defend against Villa, Wilde had been inactive for over two years and nearly at the end of his tether. Nevertheless, the match was a huge success and a crowd of 23,000 were on hand at the Polo Grounds to witness the battle of mighty mites. At the end of the second round, Villa unleashed a right hand just as the bell sounded and Wilde, who had already dropped his gloves, went down like a slaughtered steer. Though Wilde's handlers dragged him back to his corner and then sent him out for the third round, the man who had held the flyweight belt since 1916 was fighting on

Pancho Villa, the first boxer from the Philippines to win a world title, was still the reigning flyweight champion when he died following surgery in 1925. (Photo courtesy of *The Ring* magazine)

instinct alone. Wilde put up a courageous struggle, but was finally counted out by referee Patsy Haley at 1:46 of the seventh round. Villa, the former barefoot boy from the rice paddies of Iloilo, was champion of the world.

Following his victory over Wilde, Villa spent the remainder of 1923 and all of 1924 touring the United States, fighting every two or three weeks against the best flyweights and bantamweights available, sandwiching a trio of successful defenses between a slew of non-title bouts. Always hot on Villa's trail was his old nemesis Genaro, who clambered for a title shot at every opportunity. Plans for a showdown between the rivals were arranged for the summer of '24 at the Nostrand Athletic Club in Brooklyn, but Villa withdrew from the match, claiming an injured right shoulder. The New York State Athletic Commission suspended Villa, who decided to return to the Philippines for a well-deserved rest.

The first of his race to win a world title and hailed as a hero of massive proportions, he enjoyed an extended sojourn at home, eventually returning to action with a knockout over Francisco Pilapel in March of 1925 in Manila. Less than two months later, he made the fourth defense of his world title, outpointing fellow Filipino Clever Sencio over fifteen rounds at Manila Stadium. Little did anyone guess it would be Villa's last winning effort. He steamed back to the United States shortly after the Sencio victory, anxious to pick up where he'd left off the previous summer. Before getting down to the serious business of fighting Genaro, Villa accepted a non-title bout in Oakland against Jimmy McLarnin. The match was scheduled as part of the Fourth of July celebrations and Villa's purse was $12,500, a lot of money in 1925 and a good indicator of Villa's earning power, even in a non-title bout.

A few days before the fight, Villa was forced to undergo dental surgery. He was suffering from badly ulcerated teeth and a wisdom tooth was removed. Against the advice of his doctor, Villa went ahead with the McLarnin fight, ostensibly because he didn't want to handicap the promotion. Depsite the fact his swollen jaw was clearly visible to ringsiders, the weakened champ gamely lasted the distance, but was outpointed by McLarnin, who, although considered just a good prospect at the time, later went on to become world welterweight champion. Following the bout, Villa's condition grew progressively worse. The infection had spread from his jaw to his throat, and the poison was rapidly invading the rest of his body. He entered the hospital on the night of July 13, and the next morning it was decided an operation was necessary. The little giant who had endured one hundred and five professional fights without ever being knocked out, failed to survive what turned out to be a lethal dose of ether. He was only twenty-four years old and at the peak of his powers. While most books of boxing history attribute Villa's death to blood poisoning, according to newspaper accounts the day following his death, anesthesia was the knockout punch that put Villa down for the final count. He was not to be the last.

The operating room has always been a far deadlier arena than the prize ring, but during the first few decades of the 20th century it claimed a great number of boxing's finest practitioners. Beginning with Villa in 1925 and continuing over the next several years, the surgeon's mask became almost as macabre a symbol of death as the executioner's hood.

The only thing Harry Greb loved more than fighting was fucking. It was common practice for him to go a round or two in the dressing room with a floozy before going out to take care of business in the ring. When he finally retired after two hundred ninety-nine recorded professional fights—and God knows how many exhibitions and barroom brawls—he allegedly told biographer James R. Fair, "Women mean more to me than anything else on earth. If I can't see 'em, I can't love 'em, so I'm hanging up my gloves."

Greb had been blind in one eye for most of his career, and half blind in his "good" eye for at least a hundred major bouts. But that didn't stop him from becoming undoubtedly the greatest middleweight of his era. He had more nicknames than some boxers had fights, but the one that stuck and best described Greb's style was

"The Human Windmill." He threw himself into the fray with both hands churning, winging punches from every conceivable angle. Punches, however, were far from the only thing he threw. Greb was also one of the dirtiest fighters to ever pull on a jock strap. It has been said his idea of a "clean" fight was one in which he thumbed his opponent no more than a dozen times. He was the master of every foul, ranging from the aforementioned thumb in the eye to the well-placed knee to the groin. Harry elbowed, butted, tripped, and even bit his adversaries. He carved up their faces with his laces, stepped on their feet, and hit on the break. Except for his hometown Pittsburgh fans, who worshipped him, he was hated from coast to coast, booed unmercifully in every arena he fought in from New York to New Orleans. But those were rough and tumble days, and like Greb said, "Prize fighting ain't the noblest of the arts, and I ain't its noblest artist." What he was, however, was a man incapable of giving anything less than his heart and soul every time he fought. Blessed with incredible speed and inexhaustible endurance, he routinely tackled men twenty to fifty pounds bigger than himself, cutting them down to size with a withering assault. If he had had a punch to match his courage, he'd probably have been unbeatable.

Greb avoided the gymnasium as if it were a morgue, preferring instead to spend his time away from the ring in whorehouses and nightclubs. But he fought so frequently, often four, five, even six times per month, he didn't need to train. On one of the few occasions he bowed to convention and formally prepared for a match (his 1925 middleweight title defense against Mickey Walker), Harry took a harem to training camp with him to Manhasset, Long Island. But even his female companions weren't enough to satisfy his appetite. Greb regularly journeyed into Manhattan at night to chase skirts around the dance floor, rushing back to camp just in time for roadwork and breakfast. There must have been a method to his madness, because though he was sick and nearing the end of his great career, Greb rallied from behind to decision Walker in a classic punchout before 40,000 hysterical fans at the Polo Grounds.

Though he won the world middleweight crown from Johnny

The legendary Harry Greb. A true marvel of the ring, Greb was among a trio of Hall-of-Famers who died on the operating table during the 1920s. (Photo courtesy of *The Ring* magazine)

Tiger Flowers became the first black man to win the world middleweight title when he outpointed Harry Greb in 1926. (Photo courtesy of *The Ring* magazine)

Wilson in August of 1923 and held it until February of 1926, Greb's greatest pugilistic accomplishment came May 23, 1922, when he became the only man to ever defeat Gene Tunney. Greb decisioned him over fifteen blood-soaked rounds to capture the American light heavyweight title, a feat made even more remarkable by the fact that Greb weighed a mere 162½, compared to 174½ for his opponent. Tunney, who would go on to win the heavyweight crown from Jack Dempsey four years later, had the misfortune of running into Greb while the "Iron City Express" (another of Harry's nicknames) was still close to his prime. It was a massacre. Greb flew out of his corner at the opening bell and plastered Tunney with a fusillade of punches, breaking his nose in two places. Before the opening round was over, Greb had also slashed open an ugly gash over the "Fighting Marine's" left eye. Round after round, Greb punished Tunney, who lost so much blood, referee Kid McPartland was frequently forced to stop the action while he wiped the gore away from Greb's soggy gloves. Tunney doggedly lasted the course, but at the sound of the final bell, there was no doubt that Greb had won. Though Tunney outpointed Greb in four subsequent bouts over the next few years, Gene never forgot the frightening beating he absorbed in their first encounter.

"Few human beings have fought each other more savagely or more often than Harry Greb and I," wrote Tunney in his autobiography, *Arms for Living*. "We punched and cut and bruised each other in a series of bouts, five of them. The first of the five is for me an enduring memory, a memory still terrifying."

For all his cruelty in battle, Greb was a sentimental slob outside the ring. He squandered a small fortune helping broken down pugs, and was always the first to dig into his own pockets when it was time to throw a party or go out on the town. He was also extremely vain, paradoxically worried about his looks for a man who earned his living getting punched in the face. He always entered the ring with his hair plastered down with brilliantine, and also doctored his mug with powder. Greb was highly sensitive to criticism, especially when a reporter knocked him in print. It was not unusual for Harry to harbor a grudge if he didn't like what a particular scribe had written, even if he knew the writer was telling the truth. But when a friend needed help, even if he'd previously been on Greb's shit list, Harry was the first to rush to his aid.

Even when he was champ and rolling in dough, Greb never slowed his grueling pace. Between title fights, he continued to tour the country, taking on anyone, anywhere, providing there was a payday to be had and a couple of strumpets to be sampled. By 1926, the weight of hundreds of fights and countless amorous adventures had taken quite a toll, and in retrospect, it's not too surprising Tiger Flowers was able to relieve Greb of the middleweight title, February 26th, at Madison Square Garden. But even then, the verdict was considered a bum call by many observers. Referee Gunboat Smith, whom Harry had kayoed in one round many years before (after thumbing him in the eye) scored the bout for the old champ. The other two judges, however, gave the nod—and the title—to Flowers. Harry and Tiger fought a rematch in August, and while practically everybody thought Greb had done enough to regain the title, once again the ringside judges disagreed with the referee, and Tiger retained the belt on another split decision. The New York fans, who formerly hated Greb, had grown fond of him over the years, and they stormed the ring in protest, hurling everything that wasn't nailed down. Athletic commissioner William Muldoon said he thought Greb had won, but refused to reverse the decision, fearing people would think he was discriminating against Flowers, who was black.

Greb said good-bye to the ring after the second Flowers fight, and not long afterwards was involved in an automobile accident in Pittsburgh, when his car went over an embankment and rolled over several times. He injured his legs and also fractured his nose. Greb's luck had definitely taken a nasty turn. Shortly before the accident, Greb had had a cataract removed from his right eye in Atlantic City, and when he returned for follow-up treatment on the optic, he decided to also have the fractured bone removed from his nose. Some people claim Harry's vanity was the reason he chose to undergo the additional surgery, but according to newspaper accounts of the time, the fractured bone was interfering with his breathing. Regardless of his motive, it was considered a relatively minor procedure. Greb was entertaining the idea of a comeback and entered the sanitarium in good spirits on October 21, 1926.

"The operation was started under local anesthesia and later supplemented by nitrous oxide and oxygen gas," said Dr. Charles L. McGivens, attending physician. "He left the operating table apparently in good condition at 8:30 P.M. At ten o'clock this morning, his heart began to fail and he rapidly grew weaker despite the administration of stimulants."

At 2:30 the afternoon of October 22, Greb, age 32, died. A Lothario to the end, his "fiancée," Miss Naomi Braden, was at his side when he passed. Greb's death was attributed to "heart failure superinduced by shock of the operation combined with injuries received in car accident." While this is true as far as it goes, it was also noted that Greb came out of the anesthetic "fairly well, but not entirely." Once again, as in the death of Villa, anesthesia had played a role in the untimely demise of one of boxing's greatest champions.

If the link between the deaths of Villa and Greb is intriguing, then the passing of Greb's conqueror, Flowers, stretched the chain of coincidence into the realm of the bizarre. Born Theodore Flowers, August 5, 1895, in Camille, Georgia, he enlisted in the government's ship building corps at the outbreak of World War I and was sent to Philadelphia's Hog Island shipyard, where he worked as a carpenter. It was during his stay at the shipyard that Flowers attended a Liberty Loan rally, hosted by retired light heavyweight champ Philadelphia Jack O'Brien. Flowers joined in the sparring exhibitions and looked so promising, O'Brien encouraged him to join the professional ranks. Flowers took the old champ's advice to heart and embarked on a professional career in 1918, stopping Bill Hooper in Brunswick, Georgia. Hooper's manager was an Atlanta gym owner named Walk Miller, and when Miller saw the effects of

Flower's handiwork on Hooper's face, he invited Flowers to join his stable. They proved a highly successful team and stayed together throughout Flower's career.

Flowers was a religious man, a steward in Brunswick's Methodist Church, and according to one of the many apocryphal tales that enrich boxing lore, always repeated the following prayer before entering the prize ring: "Blessed be the Lord my strength, who teacheth my hands to war and my fingers to fight." Whether or not the story is true, Flowers was a gentleman and genuinely liked by practically everyone he encountered, even his opponents. In an era of hard-drinking, fast-living fighters, the man they called the "Georgia Deacon" was an exception to the rule.

Flowers boxed with considerable success all over the South and made several fruitful forays into Mexico before meeting Greb in an over-the-weight match in Fremont, Ohio, August 21, 1924. At the time, local Ohio law prohibited the rendering of decisions in bouts that lasted the distance, so Flowers' first match with the reigning titleholder is recorded as a ten-round "no decision." Some said Flowers got the better of it, others claimed Greb had an edge. Either way, Flowers' showing was good enough to give his career a considerable boost. When he stopped ex-champ Johnny Wilson later that year in his Madison Square Garden debut, Flowers was firmly established as a genuine threat to Greb's throne.

After winning the world title from Greb and successfully retaining it in a rematch, Flowers put the championship on the line against welterweight Mickey Walker, the "Toy Bulldog" who had given Greb such a rousing—albeit losing—fight the previous year. The result was a highly controversial ten-round decision for Walker before a packed house at the Chicago Coliseum.

"The decision was given to Walker after ten bloody rounds, but it was one of the worst ever handed down in the ring, and caused the Illinois Boxing Commission to hold a special meeting the following day to investigate the verdict," wrote Nat Fleischer in Volume Five of *Black Dynamite*. The commission contemplated reversing the decision, but finally decided to let the matter drop. The contract for the Walker-Flowers bout had a return clause, and it was assumed Flowers would eventually force Walker and his wily manager, Jack "Doc" Kearns, to honor it. Sadly, Flowers, the first black man to win the middleweight championship, never got the opportunity to regain the title he'd lost in such a disputable manner.

On November 16, 1927, Flowers entered the private hospital of Dr. Wilfred G. Fralick in New York City to undergo a minor operation on his right eye to remove the scar tissue which years of fighting had produced. He had fought in Harlem just twelve days earlier (stopping Leo Gates in four rounds) and was expected to be out of action for no more than three weeks. Several hours after the apparently successful surgery, the thirty-two-year-old Flowers collapsed unexpectedly and died within a few minutes. Dr. Fralick attributed his death to "status lymphaticus," a malfunction of the lymphatic system, which asserted itself following the operation. But while Flowers' latent lymphatic condition was the official cause of death, one can't help but wonder if anesthesia was once again a contributing factor. Though it was reported he had "apparently come out of the ether successfully," it was also noted that "Flowers was virtually unconscious from the time of the operation until his death."

Compared to today's methods, most surgical procedures were primitive in the 1920s, but general anesthesia was a particularly hit-and-miss proposition. Many patients fell victim to hypoxemia, an often fatal condition caused when the oxygen carried in the blood is inadequate to nourish the tissues to which it is circulated. While it is true the deaths of Villa, Greb and Flowers were all related to other medical problems, in retrospect, the common thread appears to be the powerful potions used to lull them into a state of artificial sleep. Of the trio, only Villa was considered seriously ill. Greb and Flowers could have conceivably lived for years had they not elected to undergo what amounted to touch-up surgery. Perhaps in the long run the most fascinating thing about their kindred fate is not the cause, but rather its effect. Forever linked in their failure to survive the surgeon's knife, the legends of Villa, Greb and Flowers have assumed an added dimension, gaining those layers of pathos and mystery we've always found so becoming in our fallen heroes.

4

Boxing's Original Wild Child

Private Louis Phal of the Colonial French Infantry didn't like the way his nine German prisoners were whispering among themselves. He had surprised them while they were eating and managed to capture the lot without firing a shot. Phal planned to march them back to the French line, but feared they were plotting to rush him en masse. He'd probably manage to shoot a few, but nine against one isn't the best of odds, even if you're the one holding the rifle. But thinking quickly on his feet came naturally to Phal, and he ordered the group of prisoners into a large shell hole. After the last German had descended into the muddy crater, Phal lobbed a couple of grenades in after them. A pair of thunderous concussions shook the earth. Private Phal's dilemma was solved.

Such was the nature of life and death during the bitter trench warfare that tore apart Western Europe during World War I. For most men, the squalid living conditions in the trenches and the terror of the battlefield made for a thoroughly miserable existence. For Louis Phal, however, it was just another adventure, one of the countless hair-raising episodes that punctuated a life of reckless abandon.

The massacre of the nine German soldiers earned Phal the *Crois de Guerre,* promotion to corporal, and a furlough. It was the second time he had been decorated and promoted for bravery, but Phal didn't relish the responsibility that came with an additional stripe. Just like the first time he'd been upgraded, Phal overstayed his leave, drinking wine and enjoying the delights of the local peasant girls until a squad of soldiers came to take him into custody. Once more, Phal was busted back to private, a rank he enjoyed until he was honorably discharged in 1919.

Louis Phal answered life's opening bell, September 16, 1897, in St. Louis du Senegal, the capital city of what was then a French West African colony. Little is known of his early childhood, but Phal claimed his father was a wealthy trader, dealing in aigrettes (plumes), feathers and monkeys. What is known, however, is that his life took a decided change when an affluent European woman visiting the colony became enamored of young Phal and decided he would make a perfectly darling ornament for her villa. One version of the story indicates she was French, but Phal (not always the most reliable source due to his habitual drinking) said she was a German dancer named Elaine Grosse. Whatever the woman's true identity, she apparently obtained permission from Phal's parents, for financial consideration, to take the ten-year-old lad back to Europe with her. What happened upon their arrival remains sketchy, but according to Phal, French immigration officials refused to allow Madame Grosse to take him into Germany without written consent from his parents. The consent never arrived and she finally abandoned Phal after giving him 1,000 francs.

Phal received some assistance and schooling compliments of the charitable organization La Francais Bienfassance, but was generally left to his own devices. He worked at several menial jobs, mainly as

Le Plonguer (dishwasher) at various hotels and cafes before traveling to Marseilles to become a pupil of boxer/manager Paul Latil. Phal's innate athletic ability and uncanny knack for absorbing punishment without weakening made him a perfect sparring partner for more experienced boxers. After learning the bare rudiments of his trade, he turned professional in 1912 under the *nom de guerre* of Battling Siki, engaging in eighteen bouts before volunteering for the army in autumn of 1914.

Following his discharge from the army, Siki resumed his boxing career with a couple of bouts in Toulouse and then headed for the bright lights of Paris. From January of 1920 until July of 1922, Siki went undefeated in forty-four bouts (forty-three wins and one draw). His let-it-all-hang-out, take-no-prisoners style of slugging proved popular with continental fans and Siki became a sought-after headliner, not only in Paris, but also in Rotterdam, Amsterdam, Berlin, Brussels, Antwerp and Barcelona. The majority of his opponents were nondescript performers, but though Siki was only a light heavyweight, he frequently battered much larger men into submission. Siki outpointed German heavyweight champion Hans Breitenstraeter over fifteen rounds and stopped Italian heavyweight kingpin Giuseppe Spalla in nine. Siki's most prominent opponent during these years was British light heavyweight champion Harry Reeve, with whom he fought a series of three matches. Siki won their first encounter on points, fought a draw the second time, and finally proved his superiority with a sixth-round knockout.

A lengthy string of victories was not the only thing about Siki that attracted attention. He charged through life the same way he fought—full tilt, no holds barred. Boxing's latter day wild child, "Neon" Leon Spinks, had nothing on the "Singular Senegalese" when it came to excessive behavior. Even Siki's contemporary, middleweight champion Harry Greb, a legendary hedonist, paled in comparison to Siki when it came to raising hell. Few have ever partied as heartily as Siki. He was an unremittant playboy and flagrant extrovert, who loved to parade along Paris' boulevards wearing evening dress, frequently accompanied by a pet parrot or monkey. One of his favorite tricks was to toss the monkey into a crowd, then stand back and laugh at the ensuing panic this stunt created. On one occasion, he went so far as to drag a protesting lion cub through the Montmarte district on a leash, stopping from time to time to buy drinks for both the lion and himself. Siki's nonstop drinking and volatile temper often led to unscheduled bouts outside the ring. And despite inevitable intervention by the gendarmes, Siki was incorrigible and never gave reform a second thought.

"Me Siki. Me different," was his standard reply when asked about his tempestuous lifestyle.

Despite his outrageous exploits, Siki's succes against Reeve and victories over topnotchers Marcel Nilles and Paul Journee, established him as the logical contender for the world light heavyweight title, then held by Frenchman Georges Carpentier. Though Carpentier had been destroyed in four rounds by Jack Dempsey in a bid to win the heavyweight title, he was still the idol of France. "The Orchid Man," as the handsome Carpentier was known to his legion of admirers, had regained some of his prestige by successfully defending his 175-pound crown with a one-round KO over Ted "Kid" Lewis in London. Carpentier ignored Siki's challenge at first, but eventually acquiesced when public pressure (and the possibility of a hefty payday) mounted—but not before a deal was struck. Carpentier's bout with Dempsey had created boxing's first million-dollar gate and promoters of his match with Siki wanted to protect their star box office attraction. For a price, Siki agreed to "fall down" for the Frenchman. Ignorant of the fraudulent arrangement, over 50,000 fans packed the Velodrome Buffalo in Paris, September 24, 1922, to witness Siki and Carpentier squared off in a bout destined to go down as one of the most bizarre in boxing history.

Siki was willing to live up to his end of the bargain, and for the first two rounds he pulled his punches, grinned sheepishly, and did his best to make Carpentier look good. Whether or not Carpentier was aware of the fix has never been clearly established, but when he drilled Siki with a hard right and dropped him for a brief count in

Battling Siki, Africa's first world champion as he looked in his fighting prime. A crude and powerful brawler inside the ring, Siki shocked the world when he knocked out George Carpentier to win the light heavyweight title in 1922. (Photo courtesy of Peltz Boxing Promotions)

A rare portrait of Siki taken in Paris shortly before he became champion. An extravagant character on both sides of the ropes, Siki did not live to see his twenty-ninth birthday. (Photo courtesy of Big Fights, Inc.)

the third, the challenger went berserk. While Siki didn't mind throwing the fight, he wasn't prepared to take a serious beating in the process. Carpentier had been teeing off, and Siki didn't like it. Scared and confused, he threw away the script and savagely tore into Carpentier, lashing out with roundhouse blows. Luckily for Carpentier, Siki didn't have a hand grenade tucked inside his shorts.

The startled champion tried to stave off disaster by blatantly fouling, but Siki, fighting like a man possessed, would not be denied. He continued his brutal onslaught over the next two rounds, hammering the suave matinee idol from one end of the ring to the other, smashing his nose flat and swelling his eyes shut. By the start of the sixth round, Siki's maniacal attack had Carpentier out on his feet, and the fired-up challenger wasted little time finishing the job. He jarred Carpentier's head back with uppercuts and then propelled him halfway through the ropes with a final assault to the body. That's when the fun really began.

Instead of counting out the prostrate Carpentier, referee Henri Bernstein, who was in on the fix, disqualified Siki for tripping and awarded the Frenchman the bout on a foul. Though Carpentier's feet became tangled with Siki's on the way down, it was an accident and in no way contributed to the champion's downfall. At this juncture, all hell broke loose. The crowd was understandably enraged at the referee's scandalous action and refused to leave the stadium. Some spectators rushed the ring and spat in Carpentier's face. With the situation rapidly getting out of hand, the flustered officials huddled, reversed Bernstein's decision and gave Siki the title via a knockout at 1:10 of the sixth round. In an incredible turn of events, what began as a prearranged dive, ended as Siki's greatest moment! He was suddenly Africa's first world champion and the toast of Paris. Unfortunately, he was also poised on the brink of a downward spiral that would ultimately lead to tragedy.

While the French rose to Siki and accepted him as their new hero, the news of his victory was not greeted with nearly as much enthusiasm on the other side of the Atlantic Ocean. Many Americans, the memory of Jack Johnson (the first black heavyweight champion) fresh in their minds, felt France had made a mistake permitting a black man to fight for the light heavyweight title. The editor of the *Springfield Republic* wrote that victories like Siki's might make French colonial subjects "lose their attitudes of respectful admiration for white men." The *Literary Digest* called Siki a "dark cloud on the horizon." Racist rhetoric was not restricted to the editorial pages. Sports writers continually referred to him as a "jungle beast" and crudely joked Siki had "hopped from the branches of a coconut tree right into the ring" and that he was "only one generation removed from a prominent family of Senegalese baboons."

If bigots were worried about Siki moving up in weight class and attempting to become the second black heavyweight champion, they were wasting their energy. Siki's only concern was how best to celebrate his shocking triumph over Carpentier. It was, after all, the Roaring Twenties, and Siki was the latest idol of the boulevards, the king of the cabarets. Women, always one of his many weaknesses, threw themselves at his feet. Siki was even cast in a motion picture called *Dark Alleys,* in an attempt to cash in on his popularity. Nothing was too good for Siki. But he didn't know when to quit. One endless party was a dream come true for Siki, but eventually, others grew tired of his continual indulgence and perpetual indiscretions. Matters came to a head a few months after the Carpentier fight when Siki seconded friend Ercole Balzac in a bout against Maurice Brunier. After Balzac was knocked out, a drunken Siki charged across the ring and punched Brunier's manager, Fernand Ouny. The outraged Federation de Boxe slapped Siki with a nine month suspension and temporarily revoked his title. Angered by his punishment, Siki reacted like a scolded schoolboy and further stirred up trouble by bragging about how he'd "double crossed" Carpentier after originally agreeing to "fall down." Despite the fact Siki's story was given little credence at the time, his welcome had worn thin in France. It was time to hit the road.

Siki made his first—and only—defense against Mike McTigue, March 17, 1923 in Dublin, Ireland. Boxing buffs still chuckle at the stupidity (or was it brazeness?) of a black man defending his title against an Irishman in Dublin on Saint Patrick's day. But that's exactly what Siki did. McTigue, a cunning veteran with good defensive skills, stayed away from the powerful champion for most of the twenty-round bout and won a close decision. Siki's reign as world champion was over practically before it began.

The dethroned Siki engaged in a few more bouts in France and then set sail for North America. He'd planned to reestabish himself in the United States, but years of unchecked carousing and a minimum of training had taken its toll. By the time Siki faced Kid Norfolk at Madison Square Garden on January 14, 1923, he was badly dissipated, a shell of the fearsome slugger who had un-ceremoniously ripped the light heavyweight crown from Carpen-tier's head only a year before. After a fast start, Siki faded and Norfolk won a fifteen-round decision. True to form, Siki quickly drank up his purse and soon embarked on a barnstorming tour of the country. From January 7, 1924 until November 13, 1925, he fought twenty-five times, losing just as often as he won. He appeared wherever he could get a fight; from Memphis to Min-neapolis, from New Orleans to Newark. In between sanctioned bouts, he fought in saloons, speakeasies, and on the streets, brawling and boozing his way through life like a man with a serious death wish. Sports pages across the country carried sensational headlines such as "Siki Running Wild" and "Siki Spends Night in Jail."

Nat Fleischer, editor of *The Ring,* wrote about the day he chanced upon Siki in Manhattan, standing in the middle of 42nd Street directing traffic. The ex-champ was decked out in "evening regalia, with a flowering French cape lined with purple satin, a high silk topper hat, bright red gloves and gray-suede shoes." When a policeman approached to see what all the commotion was about, a monkey leaped out from underneath Siki's cloak and landed on the officer's head. Despite a dismal won-lost record during his tour of America's boxing backwaters, incidents such as this kept Siki's name in the news and helped him garner one last major bout against Paul Berlenbach at Madison Square Garden, March 13, 1925. Berlenbach gave Siki a terrible beating, stopping him in the tenth round with the brave African still on his feet. While Berlenbach used the victory as a springboard to a title-winning bout with McTigue, by the summer of '25, Siki was back fighting second-raters for chump change.

As Siki's career continued to skid downhill, his self-destructive lifestyle continued unabated. He was seldom sober and thought nothing of pulling out of small-town matches, leaving promoters high and dry. Towards the end, considered little more than an exotic oddity, he was reduced to accepting third-rate vaudeville bookings. When his unreliable ways prevented him from obtaining official bouts, he redoubled his street battles. Brushes with the law also became an increasing problem. He was arrested for felonious assualt after pulling a knife on a New York City policeman and slashing the officer's uniform. At the time, Siki was living at 361 West 42nd Street with Lillian Werner Phal, a pretty young mulatto girl he had married while boxing in Memphis. Thanks in part to the pleas of Mrs. Phal, Siki escaped with a $5 fine. Not long after the incident, immigration authorities started proceedings to deport him. But when France announced it would not receive its former war hero, Siki applied to the U.S. for his papers of naturalization.

Siki loved to frequent the speakeasies that dotted the Hell's Kitchen neighborhood where he lived. His idea of a good time was to chug down a gallon of wine and then challenge the nearest bystander to a fight. On one memorable occasion, he wrecked a gin-mill in a drunken rage because the management had the audacity to demand payment for his libation. When Siki left the so-called nightclub, he was followed by thugs and stabbed as retribution. Of course, Siki failed to heed the not-so-subtle warning, and following a short stay in the hospital, was back on the street and up to his old pranks. Another favorite lark he enjoyed was riding all over town in a taxi and then challenging the driver to fight for the fare. Siki seemed to think he was immortal. But he wasn't.

Around 7:00 PM on December 14, 1925, Mrs. Siki encountered her husband at the door of their house. She had just finished packing for a theatrical engagement in Washington, D.C., and they were scheduled to leave the next day. "He said he was going out with the boys for a time," she said. "He said he would see me later." It was the last time Lillian Phal saw her husband alive. Exactly where Siki spent the early hours of the evening is unknown, but several people later reported seeing him rolling uncertainly along Ninth Avenue at midnight. Later, at approximately 2:30 AM on the morning of December 15, Patrolman John J. Meehan of the West 13th Street Station, came upon the fighter, who was apparently headed home after a night on the town. According to a report the next day in *The New York Times,* Meehan said Siki seemed "a trifle unsteady on his feet," but immediately hailed him.

"Hello," said Siki. "I'm on my way home."

"You'd better keep going in that direction," counseled Meehan, and Siki, with a wave of his hand, moved off.

Four hours later, Patrolman Meehan was walking his beat along Ninth Avenue when he chanced to look up 41st Street, and about one hundred feet from the corner saw a man lying face down at the curb. It was Siki. Meehan summoned a doctor, who arrived shortly along with Detectives McNamara and Sheehan. Dr. Bassatoa pronounced Siki dead from internal hemorrhage caused by two bullet wounds in the back. Judging from a pool of blood discovered a few houses away from the spot where Siki's body was found, the detectives deduced the fighter had staggered to his feet after being shot and attempted to find his way home before finally collapsing and bleeding to death. On the opposite side of the street, in front of 33 West 41st, McNamara and Sheehan found a small .32 caliber pistol, with two of the six cartridges discharged. Two bullets recovered during Siki's autopsy proved the revolver was the murder weapon. One slug had penetrated Siki's left lung and the other had lodged in his kidneys. Though Siki's murder was never solved, police theorized he had probably tried to repeat his previous speakeasy-wrecking escapades. This time, however, his assailant had made sure Siki, only twenty-eight years old, went down for the full count. Unsolved murder was not an unusal occurrence in Hell's Kitchen, and while it is generally accepted that Siki was killed by hoodlums, anything is possible. Who knows? Maybe the police, tired of all the problems Siki had created, decided to rid themselves of a nuisance. Ten days before he was slain, Siki was fined another $5; this time for slapping the face of Patrolman Louis Smith. Whoever killed Siki, they made sure his back was turned before they pulled the trigger.

Siki was a unique, larger-than-life character, even by boxing's extravagant standards. There has never been anyone quite like him. When his wife learned of his murder, she reportedly said, "He was a good boy, just mischievous. He wouldn't harm anyone." That was probably true, but only when he was sober. When drunk, Siki was mean and dangerous, a man driven by inner demons, the roots of which can only be surmised. Most likely, he was simply overwhelmed by life, exposed too young to temptation and allowed to run amok. His autopsy revealed that, although he was still an impressive-looking physical specimen, he was "suffering from adhesions resulting from pleurisy and a general anemic condition" at the time of his death.

When the news reached France, Carpentier expressed his regrets at the wasted life and senseless death of his former conqueror: "It seems a pity," Carpentier said, "that an athlete of such magnificent gifts should have met with this end. The time has passed when boxers can indulge in drinking and carousing and be champion. I only hope poor Siki's fate will be a lesson to aspiring pugilists."

Judging by subsequent boxing history, it was a lesson lost.

5

Bums and Bad Guys

They found James Ambrose dead in his cell, a gash in his right forearm, all the blood drained out of him. A violent end for a violent man. Nobody knows for certain if Ambrose was his real name. At various times he'd been known as Frank Murray, Francis Murray and Francis Martin. But to followers of the prize ring during the first half of the 19th century, he was known as Yankee Sullivan, one of America's very first boxing heroes—and a hardcore roughneck if ever there was one.

Sullivan, born in County Cork, Ireland, April 12, 1813, apparently consorted with unsavory elements of society from an early age, quickly earning a reputation as a street brawler and petty criminal. Before he was twenty-five, Sullivan graduated to more serious crime and was arrested and shipped to a penal colony in Botany Bay, Australia, to atone for his sins. The exact nature of his offense is unclear; some say it was burglary, others murder. He engaged in a few bare-knuckle bouts with other convicts while in

Australia, but soon stowed away aboard a ship bound for America. He lingered less than a year in New York City and then sneaked back into England, intent on establishing a name for himself in the London prize ring.

He succeeded in obtaining a bout with Hammer Lane, a noted London pugilist. True to his name, Lane hammered the stuffings out of Sullivan until Lane's right arm was accidentally fractured in the third round. Sullivan took full advantage of Lane's misfortune, pecking away at his injury until the brave Brit threw in the sponge, sixteen tortuous rounds later. It wasn't exactly the sort of tactic calculated to win favor with the English Fancy, and Sullivan, still technically a fugitive, soon found it advisable to hightail it back to the United States.

A bully and a braggart, he quickly found a niche in New York's Bowery, using the tainted win over Lane to bolster his standing in American pugilistic circles. It wasn't long before Sullivan found himself running a rowdy saloon called the Sawdust House. His patron's were a lively cross-section of poor Irish immigrants and assorted low lifes, united in their common love for strong drink and a good old-fashioned brawl. Prizefighting was still an underground sport, but rapidly growing in popularity. Sullivan had a series of successful bouts in and around New York City and became something of a hero; a revered member of the masculine subculture he inhabited. In those days, neighborhood gangs worked hand-in-hand with political groups, and Sully provided muscle and ballot-stuffing services for Tammany Hall politicians. He was a big man in the Bowery, and the Sawdust House a center of both political and pugilistic activity.

Sullivan's superiority was eventually challenged by Tom Hyer, a powerful butcher and a native-born American. This later point was an important one. There was considerable competition for jobs between natives and immigrants, and the tension between the two factions greatly increased interest in the fight. There were also hard feelings of a personal nature. About a year before they met in the ring, a half-drunk Sullivan had tried to mug Hyer in an oyster bar,

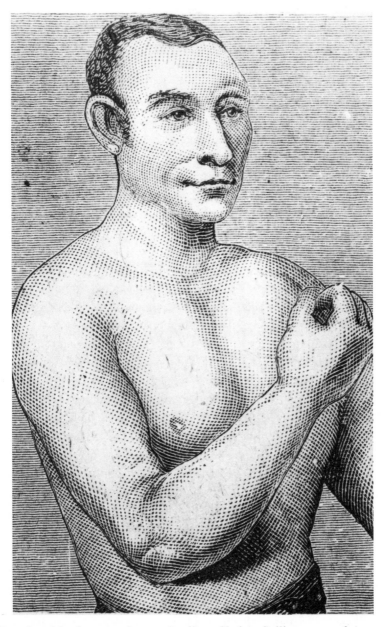

Bare-knuckles boxer and street hooligan Yankee Sullivan, one of America's first fistic heroes. (Photo courtesy of *The Ring* magazine)

only to end up getting pummeled for his trouble. It all added up to the sort of hype today's press agents would kill for, and the long-awaited grudge match finally took place in a snow-covered field at Still Pong Heights, Maryland, February 7, 1849. In the end, Hyers proved too big and too strong. He battered Sullivan into bloody defeat over sixteen bitterly-contested rounds, collecting a $5,000 side bet in the process.

The last bout of any consequence for Sullivan came against John Morrissey, a bartending bruiser from Troy, New York. Sullivan was forty-one years old by the time he fought Morrissey, but hadn't mellowed one iota. Though a big underdog, he controlled the fight for the first thirty-seven rounds, pounding Morrissey into a sickening pulp. Defeat seemed assured, but Morrissey refused to quit and was still soaking up punishment when a riot came to his rescue. Things started to get out of hand when Morrissey pinned Sully on the ropes and began to strangle him. This was a desperately illegal move, even by the rough-and-tumble standards of 1853. Naturally, Sullivan's cornermen immediately pounced to his aide and all hell broke loose. Supporters of both boxers filled the ring and slugged it out in a degrading free-for-all. As chaos reigned, the timekeeper ordered the thirty-eighth round to begin and Morrissey came to scratch. Sullivan, however, was too busy trading blows with Morrissey's second, "Awful" Orvil Gardner, to heed the call. Amid the turmoil, the umpire declared Morrissey the winner, ending one of the wildest contests of the bare-knuckle era. In a way, it was a fitting farewell, a crazy exclamation point to Sullivan's uproarious boxing career.

Not long after his infamous donnybrook with Morrissey, Sullivan headed west to California, where he resumed his nefarious political activities, throwing his weight around and fixing elections. These were lawless times, and in 1856, elements of San Francisco's merchant class decided to rid themselves of certain individuals they deemed "pests to society." Vigilante groups were formed and Sullivan was among the unlucky thugs rounded up by the self-appointed posse. A kangaroo court quickly adjourned and two men were charged with murder and hanged. Sullivan escaped the noose, but was sentenced to deportation. Four days later, he was discovered dead in his cell, most likely a victim of foul play. While the vigilantes maintained he committed suicide, several local newspapers suggested someone had given old Sully a helping hand.

Say what you will about Al "Bummy" Davis, he went down swinging.

One of the dirtiest fighters to ever butt open an eyebrow or dig a hook to the balls, Davis was a quick-tempered hothead. He fought every bout as if his life hinged on the outcome, barreling into his opponents with uncontrolled fury. If they'd have let him, he'd probably have taken a baseball bat into the ring. From the late 1930s through the mid 1940s, "Bummy" Davis was the fighter the fans loved to hate.

Born Abraham Davidoff, January 26, 1918, he grew up in Brooklyn's tough Canarsie district. The name "Bummy" had nothing to do with his reputation. It was a corruption of "Boomy," a family nickname that grew out of the Hebratic "Avrum," or Abraham. He began boxing professionally in 1937, quickly establishing himself as a favorite at neighborhood clubs. His let-it-all-hang-out style and bullheaded courage went over well with the local crowd, and it wasn't until he began fighting established boxers at major venues that his method earned the displeasure of the fans.

A dynamite left-hooker, Davis entered the big time by ending the career of Tony Canzoneri in 1939, knocking out the washed-up future Hall-of-Famer in three rounds, and then following up with a fifth-round KO over future junior welterweight champ Tippy Larkin. A points loss to Lou Ambers was only a minor setback, but in November of 1940, Davis finally ran up against someone just as tough—and dirty—as he was in welterweight champion Fritzie Zivic. While it lasted, their non-title bout was total anarchy. Zivic, a past master at every underhanded trick in the book, repeatedly stuck his thumb into Davis' eye in the opening round and knocked him down at the bell with a blatant cheap shot. Davis was infuriated

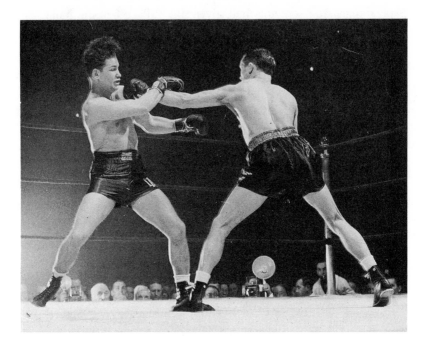

Al "Bummy" Davis (left) pulls away from a jab thrown by Fritzie Zivic during their infamous, foul-infested bout at Madison Square Garden, November 15, 1940. (Photo courtesy of *The Ring* magazine)

and stormed out for the second round with murder in his eyes. He completely blew his cool, delivering one low blow after another. The referee had no alternative but to disqualify Davis before he transformed Zivic into a soprano. In the uproar that followed, the New York athletic commission fined Davis $2,500 and suspended him indefinitely. After a stint with the U.S. Army, Davis was forgiven and his boxing license reinstated. Zivic, however, wasn't nearly so magnanimous in their rematch. He plastered "Bummy" all over the ring, stopping him in the tenth round.

Still a drawing card despite his losses to Zivic, Davis fought on for the next four years. He won most of his bouts, but was knocked out by future middleweight champion Rocky Graziano in 1945. Then, a strange thing happened. Davis launched a comeback against Johnny Jones in Brooklyn and won on a foul! The irony of the situation can only be fully appreciated in retrospect. The disqualification victory proved to be Davis' last sanctioned fight. An entirely unscheduled altercation was soon to prove his final undoing.

Davis sold a tavern he'd owned on Remsen Street in Canarsie to a man named Art Polansky. Not long after completing the transaction, the fighter stopped by Dudy's Bar and Grill to shoot the breeze with the new owner. At the time, Brooklyn was plagued by a rash of armed robberies perpetrated by a gang of thugs operating out of a large limousine. They had already robbed six taverns and shot a sixteen-year-old girl to death before arriving at Dudy's around 2:45 AM, November 21, 1945. Besides Davis and Polansky, the only other people inside the bar when the robbers got there were bartender George Miller, an unidentified off-duty cop and a drunk asleep at one of the tables.

All four intruders came through the door with their pistols drawn. One holdup man got the drop on Miller, one guarded the door and the other two trained their weapons on Davis, Polansky and the policeman. Polansky had already turned over the night's take, about $150, to the hoods when Davis spoke up.

"Why don't you leave him alone?" asked Davis. "The guy just bought the place. Give the guy a break."

"And why don't you mind your own business," snarled the holdup man, shoving his pistol in the fighter's face.

That did it. Davis snapped, jumped out of his chair and lashed out with his famous left hook. The punch smashed into the punk's face and sent him reeling backwards. The other gunmen panicked and started firing, but their shots went wild. Davis shoved a table aside and wildly rushed the four armed men, swinging haymakers and yelling curses as he charged. It was a stupid, yet wonderfully courageous thing to do, typical of the hotheaded Davis. According to a report in *The New York Times* the following day, "The guns blazed again. Three bullets hit the fighter. One went through his neck and cracked his spin, one went through his back into his left lung, and a third lodged in his right arm. But "Bummy" kept swinging with his left."

The gunmen beat a hasty retreat and sped away in their car. But Davis wasn't finished yet. Dazed and bloody, he stumbled towards his own car, apparently intending to give chase. A few steps past the barroom threshold, he staggered and fell flat on his face. Davis was dead before the ambulance reached the scene of the crime.

In another ironic twist, it was later learned Davis had planned to leave for Florida the next day to tend a string of race horses he owned. He'd originally intended to visit Polansky the previous Monday, but changed his mind because of a torrential rainstorm. The downpour had been indirectly responsible for Davis being in the wrong place at the wrong time. But it also allowed the man who had been considered a villain in the ring to die a hero.

The challenger came out of his corner at the sound of the opening bell winging punches like there was no tomorrow. He knew a quick knockout was his best—perhaps only—chance for victory. He had to gamble, go for broke. The challenger connected with a right, then followed with a left. Suddenly, the champion was on the canvas. The crowd of 16,129 at Madison Square Garden stood as one and cut loose with a deafening roar. Was it a miracle? Was the five-to-one underdog going to spring an unbelievable upset. Was Frankie DePaula about to become champion of the world?

More embarrased than hurt, the champion quickly regained his feet. He'd show this upstart who was boss. He tore into DePaula and unleashed a withering series of combinations. Three knockdowns later it was all over; the winner and still light heavyweight champion of the world . . . Bob Foster.

DePaula's moment of glory was short lived, his flirtation with the big time abruptly over. He would never box at Madison Square Garden again. It was back to his job as a barroom bouncer, back to small purses—and not too many of those. Less than two years after he'd had the world champ on the deck, DePaula was dead.

"Frankie was one of the most likeable guys you've ever seen in your life, and one of the most stupid guys you've ever seen in your life," summed up Al Braverman, the Runyonesque character who trained DePaula throughout his career. "If a friend said he was in trouble, Frankie would run down to a bar to help out, even if there was a gun waiting for him. He knocked out a helluva lot more guys in bars than he ever did in the ring."

A product of rough working-class neighborhood in Jersey City, DePaula made up for his vast deficiencies as a boxer with a thunderous punch. He could knock you silly with either hand and enjoyed a large following at the small clubs that dotted North Jersey towns such as Union City, Totowa, Teaneck and Secaucus. And when he crossed the Hudson River to fight in the Big Apple, DePaula took his rowdy fans with him by the scores. It was his ability to attract paying customers, more than his limited fistic skills, that eventually earned him a shot at the title.

As one might expect, DePaula figured training was for chumps. Who needed it? After all, a couple of good hooks and the other guy was on his face eating rosin.

"Frankie did most of his training in the shit house," said Braverman, chuckling at the memory. "He was supposed to run around the park, but he'd duck into the men's room and throw water all over himself from the fountain. Then he'd come back and say, 'Look Al, I'm sweating like a bull.' I'd say, 'Okay, how come this sweat is cold?' Then he'd holler, 'Who told you? Who ratted me out?'"

Despite his lack of dedication, DePaula won far more than he lost and seldom failed to give his fans their money's worth. In 1968, he put together a string of five consecutive knockouts, three of them in New York City. In an attempt to capitalize on his growing popularity, the Garden matched him with former middleweight and light heavyweight chamion Dick Tiger, who had recently lost his 175-pound belt to Foster and was gunning for a rematch. Tiger, nearing the end of a legendary career, was also a big favorite with the fans and over 13,000 people turned out to see the match. They were not disappointed.

The first four rounds were total mayhem. Tiger was down in the second, but rallied back to floor DePaula twice in the third. Then, just when it looked like he was finished, DePaula dropped Tiger again in the fourth. Poorly conditioned as usual, the Jersey City brawler couldn't muster the energy to finish the job, and Tiger soon regained control of the bout and eventually won a unanimous decision. Though the pace slowed considerably the second half, the savage encounter was selected as *The Ring* magazine's Fight of the Year, and despite the loss, DePaula was a bigger hero than ever.

When the time came for Foster's first title defense, it was DePaula, not Tiger, who got the call. Foster had devastated Tiger in less than four rounds and the Garden knew a rematch would do scant business at the box office. DePaula, on the other hand, was guaranteed to have the turnstiles humming.

Though he enjoyed a reputation as a fearless slugger, according to Braverman, DePaula was not exactly the bravest boxer he'd ever handled. In fact, Big Al frequenlty resorted to intimidation in order to pry the best results from his reluctant tiger.

"I had to give him a slap in the face every now and then, pull his hair, or pinch him on the inside of the thigh, to get what I wanted out of him. He feared what I would do to him in the corner more than the fight itself."

Braverman, regarded as somewhat of a Svengali when it comes to motivating fighters, devised a scheme he hoped would intimidate Foster and give DePaula a psychological edge.

"I told Frankie before we went to the weigh-in, 'Frankie, what I'm gonna do is press you on the back of the neck. When I do that, you look at Foster and say, 'I'm gonna knock you dead, you mutt.' So we go and I touch the back of Frankie's neck. All I hear is a mumble. So, I touched his neck again, and he mumbled again. I told him, 'Speak up!' He mumbled again. Frankie didn't have the guts to go through with what I told him to do. As the saying goes, the shit was running down his leg. I knew the fight was lost right then and there."

DePaula fought twice after the Foster blowout, knocking out a couple of third-rate opponents at minor venues. Who knows? He may have eventually slugged his way back into contention, but destiny was not in DePaula's corner. In 1969, he was arrested, along with his manager Anthony Jospeph Garafola and Richard Phelan, and charged with hijacking $75,000 worth of copper ingots from the Port Newark docks. In May, a jury acquitted DePaula of both theft and possession of stolen property, but could not agree on conspiracy charges against Garafola, Phelan and four other men allegedly involved in the crime. All six were facing the possibility of a new trial when DaPaula was gunned down gangland style outside the home of a young woman he dated. Two high-powered bullets lodged in DePaula's spinal column, paralyzing him.

The fighter lingered in Jersey City Medical Center for four months before finally dying September 14, 1970. According to Ira Clark, associate director of the hospital, DePaula, 31, died from pneumonia brought on by the debilitating effects of his gunshot wounds. Suspicion naturally focused on Garafola and Phelan, but no proof of their involvement was ever produced and nobody was ever charged with DePaula's murder. While the crime remains "of-

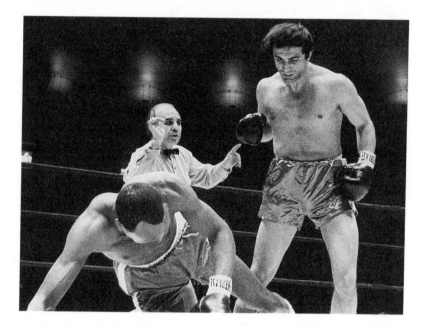

Frankie DePaula stands over Bob Foster after knocking down the light
heavyweight champion in the first round of their 1969 title bout. Foster
recovered to stop DePaula later in the same round (Photo courtesy of *The
Ring* magazine)

ficially" unsolved, street talk indicated DePaula was, for the last time, a victim of his own stupidity.

"Frankie hung with a very bad element," maintained Braverman. "They were dealing crap. The story that went around was that Frankie took a bag of crap off 'em and wouldn't pay for it. And these people finally got even with him."

In his old neighborhood, they still say DePaula might have been champion if he'd had the guts and discipline to match his punch. They say he'd still be alive today if he hadn't been stupid enough to try and cheat the hoods he hung out with. But then, if he acted like a normal, rational person, he wouldn't have been Frankie DePaula.

"He was the kind of kid you knew from the beginning was gonna end up like Swiss cheese," said Braverman, providing an epitaph for the man whose corner he worked for thirty professional fights. "By that I mean, he had to get shot. He was that kind of crazy, crazy human being."

There was no two ways about it. Heavyweight contender Oscar Bonavena was getting it on with whorehouse owner Joe Conforte's wife, Sally. People who knew Joe Conforte claim he couldn't have cared less. Sally and Joe's union was a marriage of convenience, more or less a business arrangement. What pissed Joe off was the fact Oscar was doing it at the Mustang Ranch, Conforte's legal brothel in Storey County, Nevada. Such flagrant disrespect was an intolerable insult to a proud Sicilian like Conforte, and he gave his security staff strict orders to keep the fighter off his property. Of course, Bonavena wasn't the kind of guy to be easily intimidated. He'd had Joe Frazier on the deck twice and given Muhammad Ali just about all he could handle. And besides, damn near everybody agreed that the thirty-three-year-old boxer was a real nut case.

Bonavena came roaring out of Argentina in the mid-1960s like a reincarnation of Luis Firpo, the original "Wild Bull of the Pampas." And like Firpo—who knocked Jack Dempsey through the ropes in their legendary 1923 match—Bonavena held his own with the best heavyweights of his time. He was a barrel-chested brawler with a crude hooking style and a cement block for a head. Outside of the ring, he stampeded through life doing pretty much as he pleased. Promoter Joe Hand recalled when Oscar came to Philadelphia to challenge Frazier for the heavyweight title in 1968.

"He had temper tantrums," remembered Hand, who was an officer with Cloverlay (Frazier's management group) at the time. "Part of the deal was that we were responsible for the fighters' hotel bills. When Oscar checked out of the Franklin Motor Inn, we had to pay to have his suite refurbished. He broke the sink. He broke the bathtub and put his first through the door. He was an uncontrollable type guy with a bad, bad temper."

By the time Bonavena arrived in Reno to fight Billy Joiner in February 1976, he was definitely on the skids. Nevertheless, Oscar was still rated No. 7 in the world and could look forward to at least one more big payday. After beating Joiner, Bonavena decided to stay on in Reno. He dumped manager Loren Cassina and hooked up with the Confortes. Sally soon became his manger of record, and though probably fronting for her husband, she took a *very* active interest. They definitely made an odd couple. Looking at Mrs. Conforte, it's hard to imagine the fighter being overcome with passion. She was a plain, middle-aged woman with a white beehive hairdo, and Bonavena's reputation as a "cocksman" didn't normally include squiring matronly-looking ladies. Be that as it may, he'd already squandered most of his considerable boxing earnings and was probably in the market for a "Sugar Mamma."

Bonavena became a popular, larger-than-life character around Reno, attending fight cards and mingling with the folks at various casino showrooms. He'd always been good copy, and that's one thing which hadn't deteriorated with the passage of time.

"Reno is the same as Argentina," he told *Reno Gazette* reporter Steve Sneddon. "The people are so sweet. When I'm in the hotel people say, 'Hi, Oscar.' I love Reno. Maybe I never leave."

But by mid-May, it became obvious that not everybody in the area was in love with the gregarious prizefighter. On May 16, Bonavena complained to Storey County Sheriff Bob Del Carlo that

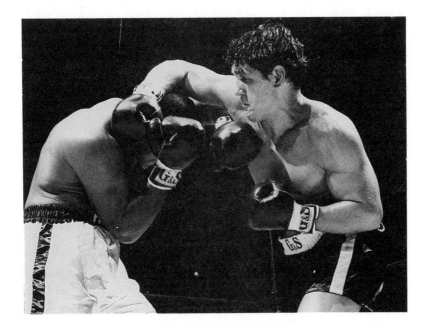

Former heavyweight contender Oscar Bonavena (right) wades into Zora Folley during their ten-round bout at Madison Square Garden, February 26, 1965. It was the Argentine brawler's first loss as a professional. (Photo courtesy of *The Ring* magazine)

his Lockwood trailer home had been broken into and some of his personal property, including his passport, had been destroyed. Six days later, Bonavena showed up at the gate to the Mustang Ranch (a fort-like compound complete with a high fence and two guard towers) at around 6:00 AM and demanded to see Conforte. Whether or not he thought the brothel keeper was involved in the break-in at his trailer is unclear. Whatever the case, Oscar was in one of his ugly moods.

John Colletti, a private investigator working as Conforte's bodyguard, met Bonavena at the gate and told him to leave. After a five to ten minute conversation with Colletti, the fighter left the bordello entrance, walked to his car and opened the door. At that point, someone yelled "Freeze!" and a split second later, a shot rang out. A bullet from a 30.06 rifle sliced through the desert air, smacked into Bonavena's chest and tore through his heart. He fell over backwards, dead on the spot. Colletti turned to his right and saw Willard Rose Brymer, another Conforte bodyguard, with a rifle in his hand at waist level, pointed toward Bonavena.

A SWAT team from the Washoe County Sheriff's Department was the first to arrive at the scene. As the brothel was about a quarter of a mile over the Storey County line, the officers were technically out of their jurisdiction. They were confronted by an angry Conforte who called them "dogs" and told them he wanted no publicity in any news media about Bonavena's death.

"It's just a dead man," Conforte told the cops. "You can't do anything about it now. So we got a dead man here. So what?"

Meanwhile, Brymer had disappeared back inside, rifle still in hand, where he was discovered in the kitchen, eating cereal and drinking orange juice. "He was sitting down, chowing down," reported ranch employee Jim Peri, Jr. "When I asked him why he shot Bonavena, he said, 'I told him to freeze. He went for his boot, and I shot him.'"

Brymer, a convicted ex-felon, was a real nasty piece of work. A few weeks before he shot Bonavena, he'd been charged with assault in an incident which had occurred near the brothel. According to the Washoe County District Attorney's Office, Brymer had stopped passersby at gunpoint, forced them to lie on the ground and then kicked them. Sheriff Del Carlo, who, along with the district attorney, were charged with policing prostitution houses and its employees, had told Conforte three days before the shooting to get rid of Brymer.

Approximately an hour after he killed Bonavena, Brymer emerged from the building and handed over the rifle. He was handcuffed by Storey County Sheriff's Sgt. Bill Tilton and taken into custody. Conforte stood by Brymer during the trial and put up his restaurant as a $250 thousand bond for his bodyguard's bail. Even while the case was being processed, Brymer couldn't stay out of trouble. He beat up a deputy who apparently pistol-whipped one of the defendant's dogs. However, no criminal charges were ever filed in that particular altercation.

The final outcome of the Bonavena case was almost as arbitrary as his death. Despite the fact another of Conforte's employees, Lloyd "Mac" McNulty, admitted to Sgt. Tilton that he had placed a gun underneath Bonanena's body before the police arrived at the death scene, Brymer was allowed to plead no contest to a reduced charge of voluntary manslaughter. As it turned out, the planting of the gun was an unnecessary precaution. Bonavena was already packing his own .38 caliber revolver.

Brymer was sentenced to serve just two years in Nevada State Prison. Shortly before his release in June 1979, he was interviewed by UPI reporter Cy Ryan. Brymer still maintained his rifle had originally been pointed at the ground when he saw Bonavena apparently going for a pistol in his boot. He said the rifle had discharged accidentally from the momentum of the upward swing. When asked how he felt about Bonavena, the thirty-four-year-old convict replied, "I can't say anything bad about him."

Nobody had a bad word to say about Roberto Medina either.

"He was the nicest kid. It was always 'Yes sir, no sir.' He was a model athlete, the kind you'd want the other kids to follow," remembered his matchmaker, Brad Jacobs.

"He was a helluva nice guy," echoed his amateur trainer Jack Rose. "He had a van and would drive the St. Petersburg Boxing Clubs all over; ten, twelve fellows, no matter where we were fighting."

"I had him over to my house for Passover and he read the prayers with my grandchildren. He was like a member of the family," recollected his manager Mike Blumberg.

It came as a tremendous shock when they discovered Roberto Medina wasn't who they thought he was. In fact, his name wasn't even Roberto Medina.

Following a successful amateur career that included winning the 1984 Florida Golden Gloves and Sunshine State Games championship, Medina turned professional in March of '84 under the banner of Tampa-based Alessi Promotions. He became a regular performer on the Florida circuit, and by July of '85 had tallied a record of twelve wins, one loss and a draw. His management decided it was time to gamble and take a step up in class. Medina was matched with Olympic gold medalist and future IBF junior welterweight champion Meldrick Taylor. The contest was part of ABC's "Wide World of Sports" program featuring four former Olympians, broadcast live from Norfolk, Virginia.

The Taylor-Medina bout turned out to be the only competitive match on the card. Though Medina was the "opponent," he stayed with the gifted Taylor throughout the entire six rounds, bravely absorbing everything Taylor could throw at him. There was no doubt Medina had lost, but his courageous stand won the hearts of the crowd and he left the ring with the sound of applause ringing in his ears. It was a moral victory if nothing else.

"I noticed on the way back to the dressing room that we were escorted by at least ten more cops than when we entered," remembered Jacobs. "At first, I just thought the extra security was because Roberto had put up such a great fight and they wanted to stop the fans from mobbing him. But when we got back to the dressing room, there were so many cops around, I realized something must be up.

Joe Garcia, known to fight fans as Roberto Medina, is led away by
authorities after losing to Meldrick Taylor in a nationally televised bout in
Norfolk, Virginia. (Photo courtesy of *The Ring* magazine)

"One of them pulled me to the side and told me that they had reason to believe Medina was an escaped convict and wanted him to go to the station house with them so they could check his fingerprints. Roberto was pretty beat up, but they wouldn't even let him take a shower. When we left the arena, we were suddenly surrounded by photographers and reporters, all of them screaming at us at the same time. You'd think the President had been assassinated. We went downtown to the jail and they took Roberto to a holding area. Then they told me they were sure he was the guy they'd been looking for."

The boxer known as Roberto Medina was actually Juan E. Garcia, a man the police categorized as a "career criminal." He had a record of sixty-one arrests in the Denver, Colorado, area alone, and had been a fugitive since escaping from a minimum security Colorado prison in 1982. Garcia had fled from a work-release program and kept going all the way to Florida, where he had started a new life as Medina.

The authorities had been closing in on Garcia for some time. They had suspected Medina was their man, but weren't sure until he took his robe off prior to the Taylor fight. A rose tattooed on his chest was the giveaway.

"When we saw that tattoo, we knew we had the right guy," said Lt. Curtis M. Todd, Jr., of the Norfolk Police Department. "Before that, the identification was iffy. He gave himself away."

Garcia's audacity was astonishing. Though the Taylor fight was his first on a major network, he had previously appeared several times on cable television.

"I figured that if I didn't get in any trouble, no one would find me. I loved boxing so much I guess I just ignored thoughts of being found out. Sometimes, you take a gamble," rationalized Garcia from his jail cell. "I guess I loved boxing so much I was willing to take that gamble. So here I am. I'm sorry I disappointed some people, but I'm not sorry I went to Norfolk for the fight. We put on a helluva show for the fans."

"If ever a fellow wanted to be rehabilitated, it was Roberto Medina," said Rose. "He was a good carpenter and worked all day during his amateur career. He was very proud and wanted people to respect him."

"He asked to see me after they cross-checked his fingerprints and booked him," said Jacobs. "He was crying and said he was sorry, and that he'd just wanted another chance."

There were a lot of other people who also thought Garcia deserved another chance. He'd led a spotless life since escaping from prison and friends and admirers launched a letter-writing campaign in his behalf. Approximately a year and a half after his recapture, Garcia was paroled. He returned to Florida to resume his boxing career, but met little success. Overmatched, he lost a few bouts and faded from the scene.

"A friend of mine gave Roberto a job selling religious statues," reported Rose. "But he started stealing the money he took in and my friend fired him. Roberto said he was so used to stealing, he just couldn't help himself."

6

Self-Inflicted Wounds

The man sat in a secluded corner of the nightclub, head bowed, his fingers pressed deep into the corners of his eyes. His debilitating headaches were chronic and seldom gave him any respite. Day after day, the agonizing pain haunted him, a legacy from his boxing career. He had been hit so hard so often, there was a displacement at the base of his skull where it had once been attached to the top of his vertebrae. In a manner of speaking former world light heavyweight champion Freddie Mills had had his head knocked off.

Sadly, endless headaches were not the only problem making Mills' life miserable. Business at his once fashionable nightclub at Charing Cross Road in London had dropped off dramatically, and the deed to his house was being held by the bank to guarantee an overdraft of £4,000. The frequent television and radio appearances which formerly padded his wallet and fed his ego had dwindled to none. And to make matters even worse, his love life was a shambles. Mills' world was falling apart at the seams, and try as he might, he just couldn't put it back together again.

It hadn't always been that way, of course. Not too long before, Mills had been one of the most sought-after personalities in Great Britain. Even after his fighting days were over, he stayed in the public eye, constantly in demand, a beloved figure who delighted everybody with his charismatic personality and mischievous sense of humor. When his long and distinguished career came to an end, he'd naturally gravitated towards show-biz and soon became a regular performer on such British television programs as "65 Special," "Sporting Fanfare," and Dickie Henderson's "Saturday Spectacular." But as the 1960s approached the halfway point, other heroes replaced him in the fickle eye of the public. Mills found his phone rang less and less. Even his nightclub, which had been launched with great fanfare in 1963 with film stars Jean Simmons and her husband Stewart Granger in attendance, had lost a considerable sum of money after a promising start. Practically every penny of the £100,000 he'd earned as a boxer was gone. For a man who had been highly successful most of his adult life, things couldn't get much worse.

The packed house at the Radford Social club in Coventry gave the former middleweight champion of the world a big cheer when he ducked between the ropes. Many had followed his career since his brilliant amateur days in nearby Leamington Spa, but that seemed so long ago, practically in another lifetime. On this particular night, the ex-champ was not even wearing boxing gloves when he entered the ring. In a scene reminiscent of Rod Serling's *Requiem for a Heavyweight,* Randolph Turpin, the man who had once beaten the incomparable Sugar Ray Robinson, had been reduced to groveling around the canvas as a professional wrestler.

Turpin's opponent that evening was "Prince Barnu," supposedly from the jungles of Brazil. In actuality, Barnu was Fred Barnes, a local junk car dealer who moonlighted on the grunt-and-groan circuit. The farce ended in a draw when both men fell from the ring and were unable to climb back within the stipulated time.

Though Turpin's £100 wrestling purse didn't seem like much

compared to the approximately £300,000 he'd grossed as a boxer, he was happy to have it, nonetheless. In fact, he needed every shilling he could get his hands on. The Inland Revenue was dunning him for delinquent income tax, and the back street cafe he ran with his wife wasn't exactly a gold mine. Turpin hoped the cafe would be a stepping stone to better things. Maybe another guest house like the one he used to own in Wales. But in truth, they were barely keeping their heads above water. There isn't much money in frying up sausage and Spam for truck drivers and factory workers. If it hadn't been for the wrestling money, they would have gone under already.

Turpin had been a magnificent boxer, at his best, perhaps the finest Britain has ever produced. The child of an interracial marriage, he had overcome prejudice and poverty to emerge as an international sportsman capable of filling major venues on both sides of the Atlantic Ocean. His prestige reached its zenith in 1951 when Turpin outpointed Robinson to win the middleweight title. His shocking victory instantly transformed him into a national hero and a throng of over 20,000 people jammed the streets outside Leamington Spa's town hall to welcome him home afterward. Less than fifteen years later, only a pitiful fraction of their numbers turned out for his funeral.

Though Mills and Turpin were two totally different kinds of men from dissimilar backgrounds, they are inevitably bound together by their common experiences: They were both pivotal figures in the boxing boom that rejuvenated the sport in Britain following World War II. Both beat American opponents to become world champions, and both lost the title in their first defense. Both also absorbed shocking punishment in the ring and suffered greatly for their valor, especially Mills. They also shared the calamity of watching the fortunes they each earned with their fists slip through their fingers. And tragically, both met wretched ends in an eerily similar fashion.

Mills grew up in Bournemouth, a seaside resort town on the southern coast of England known for its mild climate. The youngest son of Tom and Lottie Mills, he grew up in a warm family atmosphere; an energetic, good-natured boy who everyone took an instant liking to. His older brother Charlie fancied himself as a boxer and trained nightly in a shed at the back of the Turpin home on Terrace Street. Much to the horror of their mother, it wasn't long before Freddie joined his brother in the old shed, skipping rope, sparring and punching the bag. A broad-shouldered lad with a square jaw, beetle-brow and a head of thick black hair, Mills loved boxing from the start and it came as no surprise when he announced his intention of becoming a professional fighter.

He turned pro in 1936 and for the next several years kept up a frantic pace. Not only was he a regular performer at licensed cards at such venues as Bournemouth's Westover ice rink, he also put in lengthy stints with carnival boxing booths. Mills routinely took on all comers at the Chipperfield's Circus and also traveled with Sam McKeown's roving booth. The booths had always been a nursery for generations of British boxers, and world champions such as Benny Lynch. Rinty Monaghan and Jimmy Wilde were all proud alumnae of these colorful institutions. By the time Mills entered the Royal Air Force on New Year's Day 1940, he was already an established headliner with over fifty pro bouts under his belt, not to mention literally hundreds of booth encounters. He had developed a crowd-pleasing style that featured a blistering, two-fisted attack and more courage than any one man is supposed to possess. Mill's devil-may-care attitude between the ropes was probably an extension of his out-of-the-ring personality. Always eager to be liked by others, Freddie thought nothing of absorbing frightful punishment to please his fans.

The RAF made Mills a physical training instructor, which allowed him plenty of access to workout facilities. Throughout the war years, he continued to make steady progress as a professional boxer, thanks in part to an understanding brass who appreciated the

Randy Turpin (left) shakes hands with Canadian Gordon Wallace prior to their meeting in London on October 18, 1955. Wallace stopped the washed-up former champion in the fourth round. (Photo courtesy of Peltz Boxing Promotions)

A young Freddie Mills strikes a pose for the camera. Mills worked his way up from carnival boxing booths to become light heavyweight champion of the world. (Photo courtesy of *The Ring* magazine)

benefit of organized sport to the morale of a nation entrenched in a grueling war. In 1942, the government lifted the ban on outdoor sporting events and Mills was matched with old favorite Len Harvey for the British and Empire light heavyweight titles. The match was a huge success and attracted 30,000 spectators to the Tottenham Hotspur football grounds to see a battle that pitted an RAF sergeant (Mills) with a pilot officer (Harvey) from the same branch of the service. It was quite an occasion and Mills responded splendidly, sending the favored Harvey through the ropes and into the press section for a second-round knockout. It was a truly spectacular victory and announced Mills' arrival as a major attraction in no uncertain terms.

The same year Mills rocketed to the top of British boxing with his thrilling knockout over Harvey, a fourteen-year-old Turpin joined the Leamington Boys Club, along with his brother Jackie. Their eldest brother, Dick, had been a pro since 1937 and it seemed only natural for the younger boys to follow in his footsteps. Even before embarking on his amateur career, Randolph and Jackie teamed up to box exhibitions on Dick's cards. Billed as "Alexander and Moses," the youngsters delighted the crowds with their antics and often took home more in "nobbins" than Dick did in purse money. Though the "Alexander and Moses" act was supposed to be just a cute, kiddie exhibition, the boys pulled no punches and tore into one another as if their lives depended on the outcome.

The boxing section of the Leaming Boys Club was run by local police inspector John Gibbs, who took Randolph under his wing and treated him like his own son. The kindly copper knew Turpin was something special and took great pains in guiding him through a star-studded amateur career that included a multitude of national and international honors. Unlike Mills, who dealt in raw courage and swarming wide-open attack, Turpin was a "natural," the kind of once-in-a-lifetime boxer who did everything flawlessly without really exerting himself. His marvelous boxing skills were complemented by powerful, pinpoint punching. Though still an amateur, by the time he joined the Royal Navy in 1945, Turpin was already considered Britain's best bet for future world honors.

Turpin turned pro to rave revues on the undercard of the Bruce Woodcock-Gus Lesnevitch bout at Harringay, September 17, 1946, with a first-round knockout over Gordon Griffiths. Earlier that year, American Lesnevitch had thwarted Mills' attempt to win the world light heavyweight title, stopping the former Bournemouth booth fighter in the tenth round of a give-and-take brawl. The war had eventually slowed Mills' career (he had just five contests from 1943 through 1945), but his popularity never waned. During the early 1940s, he ended his association with Bob and Jack Turner, who had guided his early career, and signed with influential manager Ted Broadribb. From a financial point of view, it proved the smartest move he ever made. Broadribb had already guided Welsh heavyweight Tommy Farr (another veteran of the boxing booths) all the way to a title fight with heavyweight champion Joe Louis. He was among the shrewdest managers of his time and knew how to make plenty of money both for his fighters and himself. But many in British boxing circles considered Broadribb a callous man who cared far more about his bank account than he did his boxers. These critics point to Broadribb's proclivity for repeatedly matching Mills against men much larger than him, a habit that ultimately led to Freddie's crippling headaches.

"It was terrible the way Broadribb and (promoter) Jack Solomons grossly over-matched Mills. They were wicked to do it," said writer Harry Legge, a boyhood pal of Mills from Bournemouth, who also fought scores of professional and booth bouts. "He was only really a big middleweight. Yet he fought heavyweights weighing over 220 pounds. It was absolutely ridiculous, but Freddie was so brave, he'd go in with anyone. Mind you, Freddie made some wonderful money, but as far as I'm concerned, Broadribb was a very hard, very brutal man. He was a good manager as far as maneuvering his fighters, but he was ruthless."

It should be remembered, however, that Mills eagerly participated in these handicap matches for the same monetary reason his manager arranged them. And if Mills and Broadribb were blinded by the lure of financial gain, what can be said for the British Boxing Board of Control which sanctioned the blatant mismatches? Was that august body also more interested in counting its percentage of the gate than protecting the welfare of the participants? Of course, regardless of where one places the blame, it was Mills alone who paid the price.

Following his failed attempt to lift the world 175-pound crown from Lesnevich, Mills was outpointed over twelve punishing rounds by British heavyweight champion Woodcock. Next, he was viciously hammered by American giant Joe Baksi, who outweighed him by over thirty pounds. These back-to-back beatings would have discouraged most men, but Freddie Mills was never the sort to let physical punishment deter him. He bounced back to win seven of his next eight contests, including a fourth-round TKO over Pol Goffaux for the European light heavyweight title. Then, in July of 1948, he convincingly decisioned Lesnevitch in a rematch before a record crowd of over 46,000 elated British fans at White City stadium. England's fairground boxing booths had produced another world champion.

What should have been a joyous time for Mills was tainted by nagging worries concerning his health. Even before winning the title from Lesnevitch, he'd been plagued with blinding headaches and occasional dizzy spells. When Mills visited a Harley Street specialist at the advice of the British Boxing Board of Control, the spinal displacement at the base of his skull was discovered. Under today's strict regulations, it is almost certain he would not have been permitted to continue boxing. But less than four months after his victory over Lesnevitch, Mills was back in the ring against Johnny Ralph, another heavyweight! Though few would have guessed it at the time, it turned out to be his last victory.

The next year, Mills was matched with Woodcock again for the British and Empire heavyweight titles. As in their first encounter, Mills gave away twenty pounds and took a frightening beating before being knocked out in the fourteenth round. He took such a fearsome pounding from the crisp-hitting Woodcock, rumors briefly circulated that he'd died from his injuries. The handwriting was not only on the wall, it was scrawled all over poor Mills' battered face.

Mills had just one more fight after Woodcock, losing his world title to American Joey Maxim, January 24, 1950. As always, Freddie put up a valiant fight and took another nasty dose of punishment in the process. Not only did he lose the title, he also went home minus three front teeth. Three weeks later, at the urging of Broadribb, Mills officially announced his retirement.

In the meantime, Turpin had been rapidly advancing through the middleweight ranks. Though he displayed a somewhat nonchalant attitude towards training, his remarkable God-given ability had carried him to an outstanding record and a high spot among the list of contenders for Robinson's middleweight title. Some skeptics claim the "Leamington Licker" caught Robinson on an "off-night" when the legendary champion was weary from an extended tour of Europe. Others insist Turpin was so good on that particular evening, he would have beaten any middleweight who ever lived. But regardless of these divided opinions, nobody denied Turpin deserved the verdict. "I have no excuses to make," said the deposed champion immediately after the fight. "Turpin was the better man."

Turpin's tenure as champion of the world lasted just sixty-four days. He gave Robinson an almost instant rematch, losing the title via a tenth-round TKO before an enormous gathering of 61,000 fans at New York City's Polo Grounds. It was a fairly even contest for nine rounds, but when Robinson suffered a bad cut over his eye early in the tenth, he launched a desperation attack. His onslaught culminated with a stunning right to the jaw that sent Turpin crashing to the floor. The Britisher beat the count, and when Robinson poured on the punches, referee Ruby Goldstein stopped the fight with just eight seconds remaining in the round. Some British fans felt that Goldstein had acted prematurely and Turpin, who was even on the referee's scorecard, might very well have recuperated between rounds and come back to retain the title. Goldstein's critics pointed to the fact that American boxer George Flores had died just a few days before, shortly after being knocked out at Madison Square Garden. They figured the tragedy may have prompted Goldstein to act too hastily.

Though Turpin fought on for seven more years, he never again reached the heights he'd obtained by beating Robinson. When Robinson temporarily retired in 1953, Turpin was matched with Carl "Bobo" Olson for the vacant title. Ill-prepared and involved in a sexual escapade which would soon lead to additional trouble, he lost a close fifteen-round decision at the Garden. The other shoe dropped the day before he was to sail back to England aboard the *Queen Mary.* Turpin was arrested by New York police and charged with rape.

Miss Adele Daniels, described in some reports as a "dazzlingly beautiful" black woman, claimed the boxer had sexually assaulted her in her apartment. After having Turpin hauled into court, Miss Daniels withdrew the charges at the formal hearing, saying she intended to sue Turpin in civil court instead. The judge allowed Turpin to leave the country as scheduled, but only after Randy posted a $10,000 security deposit in a New York bank to be held until after the civil suit was decided.

The Daniels case was not the only one involving Turpin and a woman to reach the courts. His first wife, childhood sweetheart Mary Stack, had also brought charges against him, claiming Turpin beat her with a broomstick and kicked her in the stomach when she was pregnant. The charges were eventually dismissed, but not before Turpin admitted he'd slapped his wife across the face a number of times. Turpin didn't escape so easily when former policeman Frank Valentine cited him in a divorce action alleging the fighter had committed adultery with his wife, Pamela. Although Turpin once again denied the allegations, he lost the action and was forced to pay costs.

The Daniels case dragged on for several years and eventually went to trial in 1955. The ravishing Miss Daniels took the stand and told a lurid tale of how Turpin had first befriended her and then, having gained her confidence, raped her in the shower at her apartment. Before Turpin had a chance to tell the court his side of the story, a settlement was abruptly reached. This was much to the distress of Miss Daniels' attorney, who was positive he could have extracted far more money from the famous fighter than the £1,250 his client agreed upon. Boxing people and the British tabloids, both generally firm believers in the old where-there-is-smoke school of thought, figured he was probably correct. Of course, there are always two sides to every story.

"Randy wasn't half as black as he was painted, if you'll pardon the pun," said British sports writer Tex Hennessy, who has close ties to Turpin's widow and children. "The rape case in America was an enormous coverup, which only came to light a few years ago. His older brother Dick was in America with Randy at the time of the alleged rape. Randy was between marriages then, but Dick was happily married. According to what I've learned from knowing the family, Dick was the culprit."

Regardless of what really happened between the Turpin brothers and Miss Daniels, women undoubtedly threw themselves at Randolph. It is equally as obvious that he didn't handle their attentions very discreetly. Randolph was his own worst enemy in this regard and paid the price for his amorous adventures, not only monetarily, but with reams of negative publicity. Turpin was involved in so many similar incidents, he became Britain's version of Errol Flynn; his name commonly associated with sex scandals and dirty jokes. Even his second marriage to Gweyneth Price, the daughter of a Welsh farmer, was not without controversy. For some strange reason, Turpin denied any romantic association with Miss Price as late as five days before their wedding, and also failed to invite his own mother to the nuptials.

While Turpin was involved in numerous sordid episodes. Mills presented an entirely different image to the general public. He had married Ted Broadribb's daughter, Chrissie, in 1948, and on the surface at least, they were a devoted couple. After he quit the ring, however, Freddie began to stray. He fell hopelessly in love with a dancer much younger than himself and embarked on a passionate affair. Unlike Turpin, he was very careful and managed to keep the romance a secret for a number of years.

When Chrissie eventually discovered her husband's infidelity, it naturally put a tremendous strain on their relationship. The girl became the subject of endless arguments between them, but finally, Freddie reluctantly severed the relationship and gave his key to the dancer's apartment to Chrissie. She promptly threw it in the garbage pail.

The domestic front was not the only area of Mills' life causing him distress. As business at his nightclub floundered, an unsavory element began to frequent the establishment, including the infamous Kray twins, two of England's most notorious gangsters. The club's image took another pounding when the *Sunday People* published an expose, claiming prostitutes, posing as hostesses, were using Mills' place as a base of operations. Though no charges were ever lodged by the authorities, the scandal was just about the death knell for the rapidly sinking business. Mills and his partner, Andy Ho, put the club up for sale but never attracted any serious offers. Strapped for cash, Mills began to sell off much of the property he'd acquired with his ring earnings.

Mills' sad decline had reached an all-time low by the summer of 1965. Tortured by unending headaches, he struggled on, gamely trying to keep the nightclub going. In late July, he visited May Ronaldson, an old friend from his fairground days who owned a shooting gallery at the Battersea Pleasure Gardens. Mills told Ronaldson he was going to a fete in Esher dressed as a cowboy and wanted to borrow one of her rifles to complete the outfit. She was only too happy to help her old pal and readily permitted him to borrow an old rifle from her collection, but warned him that it was not in working order. Mills told her that it would be fine, as it was just for appearances, anyway.

On Saturday, July 24, Mills spent an apparently pleasant day at home and then went to work at the nightclub. He arrived around

10:30 P.M., parked his car in the alleyway in rear of the club and went inside. He stayed about twenty minutes and then came back out. He told doorman Bob Deacon he'd had a few drinks and was feeling a bit tired.

"I think I'll have a sleep in the car. It's at the back," Mills told Deacon. "Will you come and wake me in about half an hour in time for me to introduce the cabaret?"

Deacon dutifully woke his boss as instructed, but when he informed Mills there were only seven or eight patrons inside, Freddie decided to nap a little longer.

"I'm not going to come in yet, then," he said. "Wake me up in another half hour if I'm still asleep."

As far as anyone knows, this was the last conversation Mills ever had with anyone. Just before midnight, Deacon tapped on the car window. There was no response. Next, he opened the car door and shook Mills by the arm, but still was unable to rouse him. After consulting head waiter Henry Grant, Deacon left Mills alone until almost 1:00 A.M., thinking Freddie merely needed more time to sleep off the drinks. But when a gentle pat on the face failed to bring any response, Andy Ho was hastily summoned. Realizing something was seriously wrong, Ho phoned Chrissie and asked her to come over immediately. Chrissie arrived at the club as quickly as she could and rushed to the car. To her horror, she saw a bloody wound in the corner of his right eye and a rifle laying next to him, though at the time, she mistook it for the car's starting handle. Later that morning, the British public awoke to the startling news that Freddie Mills was dead.

A coroner's inquest ruled Mills had committed suicide. May Ronaldson testified she had loaned Mills the rifle and later noticed three rounds of .22 caliber ammunition were missing from the shelf where she kept it. Between the time Mills borrowed the rifle and a week or so later when he was shot, the weapon had been mysteriously repaired. Medical evidence revealed that the angle of the bullet was consistent with a self-inflicted wound and that there were

This photograph of the entrance to Freddie Mills' London nightclub was taken a few hours after the former champion's body was discovered in his car in Goslett Yard, a cul-de-sac near the club. (Photo courtesy of *Boxing News*)

Freddie Mills' funeral cortege leaves St. Giles' Church, Camberwell, London. Among the pallbearers are promoter Jack Solomons (front left) and British and Empire heavyweight champion Henry Cooper (front right). (Photo courtesy of *Boxing News*)

Fans and family donated contributions to pay for Freddie Mills' memorial stone in New Camberwell Cemetery, London. The marble boxing glove in the foreground forms the top of an urn containing a real boxing glove, sealed in plastic. (Photo courtesy of *Boxing News*)

bruises around the eye caused by the rifle barrel at the time of firing.

Despite every indication that Mills took his own life, there were many, including Chrissie, who refused to believe the sad facts. Sensational newspaper stories fueled the fire and headlines such as "Was Freddie Mills Murdered?" fanned the flames. Britain's muckraking tabloids speculated Mills was being blackmailed by hoodlums and killed when he refused to meet their demands. For many people, it was simply impossible to believe such an astonishingly brave fighter had killed himself. Yet, when all the evidence is examined, the inescapable conclusion is that Mills, tormented by excruciating headaches, plagued by financial failure, and depressed by his fading celebrity status, simply couldn't find the strength to answer the bell for the next round.

Following his loss to Olson, Turpin moved up to the light heavyweight division, winning the British and Empire 175-pound titles in 1955. But despite this modest success at a higher weight, he never again recaptured the magic he'd possessed as a middleweight. He began to lose to boxers who wouldn't have lasted more than a couple of rounds with him a few years earlier, and in 1958, after suffering a humiliating second-round knockout defeat at the hands of Yolande Pompey, Turpin hung up his gloves. Unlike Mills, there was no decade of post-boxing glory for Turpin. Though he had drawn gigantic crowds in his prime and been hailed as a hero, the frequent scandals revolving around his wildly undisciplined love life didn't exactly endear Turpin to image-conscious television and radio producers. And though generally considered a "regular bloke" by those who knew him personally, Turpin lacked Mills' outgoing personality and flair for entertaining folks with a song or a joke. It should also be admitted that a lot of doors were closed to Turpin purely because he was black.

Turpin's finances were in terrible shape by the time he retired from boxing. The divorce from his first wife had cost him in the neighborhood of £8,500 and he had also lost heavily on his guest house in Wales. His frequently foolish generosity towards others was a major downfall. When he was on top, Turpin gave away literally thousands of pounds to assorted family members, cronies and hangers-on, doling out money to almost anybody who came to him with a hard luck story. Of course, when Turpin fell on tough times himself, most of these beneficiaries and so-called friends vanished. But of all Turpin's monetary difficulties, the biggest came from the Inland Revenue. According to the tax man, Turpin owed the government a staggering £17,000.

At a hearing before the Registrar at the Shire Hall in Warwick, Turpin pleaded ignorance, claiming he'd always assumed his manager had deducted taxes from his purses. As the hearing wore on, it became all too obvious that Turpin not only didn't have the money to pay his back taxes, but also still owed other creditors a considerable amount. After hearing all the testimony, the Registrar accepted Turpin's explanation regarding his boxing earnings, and as he was bankrupt, decided to make no further effort to collect. But there was still the matter of the £10,000 he'd earned wrestling. As he had been self-managed as a wrestler, it was impossible for Turpin to claim he thought his manager had payed his income tax. From that day on, the Inland Revenue continually hounded Turpin for the taxes due from his wrestling income.

Turpin became increasingly bitter following his tax hearing, especially towards his family and others he'd given (or loaned) money to in the past. He blamed these spongers for his predicament and withdrew from his old social circles, spending practically all of his spare time with his wife and kids. When customers at his cafe wanted to talk boxing, Randolph invariably refused to be drawn into conversation about his past. He still dreamed of improving his lot, but deep down inside realized his tax burden would probably never permit him to climb out of the depressing circumstances to which his life had sunk.

Turpin was so desperate for cash, he even considered selling his championship belts. But before a deal could be consummated, he changed his mind and took them off the market. Then, just when it seemed like things couldn't possibly get any worse, the Leamington Spa city council informed Turpin they wanted to tear down the cafe and build a parking lot. The final straw came in the form of another letter from the Inland Revenue. If Turpin didn't make immediate settlement on his wrestling earnings, he would be taken to court.

On the afternoon of May 17, 1966, Turpin went upstairs to the attic of his home and shot himself in the heart and head with a .22 caliber pistol. What made the tragedy even more ghastly was the fact he also shot his youngest daughter, Carmen, age two.

Gwen Turpin never heard any shots, but said she was suddenly overcome by a strange, uncomfortable feeling, and decided to check on the two children. Only Charmaine and Carmen were home; Gwyneth and Annette were at school. The scene that greeted Mrs. Turpin when she reached the attic was horrendous. Carmen was sitting on the bed crying and Randolph was slumped on the floor next to the bed. Both were smeared with blood. Panic-stricken, Gwen picked up little Carmen and ran out of the house and all the way to the hospital. Though the girl had been shot twice, once in the head and once in the chest, she was lucky. The wounds were not fatal, and after several anxious weeks, she was allowed to return home. Her father was not so fortunate. He was already dead by the time the ambulance arrived.

The police found a farewell note pinned to the bedroom door. In it Turpin reiterated his bitterness toward those who had drained him of his money and also asked his wife to disassociate herself from everyone on his side of the family except his mother. There was much speculation as to why Turpin attempted to take his daughter to the grave with him. Gossip centered around the fact Carmen bore no outward trace of her black heritage. The other three children Turpin had with Gwen were all plainly of mixed blood, but baby Carmen was pure blonde with blue eyes and creamy white skin. Though it is possible Turpin didn't believe Carmen was really his child, those close to the family hotly dismiss the theory.

"That's a load of crap," said Hennessy. "If you line up the four girls, you'll see that the likeness is quite astonishing. Nobody knows the reason (Turpin shot Carmen), but he was obviously unbalanced at the time. What's so heartbreaking, is that if Randy could see the family he left behind now, he'd be kicking himself."

As was the case when Mills died, rumors of murder also circulated after Turpin's death. There had been an incident a few years earlier concerning £20,000 Turpin had allegedly stashed away for a rainy day. Supposedly, Turpin, in desperate need of funds, had telephoned certain individuals and asked for his hidden money. As the story goes, he was then "visited" by four members of the underworld, who "persuaded" him to forget all about the money. Acquaintances of Turpin recalled seeing him badly beaten around the time in question, but said Randolph had attributed his injuries to a wrestling melee with rowdy fans. In any event, the coroner's inquest ruled Turpin took his own life; a decision based on fact rather than conjecture.

Turpin's suicide came less than a year after Mills'; the second blow in a stunning combination that shook the British boxing establishment to its foundations. While Turpin's woes had received wide coverage in the press, most citizens were under the impression Mills was still leading a charmed existence when he took his life. Questions were raised by the news media and in Parliament. Were Mills' and Turpin's mental faculties impaired due to the punishment they had absorbed in the ring? Was boxing to blame? While Mills' physical problems were well documented and certainly a contributing factor in his death, the verdict is not so clear cut in Turpin's case. Though he did not suffer from headaches like Mills, he lost a number of bouts by knockout the last few years of his career which could have conceivably caused brain damage. His personality did undergo a marked change toward the end. No longer carefree and impulsive, he became sullen and moody. This depressive behavior, of course, could just as well have been due to the woeful circumstances of his personal life as any boxing-induced injury.

In the final analysis, boxing was merely the stage upon which
Turpin and Mills played out their lives of triumph and tragedy. If
there is a villain in their lamentable tales, it is the fickle nature of
fame and fortune. Boxing is a brutal sport, but nowhere near as
vicious as the game of life.

7

Tough Guy

Some people who knew Gus Dorazio claimed he had a crude, calculating manner about him, a kind of animal cunning that undoubtedly served him well inside the ring. Even when he was being nice, Gus had a habit of looking at folks in a way that made them feel like he was sizing them up for a cheap shot. Others figured he was just an overgrown kid, a bit punchy, perhaps, but basically an okay guy. But regardless of one's opinion of the late Philadelphia heavyweight, it's impossible to deny his affinity for trouble.

Dorazio was a charter member of Joe Louis' "Bum of the Month Club," one of a collection of no-hopers Louis fought during his barnstorming tour of the country prior to World War II. When Louis' road show scheduled a pit stop in the City of Brotherly Love, Dorazio, a popular hometown pug, was selected as the heavyweight champion's designated victim.

A pro since 1939, Dorazio really had no business being in the same ring as Louis. Sure, he'd out pointed the promising Bob Pastor, But Arturo Godoy, light heavyweight champion Billy Conn and others had already whipped the Philly tough guy. Gus's main asset was his reputation for always marching straight into the teeth of his opponents' best punches. Anybody with half a brain knew Dorazio was doomed.

Despite the blatantly one-sided nature of the match (the official odds were twenty-to-one), a crowd of 15,902 shoehorned into the Convention Hall, February 17, 1941, to see Dorazio try his luck against the mighty "Brown Bomber." It was enough for Philadelphia fans that one of their own was fighting the already legendary champion. So what if he didn't have a chance? They knew that Gus would go down swinging.

Some ringsiders even claimed Dorazio won the first round. But when he launched a wild left in the second, Louis struck with cobra-like quickness. Joe drove a short right inside Gus's looping swing and dropped the local favorite face first to the canvas. Except for a slight twitching of his legs, Dorazio lay motionless as referee Irving Kutcher counted him out 1:30 into the round.

Like so much of Dorazio's life, the Louis fight was not without controversy. Although reporters were unanimous in their praise of both Louis and the knockout punch, State Senators John J. Haluska, H. Jerome Jaspan and Anthony J. DiSilvestro charged Dorazio had gone into the tank and characterized Louis' victory as a "complete frame-up."

"I'm convinced this man Dorazio took a perfect 'dive'," Haluska claimed on the Senate floor in Harrisburg. "(Either) Dorazio sold out for consideration or he was unfit to meet the champion."

Leon L. Rains, chairman of the State Athletic Commission, considered himself the main target of the Senators and countered their charges with a few of his own.

"It was all trumped up before they even saw the fight," Rains told the press. "They came here with three plans in mind. If the fight went eight rounds or more they were going to charge Louis carried Dorazio. If Dorazio was cut up, they were going to insist I be fired for permitting a butchery. If it went a round or two, they were going to charge a fake. And that's what they did."

Smart alecks claimed the politicians were pissed because they'd

Gus Dorazio (on scale) and Joe Louis weigh-in for their 1941 heavyweight title bout in Philadelphia. Dorazio went down and out from a sweet right hand in the second round. (Photo courtesy of Peltz Boxing Promotions)

Gus Dorazio ponders a question from the judge during his arraignment at Philadelphia's Central Court for "numbers" writing in 1945. At the time, Dorazio was free on bail while awaiting his draft-dodging trial. (Photo courtesy of Peltz Boxing Promotions)

shelled out $23.40 for ringside seats and felt they'd been short-changed. But columnist Otts Hulleberg spoke for the majority when he wrote, "Gus took a dive all right, a dive to the floor from one of the sweetest, and shortest, rights that ever hit a chin. Remember Schmeling? He also took a 'dive,' and in the first round. Virtually all of the Bomber's opponents have taken similar 'dives' after meeting with Joe's murderous punches. To Dorazio's credit...he never took a backwards step."

Years later, Dorazio, then in his mid-sixties, insisted that not only was the KO legitimate, but that with a litle bit of luck, he could have beaten Louis.

"I still dream of that fight," said Dorazio. "I was sure I could beat Louis, and in the first round I hurt him. I know I could have beat him if I hadn't left my feet throwing a hook and he nailed me. I could have handled him—honest."

Dorazio was just a pawn in the political hubbub following his loss to Louis, but there were numerous other occasions when he was far from an innocent bystander. Gus was never bashful when it came to bending the law to suit his needs. The first major scandal involving Dorazio came in 1945 when the FBI arrested him as a draft dodger.

As if the draft-dodging beef wasn't enough, a week after federal authorities freed Dorazio on $1,000 bail, the vice squad nabbed him for taking numbers bets from stevedores at the Philadelphia waterfront. Though it was a nickel-and-dime bust, the affair was a pretty good indication of Gus' petty-criminal mentality. Getting arrested was beginning to be a habit with Dorazio, and when Magistrate Thomas A. Connor asked him if he had anything to say, Gus stifled a yawn and nonchalantly drawled, "No, nothing, now."

At the fighter's draft-dodging trial, board clerks Margaret Furia and Helen McHugh testified Dorazio had been reclassified 2-B (deferred as an essential worker) in 1944 after William J. Savage, owner of the Union Welding Co., presented information to the board indicating Gus was employed by his company as a welder forty-eight hours a week. In fact, Dorazio never worked at Union

Welding, and had actually netted $4,560 in boxing earnings during the period he was supposed to be doing his bit for Uncle Sam. The feds had him dead to rights and all Dorazio could do was throw himself on the mercy of the court and hope for the best.

On October 15, 1946, U.S. District Court Judge Guy K. Bard, sitting as judge and jury in the case, convicted Dorazio of falsely representing himself as a war worker to evade the draft and sentenced him to a year and a day in federal prison. Savage, who had taken refuge in a sanitarium, was convicted of aiding and abetting Dorazio.

"I am giving him (Dorazio) a break," said Judge Bard, "not so much because he is a good father and a good husband, but because when he later was classified 1A by his board, he was turned down for military service because he was physically unfit. Actually, the Army didn't lose anything."

The felony rap effectively put an end to Dorazio's already deteriorating boxing career. He lost four out of the seven bouts in 1944 and was inactive during 1945 while serving his sentence. The over-the-hill brawler gave it one last try in '45, losing to Red Applegate via a fifth-round knockout.

Before Dorazio burned out as a fighter in his mid-twenties, he won the hearts of many fans with his let's-get-it-on attitude. A couple of years before Dorazio's retirement, sports writer Cy Peterman summed up the general feeling toward the rough-hewn slugger. Gus had just upset up-and-coming Harry BoBo, and Peterman was trying to help him obtain one more big payday before hanging up his gloves.

"(Dorazio is) a willing workman who made the utmost of limited fighting talents," wrote Peterman in the *Philadelphia Inquirer*. "No killing puncher, no fancy Dan with rapier jabs, Gus waded in and took his share to ladle out the blows. He deserves one good slice 'ere he's done, portions of the luck that less deserving starters— many fakes and stiffs and utter bums—have been paid for far less effort."

Unfortunately, the admirable qualities that allowed Dorazio to overcome certain natural disadvantages in the ring did not carry over into the rest of his life.

Like some menacing character in a B-movie. Dorazio turned his brute strength to less socially-acceptable pursuits. He became a union goon and enforcer for loan sharks. If there was a labor problem, Gus provided the muscle to keep troublemakers in line. When a client reneged on his debt to a loan shark, Gus was the guy who exacted brutal retribution. He was the classic ex-pug turned thug, the last guy you wanted to run into in a dark alley or barroom lavatory. It was a situation that eventually led to tragedy.

On January 7, 1949, Albert Blomeyer and Alexander Amberg had just left their place of employment at C. Schmidt & Sons when they were approached from behind by Dorazio, who worked as a bottler at the same brewery. According to witness Alois Witt, Dorazio started swinging at Blomeyer, who retreated into the brewery with Dorazio in hot pursuit. When the ex-fighter caught up with Blomeyer, he locked his co-worker's head in the crook of his left arm and repeatedly punched him in the face with his right fist. It was a particularly savage attack, undeniably calculated to inflict serious damage. Dorazio may have been washed-up as a professional boxer, but was still way too much for the average man to handle in a street fight.

When Witt attempted to intervene, Dorazio turned on him and delivered approximately fifteen blows to his face and body. Next, assistant brewmaster William A. Hipp rushed from his office and tried to stop the sickening beating. He was also punched and told he better keep quiet or Dorazio would see to it he "wouldn't walk again." Finally, the enraged Dorazio was overpowered by a gang of truck-loaders who rushed to the rescue from a nearby platform.

Blomeyer and Witt were taken to St. Mary's Hosital, where Witt was treated for a fractured nose and Blomeyer for apparently superficial bruises. The two men then went to the Labor Lyceum, found it locked, started home by trolley, but switched to a taxi cab at

Blomeyer's suggestion. After reaching home, the thirty-three-year-old Blomeyer was unable to speak. Witt helped his friend to a chair, waited about fifteen minutes and then departed. Later that evening, Blomeyer's wife called a doctor who took the comatose brewery worker to Women's Homeopathic Hospital. Shortly before midnight, Blomeyer died of a compound skull fracture.

After Detectives James Martin, Thomas Blong and Martin Curran arrested Dorazio at his home in the Yeadon section of Philadelphia, he told them, "People had been taunting me. They called me punch-drunk. They called me on the phone to heckle me. I just got the notion to get even with someone." It wasn't long, however, before the police deduced "union trouble" was the most probable motive for Blomeyer's fatal beating.

At the time, inter-union strife plagued the brewing industry. There was a fierce rivalry between the CIO and AFL for control of the employee's loyalties and both Blomeyer and Witt were CIO shop stewards. The day Blomeyer was killed, they had been circulating a petition among workers in an effort to collect enough signatures to meet the National Labor Relations Board's criterion for an election. Needless to say, the faction Dorazio allegedly represented took dim view of such activities.

Dorazio's trial was a brief, three-day affair. His lawyer, William A. Gray, attempted to show that the onetime heavyweight contender had acted in self-defense. But the eyewitness testimony against Dorazio was overwhelming and the jury of eleven women and one man didn't have too much to debate. After only forty-five minutes of deliberation, they convicted Dorazio of second-degree murder. Judge Edwin O. Lewis gave Dorazio from two and a half to five years in prison, a rather lenient sentence considering the seriousness of his offense.

Dorazio remained free on $10,000 bail while an appeal was lodged with the State Supreme Court in an effort to secure a new trial. The defense claimed Blomeyer died as a result of hitting his head when he fell, not from blows struck by the former heavyweight contender. Defense attorney Frank J. Anderson argued Dorazio had been improperly tried, and that he should not have been charged for any greater crime than manslaughter.

Assistant Director Attorney John F. Kane vigorously opposed the plea for a new trial and called Dorazio a "paid union goon" who had threatened to send one man home in an ambulance and another in an undertaker's wagon. On June 26, 1950, the State Supreme Court denied Dorazio's appeal and upheld his sentence.

"The events show a brutal, persistent attack upon a helpless, non-resisting victim," declared Justice Allen M. Stearne. "They show a measure of depravity and hardness of heart, a recklessness of consequence and a mind regardless of social duty, which imports malice."

Judging by his subsequent actions, Dorazio's second stretch in the slammer did very little to reform his overall outlook on life. In September of 1956, he was arrested again after a free-for-all at the Surf Club, where he worked as "night manager" (read bouncer). According to published reports of the incident, five men entered the club about 12:30 AM and created a disturbance when two of them began to dance together—not exactly the smartest move to make at a hardcore, macho hangout in the late 1950s. Club manager Michael Sokoloff, who as a boxing manager was known as Mike Bananas, walked over to the men and told them he would refund their money and asked them to leave.

"Don't give them back their money," chipped in Dorazio belligerently. "Just let them get out of here."

With that, someone started swinging. A melee ensued and before order was restored, the five unwanted customers all wound up at Graduate Hospital, where they were treated for an assortment of cuts and bruises. After everyone was patched up, the next stop was the 12th and Pine Streets police station, where Dorazio, Sokoloff, bartender William Shafer, and the five injured patrons were hauled before Magistrate Michael Davis.

Despite the fact Dorazio was accused of using a blackjack (a charge he vociferoiusly denied), when Magistrate Davis asked if anyone wanted to press charges, nobody stepped forward and the case was promptly dismissed. Unlike Dorazio's previous scrapes with the law, the rumble at the Surf Club was considered mildly humorous. The headline in the *Philadelphia Inquirer* the following day read: "Dorazio Scores TKO in Court After Brawl." However, the next time Gus made the newspapers, nobody was laughing.

On February 22, 1961, Dorazio and Rocco Turra were arrested and charged with stealing $5,000 in cash and jewelry from a theatrical booking agent. This was considered a far more serious breach of etiquette than mopping the barroom floor with members of a sexual minority.

Six days earlier, Mrs. Betty DeSantis and Mrs. Nancy D'Orsi had gone to the residence of ticket agent Anthony Spaggs at 1214 Spruce Street. Spaggs was in Florida at the time and the two women had been hired to clean the apartment in his absence. But when they arrived, the cleaners discovered far more than they had bargained for.

According to testimony given by Mrs. DeSantis, when the two women entered the apartment they were confronted by Dorazio and Turra, who was holding a gun. She said Turra told her to, "Turn around and be quiet or I'll blow your brains out."

The women were then forced to lie on the floor, where they had their hands bound with electrical cords. Once Mrs. DeSantis and Mrs. D'Orsi were secured, the robbers took a metal box containing $1,500 in cash and $3,500 in jewelry from a closet. Before leaving, they also stole an additional $150 from Mrs. DeSantis' purse.

When police asked Mrs. DeSantis to identify the suspects, Turra said: "Take a good look at me. Are you sure I'm the man?"

After she said she was, Turra snarled, "Remember, I won't be in jail forever."

At Dorazio and Turra's trial, Mrs. DeSantis stuck to her story, But Mrs. D'Orsi said she could not identify the assailants. Gus claimed the date of the robbery was also the day his father was buried, and that he had spent the entire evening at home. Several witnesses were produced to verify his alibi.

Without Mrs. D'Orsi's collaborating testimony, the prosecution's case was weak, and after an hour's deliberation, the jury acquitted both Turra and Dorazio of all charges. Whether or not Turra's threat to Mrs. DeSantis had indirectly intimidated Mrs. D'Orsi is a matter of speculation. Who knows? Maybe Dorazio and Turra had been victims of the old round-up-the-usual-suspects syndrome. Regardless, the burglary rap marked the last time Dorazio had a major run-in with law enforcement officials. He was forty-five at the time and probably getting too old for the kind of anti-social behavior that had marred most of his adult life.

The last fifteen years of his life, Dorazio needed a one-handed walker to help him move about, the result of a chronic, lower-back problem that prevented him from working. Nevertheless, the look in his eyes and the sound of his crushed-stone voice told you he was still a tough guy. Toward his death in September 1987, he was confined to a wheelchair. A lot of people would say Dorazio's karma had finally caught up with him, but let's not be too hasty to judge.

"I remember Gus before he went in the amateurs," said Willie O'Neill, a veteran observer of the Philly fight scene. "He used to sell candy apples around the neighborhood. He was a nice kid, but not too bright. I used to take one of his apples and pretend I wasn't going to pay for it. It was easy to mess with his head, you could talk him into most anything. He was convinced he could beat Louis, he really was. He told everybody in South Philly how he was going to knock out Louis—and Gus couldn't punch! It was a shame, but they kept throwing him in again and again with all the best heavyweights. Gus wasn't afraid of anybody, but after a while, the beatings he took made him punchy."

Though his name no longer stained neighborhood police blotters, Dorazio didn't entirely fade from the headlines the last few years of his life. When actor Sylvester Stallone invented the character of

Rocky Balboa for the 1976 movie, some writers drew parallels between the celluloid boxer and Dorazio. Like the former Philadelphia heavyweight, "Rocky" was given a one-in-a-million shot at the heavyweight and also worked part-time as a strong-arm man. But "Rocky" was a softy at heart and deplored the rough stuff outside the ring. Dorazio, on the other hand, wasn't so squeamish.

8

The Champion Nobody Wanted

Geraldine Liston was far too preoccupied to relax during the flight from St. Louis to Las Vegas. It was January 5, 1971, and her New Year's holiday with relatives had been cut short by the nagging worry that something was wrong at home. Terribly wrong. She'd repeatedly tried to contact her husband by telephone, but nobody answered. The new year was definitely off to a bad start.

She felt a little better during the short drive from the airport to their split-level home near the sixteenth hole of the Sahara-Nevada Golf Course. Though it was only around 8:45 PM, she told herself he'd be home when she arrived. Then, she'd really give the big bum a piece of her mind. The nerve of him, probably out whoring around while she worried herself half sick.

But when Geraldine saw a week's worth of newspapers piled outside the front door, her stomach turned a somersault and her apprehension quickly dissolved into fear. The first thing she noticed, after unlocking the door, was a sickening odor which permeated the house. The stench engulfed her like a blanket, and even before she found him in the master bedroom, she must have realized the truth.

There, laying on his back, slumped partially on the bed and dressing table at the foot of the bed, was the body of Charles "Sonny" Liston; husband, father, ex-con... and the former heavyweight champion of the world. He was naked except for a teeshirt, a ribbon of thick, black blood coagulated around his nostrils.

During his lifetime, Liston had been an enigma, the prototype tough guy who hid his feelings behind a sullen stare and a curt comment. He was haunted by his past and tormented by a reputation he was never able to shake. Despite countless attempts at penance and purification, in the general public's mind, Liston remained a troublemaker to the end.

To much of white America during the 1960s, Liston personified the "bad nigger," a threatening stereotype rooted in paranoia and ignorance. To numerous law enforcement officials throughout the country, Liston was simply a hood, a common ruffian who had been lucky enough to win the heavyweight title. To the majority of boxing fans he was a disgrace, a fighter who had committed the unpardonable sin of surrendering the championship while sitting on his stool.

But was Liston merely a brooding ex-con, a brute who delighted in bullying those weaker than himself, a miscreant who got exactly what he deserved? Or was he a man trapped in a guise of his own creation, hounded to the point he was unable to shed the image he'd assumed as a vehicle for survival?

For Liston, survival was always a struggle. He was born in the Arkansas boondocks, May 8, 1932 (though the precise year is open for debate) in St. Francis County near Forest City, about twenty miles from Little Rock. His father, who worked on the cotton farm where Sonny was born, sired about twenty-five children by two women. Sonny was among the thirteen offspring born to his second wife.

From the cradle, poverty and hunger were a way of life for Sonny.

A field hand by the time he was twelve, Liston's lone blessing in a childhood filled with hardship and deprivation was his size and prodigious physical strength. Even they became a curse when his mother relocated to St. Louis and enrolled the thirteen-year-old Liston in school for the first time.

"My mother put me in school and, after I started going, the other kids would see me coming out of the small kid's room. And I was such a large boy, they made fun of me and started laughing," Liston revealed many years later while testifying before Senator Estes Kefauver's antimonopoly committee.

Liston responded to the ridicule the only way he knew—with his fists. Schoolyard brawls and hooky rapidly replaced English and mathematics on his curriculum. In Liston's own words, "hooky led to other things," and eventually landed him in the house of detention. According to Sonny's reckoning, he was "about four-teen" at the time of this, his first of numerous incarcerations. Once on the streets again, the teen-age Liston seemed almost in a hurry to get back behind bars. In June of 1950, he was found guilty of sticking up a gas station and sentenced to five years in the Missouri State Penitentiary at Jefferson City.

Liston's experiences during this stretch in the slammer had a profound influence, and in many ways determined the course of his life. Encouraged to take up boxing by penitentiary chaplain Father Stevenson, Liston had finally found a conduit for his natural athletic ability. But more importantly, he found an outlet for his anger and aggression. Liston immediately displayed prowess in the ring and soon became prison champ; a con feared and respected by fellow inmates. Sonny basked in his newfound status. He enjoyed the adulation that came with being a big man on campus and readily adopted the mannerisms of "Cock of the Yard," a lifetime role which, along with his overall jailhouse mindset, eventually imprisoned him as surely as the walls of Jefferson City.

With the help of Father Stevenson, Liston was paroled after serving twenty-nine months. He soon won the National Golden Gloves and quickly graduated to the professional ranks. In his debut, September 2, 1953 at the St. Louis Arena, Liston established the pattern most of his bouts were to copy: impassively bludgeoning Don Smith into submission in just thirty-three seconds.

Liston's original manager, Frank Mitchell, was the first in a long line of mob connected characters to guide Sonny's career. Next, came labor racketeer John Vitale, for whom Liston moonlighted as a head-knocking goon. When Vitale had trouble with his black employees, Sonny kept them in line. As mean as Liston was in the ring, he was even meaner on the street. It was a life-style that was bound to catch up with him sooner or later. In May of 1956, after winning fourteen of fifteen pro bouts, Liston's boxing career was interrupted when he was convicted of "assault to kill." The beef revolved around an altercation with a racist St. Louis cop who was dumb enough to point a gun at Liston and not pull the trigger. Sonny took the gun away and broke the cop's leg. The bust cost Liston five months in the St. Louis Workhouse and he didn't return to the ring until January of 1958, when he picked up where he left off and bowled over Bill Hunter in the second round.

By March of '58, Liston had signed a five-year contract with Pep Barone, another dubious individual and friend of Frank (Blinky) Palermo. A close associate of underworld boxing czar Frankie Carbo, Palermo was eventually indicted by a federal grand jury on five counts of interstate transmission of threats to injure boxing promoter Jackie Leonard and manager Donald Nesseth. Liston had become a valuable property, and the underworld saw in him a superb chance to wrest the heavyweight title away from Floyd Patterson and his manager, Cus D'Amato. Congressional records later revealed that Liston's contract was divided up in the following manner: Mitchell was totally out, but Vitale retained twelve percent; Palermo also got twelve percent; while Barone got twenty-four percent as manager of record. Carbo received a controlling fifty-two percent.

Liston was then approaching his fistic prime. Standing 6'1" and weighing around 210 pounds, he was a devastating fighter, perhaps one of the greatest heavyweights of all time. While critics have always maintained Liston "couldn't wipe his ass with his right hand," nobody denied the power emananting from his left. Sonny's jab was awesome, a jarring, telephone pole of a punch which softened adversaries for the *coup de grace,* usually a compact left hook. He tallied eight wins in '58, among them a pulverizing first-round knockout over Wayne Bethea that catapulted him into the ranks of contenders.

From February 1959 through July of 1960, Liston scored eight straight knockouts. Included among his victims were such outstanding boxers as Cleveland Williams, Nino Valdez and Zora Folley. Cagey Eddie Machen broke the knockout string, but still lost a ten-round decision. Liston was the obvious choice to challenge Patterson. But D'Amato continually ducked Liston, shrewdly citing Sonny's nefarious past and continuing relationship with various members of organized crime as an excuse. In actuality, he was protecting his fighter, for Cus knew Patterson didn't stand a chance against the marauding Liston.

It was during this period that Liston moved to Philadelphia, where he lived with Geraldine in a two-story house at 5785 Dunlap Street. As far as the Philadelphia police were concerned, Liston was a marked man. To their way of thinking, Sonny's fracas with a brother officer in St. Louis made him fair game for any cop in the country. Unknown to Liston, every Philly squad car had his photograph taped to the sun visor. The harassment ranged from a two-bit loitering rap to the infamous "Lark in the Park."

One evening in June of 1961, Liston was returning home from the gym, accompanied by his friend Isaac Cooper. While driving through Fairmount Park, the pair spotted a well-turned out black woman in a new Cadillac. Thinking she was probably a prostitute, the amorous pair pulled alongside to get a better look. They were just about to strike up a conversation when Liston noticed a police cruiser approaching. Wary of another confrontation with the long arm of the law, Liston pulled away, hoping to avoid any hassle. He should have known better. The innocuous incident rapidly escalated into a full-blown police production, complete with an alleged car chase and eventual arrest.

The woman in the Cadillac, probably concerned for her own welfare, told the police she had only stopped because Liston claimed to be a cop. The District Attorney's office piled on the charges against Liston, including "impersonating a police officer" and "resisting arrest." At the trial, Liston's lawyer, Morton Witkins, punched holes in the D.A.'s case, producing a traffic engineer who proved the cop's version of the supposed "chase" physically impossible. The bogus charges were dropped, but the negative publicity further stained Liston's already tarnished image.

In a cosmetic attempt to shed himself of underworld ties and placate the Pennsylvania Athletic Commission, Liston bought back his contract from Barone and acquired Philadelphian Georgie Katz (who had successfully handled welterweight contender Gil Turner) as an interim manager. In another ploy to cleanse himself, Liston spent some time in Denver with Rev. Edward Murphy, a Jesuit priest who became Sonny's "spiritual advisor" and taught the illiterate fighter to write his name.

His unsavory reputation notwithstanding, Liston had become a popular TV attraction, and boxing fans, tired of Patterson's round-robin series with Ingemar Johansson, clammered for a Liston-Patterson bout. As the story goes, even President John F. Kennedy urged Patterson to defend against the number-one contender.

When Patterson put the title on the line against inept Tom McNeeley, December 4, 1961, in Toronto, Liston was pitted against German no-hoper Albert Westphal in Philadelphia as part of a closed-circuit doubleheader. Patterson prevailed with a four-round knockout, while Liston dispatched Westphal (whom Sonny referred to as "Quick Fall") in a grand total of one hundred eighteen seconds. The time was ripe for the long-awaited showdown, and Patterson, an honorable man, went against D'Amato's wishes and agreed to finally give Liston his chance.

Before the match could be signed, a site had to be selected. New

York City was the first choice, but Liston had been refused a boxing license by the Empire State in the past. Hoping his relatively good behavior over the past few years had softened the New York Athletic Commission's stance, he applied again, April 17, 1962. Once more, his request was refused.

"The history of Liston's past association with Vitale, Palermo, Mitchell and others is a factor which can be deterimental to the best interest of professional boxing and to the public interest as well. We cannot ignore the possibility that these long time associations continue to this day. The wrong people do not disengage easily," wrote Major General Melvin L. Krulewitch, chairman of the N.Y.S.A.C.

But the fight New York City shunned as if it was a contagious disease, Chicago coveted with scavenger-like enthusiasm. After ten years as a professional boxer, and over two years as the top contender in the heavyweight division, Liston at long last climbed into the ring to fight for the world championship on September 25, 1962. Sonny's moment of truth was painfully brief—for both Patterson and the gathering of 18,894 in Comiskey Park, who paid $665,420 for the privilege of witnessing what was the third quickest knockout in heavyweight championship history. Just under two minutes into the opening round, Liston tagged Patterson with a clubbing left hook to the head. Patterson went down and out 2:06 into the bout.

Opinions on the massacre were divided.

"It was a terrible hoax," said ex-heavyweight king Gene Tunney. "The people who paid to see that fight were burglarized—and shows like that one are rapidly killing boxing. Patterson was so frightened he didn't even box."

Maybe Patterson was frightened, but according to Nat Fleischer, editor of *The Ring* magazine, the knockout was far from a hoax.

"A couple of rights to the body, two jarring lefts to the side, and then came a stunning left that landed high on the forehead. Seconds later Sonny landed a second left, this time a hook that crashed with T.N.T. power and hit Patterson on the jaw. He crumpled to the canvas," reported Fleischer. "It was as clean a punch as could be wished for by Sonny, who following a look of surprise, backed away at the command of referee Frank Sikora, who began the count."

For Liston, winning the heavyweight title was no panacea. To begin with, the IRS seized the entire proceeds from the Patterson fight. In an unprecedented move, government tax officers slapped liens totaling nearly $3.9 million on the fight promoter, Championship Sports, Inc. The corporation had failed to file a tax return for the previous year and Uncle Sam wasn't taking any chances. For once, Liston was completely innocent, but suffered nevertheless.

But money isn't everything. Liston was sure that winning the title had erased all his old sins and that from then on everything would be sweetness and light. On the flight home to Philly after toppling Patterson, Sonny was full of idealism. He wanted to help the kids of America and be an example they could look up to. He was so positive there would be a formal reception waiting for him when he arrived, he spent most of the flight rehearsing his speech. What Liston didn't know was that Jack McKinney, boxing writer for the Philadelphia *Daily News,* had been on the phone desperately trying to get a representative from City Hall to welcome Liston upon his return. His efforts fell on deaf ears. When the plane landed, not a soul was there to meet him.

"It was one of the saddest things I've ever seen," said McKinney, who had become friendly with Liston and even sparred a few rounds with him. "Sonny didn't say a word, his Adam's apple just moved a bit. But he was crushed. He never really recovered from that moment."

Even the press continued to hammer away at Liston. Larry Merchant, later boxing analyst for the HBO cable network but then sports editor of the *Daily News,* couldn't resist taking a sarcastic dig at Liston's past. "A celebration for Philadelphia's first heavyweight champ is now in order," wrote Merchant. "Emily Post probably would recommend a ticker-tape parade. For confetti we can use shredded warrants of arrest."

Philly's Finest were also unimpressed by Liston's pugilistic accomplishments, and when the new champion was issued a summons for driving "too slow," he gave up on the City of Brotherly Love and moved to Denver. But before leaving he leveled the city with a parting shot that will probably outlast the memory of his boxing career.

"I'd rather be a lamppost in Denver than the mayor of Philadelphia," cracked the disgruntled champion as he headed west.

The rematch with Patterson the following July in Las Vegas proved little more than a replay of their first encounter. Patterson lasted until 2:10 of the opening round, exactly four seconds longer than in his previous effort. There was, however, a training camp incident which provided a revealing insight into Sonny's personality.

Liston conducted public workouts every afternoon at the Thunderbird. At the time, a brash young heavyweight by the name of Cassius Clay was campaigning for the next shot at Liston's title. Clay, already a consummate showman, would regularly pay his way into the workouts and heckle Sonny as he went through his paces. Judging by the deadpan he maintained, one might think Liston hardly noticed his tormentor. But he did. One night, accompanied by his cronies, Liston spotted Clay bent over a craps table inside the casino. He crept up behind Clay and tapped him on the shoulder. When Cassius turned around, Liston slapped him hard across the face. Flabbergasted, it was all Clay could do to stammer, "What did you do that for?"

"Because you're too damn fresh," growled Liston as he stalked away, convinced Clay was a sissy. To Sonny's jailhouse mentality, if you confronted a guy and he backed down, he was a punk and you didn't have to worry about him anymore. It was a miscalculation that was to soon cost Liston his title.

Practically nobody gave Clay a prayer of beating the man he had mischievously nicknamed the "Big Ugly Bear," especially Liston. Sonny was certain of his own invincibility and had begun to slack off in his training. Beginning with the Patterson rematch, he only boxed with sparring partners who made him look good. Upon arrival in Miami, his sexual habits proved far more strenuous than his training routine. Besides Geraldine, whom he'd always slept with right up to, and including, the night before a fight, Liston was also keeping company with two other women. Writer Hal Conrad, who was working as a publicist for Liston's latest managers, Jack and Robert Nilon, was worried about the champ's conditioning and urged him to buckle down before it was too late.

"He told me, 'Don't worry, Hal. I'll put the evil eye on this faggot at the weigh-in and psych him right out of the fight,'" remembered Conrad.

As it turned out, it was Liston who was upstaged at the weigh-in. Clay went into his crazyman act, disrupting the entire proceeding with his bizarre antics. What effect Clay's histrionics had on Liston is difficult to ascertain, but one thing is certain, the champion was prepared for no more than a three round fight when he entered the ring at the Miami Beach Auditorium the evening of February 25, 1964.

Clay, who as Muhammed Ali would soon become an international superstar, was considered by most observers nothing more than an ostentatious braggart prior to his first fight with Liston. Many so-called experts dismissed his blinding hand and foot speed as superficial flash that would disintegrate the first time Liston sunk a hook into his belly. Sure, Clay was undefeated in nineteen pro bouts since winning a gold medal at the 1960 Olympics. But who had he beaten except a bunch of old men and an assortment of stumblebums? The overwhelming consensus was that Sonny would button his lip and send him home to Louisville in a baggie.

Liston was installed as a prohibitive seven to one favorite, but once the first bell sounded, the only one who looked more foolish than the odds makers was the defending champion. Clay danced around the ring, easily avoiding Liston's best punches. By the end of the third, Liston was cut under his left eye and running low on gas. Clay was gaining confidence every time Sonny missed and was also starting to find the range for his own, rapier-like counters. Liston did slightly better in the fourth, and when Clay returned to his corner, he complained to trainer Angelo Dundee that he couldn't see.

"I can't see, Angelo! My eyes are burning," yelled Clay. "Cut the gloves off. We're going home."

"No way," snapped Dundee. "Get in there and fight. If you can't see, keep away from him until your eyes clear."

Dundee literally shoved the protesting Clay out for the fifth round. Cassius did his best to follow Dundee's advice and called upon all of his marvelous athletic ability to survive the round. Though Clay managed to escape a knockout blow, Sonny worked him over well enough, especially to the body. His eyesight fully recovered by the start of the sixth, Clay dazzled the disheartened and spent champion with pinpoint combinations. When Liston returned to his corner at the end of the round, he plopped on his stool a beaten man.

"That's it," grunted Liston as his cornermen climbed between the ropes. Maybe they didn't hear him, maybe they didn't understand his meaning. Whatever the case, they continued getting him ready for the seventh round. Liston just sat there staring straight ahead, but when trainer Willie Reddish slipped his mouthpiece back in, Liston spit it out.

"That's it, I said," growled Liston.

As the bell sounded for the seventh round, Jack Nilon and Reddish, explained to referee Barney Felix that Sonny had injured his left shoulder and couldn't go any further. Liston's title was gone, his reputation as an invincible fighter forever ruined.

The controversy created by the less-than-satisfactory conclusion created two pieces of fiction that have become part of boxing lore. First, was Liston's alleged injury. The defrocked champion's personal physician, Dr. Robert Bennett, said it appeared Liston had injured a nerve or pulled a tendon. A selection of various other doctors inspected the shoulder and declared Liston injury was legitimate. As evidence they pointed to the fact Liston's left arm and shoulder were "swollen" to such an extent they measured two inches larger than those on the right side of his body. In truth, the

The first bout between Sonny Liston (right) and Muhammad Ali, then known as Cassius Clay, February 25, 1964, at Miami Beach. Clay won the world heavyweight title under highly controversial circumstances. (Photo courtesy of *The Ring* magazine)

Ex-heavyweight champion Sonny Liston sits in a Denver police patrol wagon after being arrested for driving under the influence of alcohol, December 25, 1964. (AP photo)

injury was a hoax, a fabrication created to make Liston's capitulation more palatable. Liston's left arm and shoulder had always been bigger than his right, a legacy from his early days in the cotton fields. Other symptoms, such as Liston's claim that he did not have any feeling from the left side of his neck down to his elbow, were strictly subjective and impossible to prove or disprove.

So, what really happened? The answer is deceptively simple: The poorly conditioned Liston was demoralized, close to exhaustion, and getting slapped silly by a younger, fresher and highly talented boxer. In the harsh parlance of the fight game, "he quit like a dog."

The other generally accepted myth is that it was liniment used on Liston's shoulder which found its way into Clay's eyes, temporarily blinding him. The reality was far more repulsive. It was a deliberate attempt to blind Clay. Liston's cutman, Joe Polino, had long carried a "special potion" tucked away, to be used as an emergency bailout should Liston have undue difficulty with an opponent. In all likelihood, it had been used only twice before the Clay fight, in Liston's first bout with Cleveland Williams, and again during Sonny's difficult match with Eddie Machen. Whose idea it was to put this cowardly tactic to use against Williams and Machen is unclear, but according to Polino, it was *Liston* who requested it against Clay. After "doctoring" Sonny's gloves between the third and fourth rounds, Polino threw the evidence as far under the ring as he could. The fact Liston was unable to dispose of the virtually sightless Clay during the fifth round, speaks volumes for Clay's courage and defensive skills. Investigations into the bout were carried out by a variety of agencies, including the U.S. Senate, but none uncovered any illegalities.

The contract for the Clay-Liston bout had a return clause, and after the usual amount of wrangling, a return match was scheduled for November in Boston. Stung by the criticism resulting from his dismal showing in the first bout, Liston threw himself into training as never before. By all accounts he looked a new man. What would have happened had the rematch taken place on the originally scheduled date is anyone's guess. But a few days before the fight

Clay, who by then had changed his name, first to Cassius X and then to Muhammad Ali, suffered a double hernia and the bout was postponed.

Due to Liston's inability to obtain a boxing license in many jurisdictions and Ali's controversial conversion to the Muslim faith, the promoters had to scramble for a venue willing to accept the rescheduled return match. They settled for the highly unlikely city of Lewiston, Maine, a drab textile center of about 40,000 inhabitants. The travesty which unfolded there on May 25, 1965 before a scant crowd of 2,434 is recognized as one of the most notorious affairs in a sport overloaded with ignominious episodes.

Liston, a slight favorite at six to five, flopped to the canvas moments into the opening round after fielding what has become known as Ali's "phantom punch." The referee, former heavyweight champion Joe Walcott, failed to pick up the timekeeper's count and permitted the fight to continue despite the fact that well over ten seconds had elapsed before Liston regained his feet. Finally alerted to his error, Walcott stopped the bout with both fighters on their feet and boxing, as cries of "Fix!" filled the minor league hockey arena. Though the time of the knockout was announced as one minute of the first round, films of the fight show that 1:42 had elapsed by the time Walcott declared Liston out.

The ensuing uproar threatened to bury boxing once and for all. Most people, whether they'd seen the bout or not, were sure Liston had thrown the fight and no punch had landed. Others, including Nat Fleischer, maintained Ali had connected with a bonafide blow and the knockout genuine. Everybody agreed the proceedings had resulted in still another black eye for boxing.

In fact, as careful examination of the films indicates, Liston had been hit, though certainly not hard enough to cause a one-punch defeat. He had simply taken the first opportunity that came along to go into the tank. The larger question is why. The answer is fear. During training, he had been visited by a couple of tough guys claiming to be representing the Black Muslims. Their message was brutally simple: if Liston regained the title, there would be a bullet waiting for him. Whether the threat was genuine, or whether the men were actually Black Muslims, is not known. But Liston certainly took them seriously. So did Lewiston police chief Joe Farrand, who had heard the widespread rumors of death threats and ordered spectators searched on their way into the arena.

"I don't think Sonny was interested in winning his second fight with Ali," said Liston's cornerman Teddy King, who confirmed reports of the so-called Black Muslims' unwelcome visit. King also remembered an incident immediately following the fight which indicated the phony nature of Liston's performance.

"We had just got back to the hotel after the fight. I was outside Sonny's room and overheard Geraldine laying him out for quitting," said King. "She was really letting him have it, and Sonny just stood there and took it like a little kid. When we came in the room, he said, 'Tell her I got hit, Teddy.' I didn't know what to say, so I just kept my mouth shut and nodded."

While back-to-back disgraces should have ended Liston's career, they didn't. Over the next four years, he won fourteen straight bouts, reestablishing himself as a contender. In December of 1969, he faced Philadelphia Leotis Martin in a nationally televised bout emanating from Las Vegas, where Sonny had resided for the past several years. If he had won, a title bout with champion Joe Frazier at Madison Square Garden was a strong possibility. Martin, a hard-luck boxer with a murderous punch, survived an early beating to knock out Liston in the ninth round of a punishing fight. Liston's last hope for regaining the title was gone.

He fought once more the next year, stopping Chuck Wepner, a ham-'n'-egger known as the "Bayonne Bleeder," in the tenth round of a bout held at a small, smoke-filled club in Jersey City. Liston's long, controversial boxing career was over. By the end of the year, he would be dead.

Despite his reputation, Liston was not a bad man in the strict sense of the term. A misunderstood loner, he could be moody and difficult to get along with at times, but there was also another side to Liston. He loved kids, adopted several (both black and white),

Sonny and Geraldine Liston arrive home at Philadelphia International Airport during Sonny's reign as world champion. "I'd rather be a lamppost in Denver than mayor of Philadelphia," cracked Liston after relocating in Colorado.

Liston's split-level home in Las Vegas, where his wife discovered the former heavyweight champion's body, January 5, 1971. The exact cause of Liston's death remains a mystery. (AP photo)

and had great empathy for those down on their luck. Teddy King recalled the time Sonny handed out food to bums along Chicago's skid row. It was his surly manner, as much as anything else, that alienated people.

"If Sonny liked you, you were okay," remembered Milt Baily, another second who worked Liston's corner during his salad days. "But if he didn't like you, to hell with you. That's just the way he was."

To an extent, Liston's gruff manner was a put-on. Unknown to most, Liston was also a sensitive man, especially about his age. He was deeply hurt by the way he was treated after winning the championship, and resented the way police harassed him. Lusty and ribald by nature, he was, nevertheless, henpecked by Geraldine, a domineering woman who definitely wore the pants in the Liston household. Like most human beings, he was neither sinner nor saint, just a complex jumble of both. Unfortunately for Liston, old habits die hard and he continued to consort with shady characters during the last few years of his life. Exactly what illegal activities he was involved with, if any, is open to opinion. But as King said, "Sonny was the kind of guy always ready to do something bad."

Las Vegas gym owner Johnny Tocco, who trained Liston for his last two fights, said although he did not believe Sonny used hard drugs, he might have been "hustling junk" for others. Jack McKinney, who had left the boxing beat by the time of Liston's death, heard rumors Liston had "tried to move in on some loan sharks from East Vegas, who he'd been working for as a collector." His flagrant association with a white prostitute had also been unpopular in Las Vegas. Whatever the story, practically all sources agree Sonny did not spend his last years baking cookies for the church social.

According to Captain Gene Clark of the Las Vegas sheriff's office, one-fourth of an ounce of heroin was found in a balloon in the bedroom where Liston's body was discovered. A small quantity of marijuana was also found in the house. Early newspaper accounts suggested a possible overdose, and sheriff's deputies said Sonny's corpse had puncture marks on both arms which "could" have been caused by a needle. The mystery deepened when Clark County -coroner Mark Herman ruled Liston died of natural causes due to "lung congestion brought on by a poor oxygen and nutrient blood supply to the heart muscles." True, traces of morphine and codeine which would normally result from a breakdown of heroin in the body were found, but "not sufficient amounts" to cause death.

Did Liston die of natural causes? Did he take an accidental overdose? Or were more sinister forces at work? The most common view among boxing people is that Liston had fallen from grace with the Las Vegas underworld and been given a "hot shot," the street name for an intentional overdose, often administered at gun point.

One far-out story—advanced by the tabloid television show "Unsolved Mysteries"—claimed Liston was bumped-off for reneging on a deal to throw the Wepner fight. But in an interview published in *Boxing News,* Wepner's manager, Al Braverman, called the hypothesis "absolutely the biggest God damned horseshit I've ever heard."

Those subscribing to the "hot shot" theory feel the coroner's report was watered down for some reason, perhaps to avoid further adverse publicity for a city that depends on tourist dollars for its livelihood. Moreover, they point to the fact Liston had an abnormal fear of needles, and although known to drink vodka on the rocks and maybe take a puff of marijuana, was never associated with heroin use.

Tocco, who was close to Liston during his final years, thinks the "hot shot" theory could very well be accurate, but doesn't completely discount natural causes. Liston had been involved in a traffic accident Thanksgiving Day and spent a few days in Nevada Memorial Hospital. Maybe his injuries were more serious than anybody knew. Tocco remembers visiting the former champion in the hospital and Sonny showing him where doctors had inserted needles in his arm. But it is highly unlikely those marks would still be present five or six weeks later.

Liston's sudden death was the brutal final chapter in a life shrouded in mystery and filled with unanswered questions, a poetically fitting ending for a classic anti-hero. For while Liston's escapades, both in and outside of the boxing ring, had been the object of public scrutiny for years, he nevertheless carried countless secrets to his grave.

9

They Died With Their Gloves Off

Things always seemed to happen so fast for Davey Moore. NBC-TV labeled him one of "Tomorrow's Champions" the moment he turned pro in November of 1980. Just eight victories later, Moore found himself in Tokyo challenging Tadashi Mihara for the WBA junior middleweight championship. Most experts thoughts he'd been thrown in over his head and destined for a fall. But Moore fooled them, winning the title with an eighth round technical knockout.

Moore had no time to bask in the glory of his accomplishment or rest on his laurels. Two months later, he was shipped off to South Africa to defend against Charlie Weir, a slugger with a proclivity for foul tactics and a rabid local following. It was another tall order for Moore, especially considering he'd be boxing a white man in Johannesburg. But once again, the young warrior from the Bronx rose to the occasion and stopped his challenger in the fifth round. That was the easy part. The hard part came after his hand was raised in victory. A gang of racist goons, enraged by Weir's downfall, tried to mug Moore on the way back to his hotel. It was like something out of a bad movie, but all too real. Luckily, Moore and his cornermen fought off their attackers and made it back home to the United States in one piece.

Life continued to zoom by for the new champ. By 1983, Moore's beaming face and trademark victory lap around the ring had become increasingly familiar sights to American TV audiences. He'd racked up two more successful title defenses, but it still wasn't enough. If boxing's power brokers were determined to use up Moore as fast as possible, he was their ever-ready accomplice. Roberto Duran was anxious to win a third title and Moore jumped at the chance to give it to him.

Duran was already a boxing legend with more than eighty bouts under his belt, a fierce, deadly-punching ring artist who knew tricks that were never in the book. Despite the fact he was the titleholder, Moore, with only a dozen professional bouts to his credit, was a comparative novice. He had never fought anyone within sniffing distance of Duran in terms of overall class. It was suicide, but you couldn't tell Davey Moore that.

"I advised Davey not to fight Duran," said Ben Cognetta, a longtime friend of Moore's, who later became his manager. "I knew he didn't have enough experience. But he took it anyway. There were two reasons: Number one was the money. Number two was recognition. Even though he was the champ, he thought nobody knew who Davey Moore was. And that bothered him."

The match drew a capacity crowd of over 18,000 fans to Madison Square Garden to witness what amounted to an obscene massacre. Moore was unmercifully beaten by Duran before referee Ernesto Magana belatedly stopped the inhumane slaughter in the eighth round. The fact Moore had undergone dental surgery only a few days before the bout made matters even worse. At the conclusion his face was grotesquely swollen, battered practically beyond recognition. Despite the fact everyone made a lot of money, it was a shameful night for boxing.

Moore's descent was just as rapid as his rise. He won three out of four fights over the next three years, finally obtaining a shot at Buster Drayton, who held the IBF version of the junior middleweight crown. They met at Juan-les-Pins on the French Riviera, and while Moore gave his usual valiant effort, Drayton hammered him into another knockout defeat. Though he didn't know it at the time, Moore was finished as a world-class boxer.

As his fortunes continued to plummet, Moore embarked on one last comeback. He didn't have much choice. During his six-figure-purse days he purchased a home in an exclusive neighborhood in Holmdel, New Jersey, where he lived with his girlfriend and their son. He was behind on his mortgage payments and the bank was preparing to foreclose. Most boxing people considered Moore washed-up, but ex-champs always retain a modicum of marquee value. Moore knew he'd be able to squeeze a few more paydays out of his weary body.

Cognetta, however, felt Davey had the potential to be more than just a stepping stone for an assortment of punks and prospects looking to add a former champ's name to their resumes. Cognetta knew Moore had never really been given a chance to learn his trade properly. He'd been rushed from the start, thrown to the wolves for the sake of the almighty dollar, a victim of television's insatiable appetite for fresh meat. Cognetta's plan was to have Moore start all over again, acquire the skills he'd long neglected.

"Davey's idea of boxing was to go in the ring and try to crack the other guy before he got nailed himself. He didn't even think about defense," said Cognetta. "So, I sat down with him and told him what I wanted him to do. I stipulated he had to agree to go along with the program before we signed a contract."

Moore figured it was worth a shot and began private sessions with trainer Johnny Persol, the former light heavyweight contender. Moore was embarrassed to work out when other boxers were in the gym. After all, he'd been a world champion and didn't want anyone to see him learning such basic moves as how to throw the jab properly, or tie a guy up when hurt.

The battered face of Davey Moore (left) is clearly evident in this photograph of his losing bout against Roberto Duran at Madison Square Garden, June 16, 1983. (Photo courtesy of *The Ring* magazine)

"Davey was a very bright guy," said Cognetta. "He had a very quick mind and he was starting to come around, learn the things Persol and I wanted him to learn. You know, he won the last two fights on his comeback...stopped Hector Rosario and Gary Coates."

The last time Cognetta spoke to Moore, both men were in a joyous mood. He'd phoned to tell the boxer about a contract he'd just signed for a series of three bouts in France. It was the best news Moore had received in quite a while.

"It was for decent money, and I figured that with those three fights, he could be right back in line for a title shot," remembered Cognetta. "When I told him, Davey said, 'Great, now I'm really going to work.'"

A short time after speaking with his manager, Moore drove to a nearby store to buy some groceries. It was a rainy June afternoon, but his spirits must have been high, his mind filled with thoughts of his upcoming European campaign. His future was suddenly looking a bit brighter. It wasn't the good old days before Duran, but it would do. He was only twenty-nine years old, still young enough to dream of becoming champion again.

When Moore arrived back home, he parked his Montero, a jeep-like vehicle, in the driveway. The driveway was built on a steep slope, and as Moore prepared to carry the groceries into the house, he noticed the jeep rolling backwards toward the street. In an effort to stop it, he jammed his muscular back against the automobile, hoping to hold it in place until he could figure out what to do. The next thing Moore knew, his feet slipped on the rain-slickend driveway and flew out from under him. He was in a sitting position when the jeep rolled over the top of him, folding his body in half like a jacknife. The jeep kept rolling with Moore trapped underneath. He was practically broken in two.

Moore had acted instinctively, attacking the runaway jeep the same way he'd gone after his opponents in the ring. He forgot all about his jab, all about defense. He died the way he fought—full speed ahead, damn the consequences. When medical help arrived,

Moore was already dead. Like everything else in his life, it had all happened so fast. Davey Moore never had a chance.

Davey Moore was not the first boxer to be crushed under the wheels of an automobile. A similar accident occurred in 1921 when Auslin Rice was run over by his own truck in New London, Connecticut. Then there was the original Joe Walcott, the legendary "Barbados Demon," who held the world welterweight title from 1901 to 1904. Walcott, who stood just a fraction of an inch over five-foot-one and seldom weighed over 142 pounds, was renowned as "giant killer" because of his uncanny ability to beat men much bigger than himself. His list of victims even included heavyweight Joe Choynski, who once held heavyweight champion Jim Jeffries to a draw.

Walcott, one of the premiere boxers of his era, was a particularly sad case. He earned large sums of money during his career and owned a fine home in Malden, Massachusetts. But once his fighting days were over, Walcott fell on hard times and ended up working as a porter at Madison Square Garden, mopping up for pugs who couldn't have carried his jock strap a decade or two before. In the end, it was another catch-weight bout that did him in. Walcott may have been a giant killer in the ring, but the former champion was no match for a couple of tons of moving metal. In 1935, he was struck and killed by an automobile near Massillon, Ohio.

Undoubtedly the strangest death of this sort was suffered by two-time light heavyweight champion Victor Galindez. The burly Argentine boxer was a free spirit, an incorrigible thrill-seeker who lived his life on the edge of danger, always on the outlook for new ways to cheat death. A month before he fought Len Hutchins for the vacant WBA light heavyweight title in 1974, Galindez tore up his right knee in a car wreck. A week before the fight, he twisted his right ankle while riding a horse. His management wanted to postpone the fight, but Galindez wouldn't hear of it. He was worried he might never get another chance. As if his knee and ankle injuries weren't enough, the irrepressible lug gulped down a large

The orginal Joe Walcott, known to his fans as the "Barbados Demon."
Though Walcott weighed less than 150 pounds, he beat many light
heavyweights and heavyweights. (Photo courtesy of *the Ring* magazine)

portion of Frogs a la Provencal after the weigh-in, which hit his stomach like an atom bomb.

"With a sick stomach, with a badly injured knee and a swollen ankle, I got into the ring," recalled Galindez many years later, "What a crazy man I was."

Despite a multitude of handicaps, the hobbled Galindez bludgeoned Huntchins into a thirteenth-round knockout and won the title. He was a wild and crazy guy all right, but he also knew how to fight. It was the beginning of a lengthy run of success. Galindez made several fortunes with his fists, investing his purses in real estate and high-performance cars. He bought a chalet and nine apartment buildings in Buenos Aires. He lost the lot when he divorced his first wife, but the setback hardly fazed him. Galindez simply kept fighting and soon replenished his bank account. He bought more apartments and another chalet. But above all, he bought cars; lots of cars. At one point, he owned four Torinos, a Camaro, a Corvair, a Tullieta, four Peugeots, four Fords, a Chevy pickup, five Mercedes Benzes, one Corvette, one BMW, one Yamaha motorcycle and two Kawasaki motorcyles. He had to fight on a regular basis just to keep them filled with gasoline.

According to those who knew him well, Galindez was obsessed with leopards. They were wild and fast, hard to capture, ferocious fighters—just like Galindez. He even upholstered the interior of his first sports car with leopard skin. And like the big cat, Galindez seemed to have nine lives. His medical chart was almost as long as his boxing record. During his career, he'd suffered multiple injuries from a motorcycle accident; severely lacerated his elbow in a fall by a swimming pool; dislocated his elbow winning a fight, and broken his jaw. His bushy eyebrows were ripped open in practically every bout. But none of these disasters seemed to bother Galindez. In many ways, he was just like a big kid, sure of his immortality, impervious to the punishment his body was absorbing.

Galindez, with his swaggering charm and bruising ring style, was a national hero in Argentina. But the economic structure of boxing made it necessary for him to make frequent trips abroad to defend his title. He became a popular attraction around the world, fighting in the United States, South Africa and across Europe. By the summer of '78, he'd made ten successful defenses of the light heavyweight title, beating such outstanding challengers as Yaqui Lopez, Richie Kates, Eddie Gregory and Pierre Fourie, as well as many lesser lights. When he climbed into the ring to face Mike Rossman on the evening of September 15, 1978, Galindez hadn't lost a bout since 1971, an unbeaten streak of forty-three fights.

Not that all of Galindez' victories were easy. He fought a running battle with the scales for many years. It had always been a terrible struggle to melt his chunky body down to the division limit of 175 pounds, and he frequently entered the ring drained by the effort. The day of the Rossman fight, Galendez was forced to jump rope for seventy minutes in his hotel's boiler room—and still needed two trips to the scales before making weight! Rossman, who fought better than he ever had before, or ever would again, won the title when the referee stopped the fight in the thirteenth round.

The loss of the title was a shattering blow to Galindez. He'd held it so long, he'd forgotten what it was like to not be champion. Stung by defeat and his loss of prestige, he vowed to regain the title. Then came the famous incident when Galindez refused to come out of his dressing room for a nationally televised rematch with Rossman. Officially, it was because of some silly beef over judges. Off the record, some whispered Galindez wasn't in shape; others figured it was all a case of gamesmanship. In any event, he left Rossman in a snit and Howard Cosell practically speechless—practically.

It was all very disconcerting, but less than a year after he lost his precious title, Galindez lived up to his promise. He regained the championship, bullying Rossman into a tenth-round surrender in New Orleans. It was to be his last moment of greatness. Age, injury and so many tough battles were starting to catch up with Galindez. In the first defense of his second reign, a left hook from Marvin Johnson broke his jaw and knocked him cold. The leopard was losing his teeth.

Convinced he could still campaign successfully in the heavier,

Former two-time light heavyweight champion Victor Galindez gives the thumbs-up signal just before the start of his first—and last—auto race. (Photo courtesy of *The Ring* magazine)

newly-created cruiserweight division, Galindez embarked on a comeback in June of 1980 against Jesse Burnett, a fighter he'd beaten several years before in Copenhagen. Little of the old fire was left, however, and Burnett won the decision. Still, Victor refused to give up, refused to admit it was over. He went back into training a month later, positive he could rekindle the flame. It was not to be. During a sparring session with Antonio Musladino, Galindez experienced a sharp pain in his eyes, and it was discovered he'd suffered a pair of detached retinas. While an operation corrected the problem, boxing was forbidden.

A relatively young man of thirty-one, Galindez looked for new ways to satisfy his craving for adventure. He was in reasonably good shape financially, but needed something to stimulate him, something to replace the electrifying rush he experienced in the ring. As it turned out, he didn't have to look any further than his bulging garage for inspiration.

"I wanted to become a boxing champion. I became one," Galindez bragged to a reporter for Argentina's *Gente Magazine.* "I'd now like to become a champion auto racer. It's less dangerous than boxing. Racing is a lot safer. You don't have to take punches in racing."

"He's crazy," said his second wife. "He's not happy unless he's doing something dangerous."

Crazy or not, Galindez hurled himself into the sport with the same sort of enthusiasm he'd shown for boxing. He soon enlisted the aid of a mechanic/driver friend named Antonio Lizeviche, who helped him obtain his racing license. They entered their first race together on October 26, 1980, at 25 De Mayo, a town about two hundred miles southwest of Buenos Aires. Lizeviche, a former Formula One racer, was the driver, Galindez his co-pilot. A news photograph taken just before the start of the race shows Galindez wearing helmet and goggles, giving the "thumbs up" signal out the window of his souped-up Chevrolet. He looked happy again, his competitive juices flowing just the same as before the sound of the opening bell.

If Galindez knew he had to die in a racing accident, he would probably have wanted to go out in a spectacular smashup, preferably on the final lap, headed for the checkered flag. But it didn't happen that way. According to reports, Galindez and Lizeviche's car had engine trouble early in the race and pulled over to the side of the track. Both men got out of the vehicle and despite warnings to "stay in your car" shouted by other drivers, they began to walk back to the pits as oncoming cars wizzed by at close to one hundred twenty-five miles per hour. Then it happened. Car number 71, driven by Marcial Feijoo, spun out of control and hit the rear of the car along side of it. Feijoo swerved away and slammed into Galindez and Lizeviche, killing them both instantly.

Galindez's body lay in state in Luna Park, the site of so many of his boxing triumphs, and the venue where he first won the world title. Thousands of admirers filed past his casket, paying their final respects to the boxer who had given them so many magic moments. Perhaps some of them even envied the life he'd lived; the glamor, the money, the excitement. Yes, Galindez sure had been a wild and crazy guy; a brave one too. But it is doubtful any of his mourners would have traded places with him. Galindez' last ticket to adventure was strictly a one-way trip.

Many other boxers have perished in more orthodox traffic accidents. Among the earliest was William Lawrence Stribling, Jr., better known as Young Stribling. One of the few world-class boxers to campaign successfully in every weight class from bantam to heavyweight, Stribling was among the most popular athletes Georgia has ever produced. Damon Runyon called him "King of the Canebreaks," a sarcastic reference to Strib's early days touring rural tank towns. But by the morning of October 1, 1933, Stribling was an international celebrity, one of boxing's most prominent personalities.

Stribling had seldom felt happier. And why not? He was healthy, wealthy and married to a wonderfully sexy woman who had just presented him with a brand new son. Still movie-star handsome after two hundred eighty-six professional fights, he was a charmer leading a charmed life. The boxer had risen early and shot a round of golf at the Idle Hour Country Club, just a few miles outside of Downtown Macon. Around noon, he left the links, fired up his motorcycle and roared off down Forsyth Road toward Macon Hospital to visit his wife and baby. It would be feeding time soon, and he didn't want to miss it.

The warm autumn air felt fantastic as it zipped by Stribling's face, and he couldn't help smiling as he rode and reflected on what a fantastic adventure his life had been. So what if he hadn't won a world title yet? He was only twenty-eight, there was still plenty of time. The way Young Stribling figured it, he was just about the luckiest guy in Georgia.

Stribling had just passed the Buck Ice and Coal Company, when he noticed his longtime friend Roy Barrow driving down the road traveling in the opposite direction. At exactly the same instant Stribling turned to wave at his old buddy, bond salesman R.V. Johnson, who was trailing Barrow's car, decided to pass on the left. Stribling caught sight of Johnson's oncoming car out of the corner of his eye and attempted to swerve into the ditch. But he was a split second too late and his motorcycle smashed into the front fender of Johnson's car. The impact threw the fighter over the handlebars and sent him tumbling onto the side of the road. Miss Francis Jones, a registered nurse, was riding with Barrow. She rushed to Stribling's aid and fashioned a tourniquet from her cape in an attempt to stem the geyser of blood squirting from his leg. Poor Strib's left foot was almost completely severed at the ankle.

The mortally injured fighter was rushed to the same Macon hospital where his wife, Clara, had given birth to their son ten days earlier. A team of surgeons amputated Stribling's foot and battled to save his life. Telegrams poured in from all over the world, including many from former opponents: "I couldn't keep you on the canvas, Bill, and this won't either," cabled Max Schmeling, whom Stribling had unsuccessfully challenged for the world heavyweight title two years earlier. But it was hopeless. Stribling was failing fast, and

Young Stribling as he looked in 1924, the year he challenged Paul Berlenbach for the world light heavyweight championship. (Photo courtesy of *The Ring* magazine)

with his family gathered at his bedside, he died as the sun rose on the morning of October 1933.

When it comes to death on the highway, prize fighters have never taken a back seat to anyone, not even country & western singers or rock 'n' roll stars. The biggest name to cash in his chips in an auto wreck was Jack Johnson, the first black heavyweight champion and a notoriously bad driver.

The pandemonium of his championship days and highly-publicized love life long past, the old champ's lone flirtation with danger in his waning years came behind the wheel of a Lincoln Zephyr. He'd always been fascinated by speed and once challenged Barney Oldfield, the fastest auto racer of the time, to a match race. Oldfield, in a sixty-horsepower Knox, blew the "Galveston Giant's" doors off, but failed to dampen his enthusiasm for driving like a maniac. The boxer's list of "moving violations" was almost as long as his fight record. He'd been repeatedly fined for speeding, driving on the sidewalk, failure to stop at a red light, passing illegally, and just about anything else you can think of involving the reckless handling of an automobile.

On the afternoon of June 10, 1946, Johnson was traveling with companion Fred Scott from Texas to New York City along a stretch of U.S. Highway No. 1, just south of the Franklinton line, twenty miles north of Raleigh, North Carolina. The ex-champ had just completed a tour of personal apperances and was on his way to see the Joe Louis-Billy Conn rematch. He never made it. The sixty-eight-year-old Johnson lost control of the powerful car he was driving, causing it to crash into a light pole and overturn. Both passengers were thrown from the car, but only the elderly boxer was seriously injured. He was taken to St. Agnes Hospital in Raleigh suffering from internal injuries and shock. A few hours later, Dr. W.D. Allison announced that Jack Johnson was dead.

As the decades of the 20th century flew by like Berma Shave signs along the highway, boxing's road-related body count continued to mount. Numerous fighters, the famous and the not-so-famous,

Jack Johnson and his wife, the former Etta Duryea, in Havana, Cuba. Duryea committed suicide in 1912, but Johnson lived on until 1946 when he died in a car wreck. (Photo courtesy of *The Ring* magazine)

lost their lives amid the sounds of screeching brakes and crunching metal. The list goes on and on. Champions, contenders and just plain pugs, all reduced to a common denominator; fellow travelers who never reached their destination.

Australian fans were positive they had a future world champion in Dave Sands, whose real name was David Richie. The personable, stiff-punching Aborigine was one of six boxing brothers and a gifted athlete. He'd already won the British Empire middleweight title (and every Australian belt from middleweight to heavy) by the time he journeyed to Chicago in 1951 to box Carl "Bobo" Olson. Sands decisioned the future middleweight king over ten rounds, impressing American observers with his all-round ability. His performance would probably have led to a world title challenge if fate hadn't stepped in and shattered yet another set of dreams. Sands, age twenty-six, was killed August 11, 1952, when the truck he was driving overturned in Dundog, Newcastle, New South Wales.

Canadian welterweight Johnny Greco, who'd made a big hit in New York during the mid-1940s, lost his life in a 1954 highway accident in Montreal. Three years later, American welter Eddie Murdock suffered a similar fate in Mojave, California. In the 1960s', "Irish" Bob Murphy, Bobby Horn and Chic Calderwood joined the ranks of main-event boxers who crashed heaven's gate behind the wheel of an automboile. The trend continued the following decade when Japan's Masao Ohba, holder of the WBA flyweight title, died of injuries suffered in an auto accident outside Tokyo, January 24, 1973. Ohba's death was a particularly stunning blow to the sport in Japan. Considered the country's finest ringman since Fighting Harada (who held both the flyweight and bantamweight world titles in the '60s), Ohaba had been the one-hundred-twelve-pound champion since October 1970. He'd made five successful defenses; the last a twelve-round knockout over Chartchai Chionoi, just twenty-two days before he died at age twenty-three. While Japan has produced numerous titleholders since, few, if any, have been in Ohba's class.

The great Japanese flyweight Masao Ohba was still world champion when he was killed in an automobile accident outside Tokyo, January 24, 1973. (Photo courtesy of *The Ring* magazine)

The year 1977 saw Dominican welterweight Fausto Rodriguez and his family wiped out in a wretched two-car crash during a rainstorm outside Santo Domingo. American Rodney Bobick (brother of heavyweight contender Duane) died in a one-car smashup near his home in Bowlus, Minnesota. The next year, Jamaican Percey Hayles, who lost his bid to capture the junior welterweight title from Carlos Hernandez in 1956, was killed when a motorist ran over him as he rode his bicycle home one sweltering August afternoon.

South African Arnold Taylor was a face-first slugger, but lacked the heavy punch to compliment his courage. Always a crowd-pleaser, Taylor found his bravery finally rewarded when he won the world bantamweight title from Romeo Anaya, November 3, 1973, in an unusually brutal affair. As one might expect, Taylor didn't hold the title long. Less than a year later, he was out pointed by Korean Soo-Hwan Hong in his first defense. Taylor kept plugging for another couple of years, but called it a career following a knockout loss to Vernon Solis in 1976. While Taylor's fans had been used to seeing him shed blood in the ring, the cheers turned to tears when he spilled his guts all over the highway. Five years after his last fight, the thirty-six-year-old former champ was rubbed out in a motorcycle accident.

Mexico's splendid featherweight Salvador Sanchez spent a significant portion of the $2 million he earned as world champion on nine cars. His favorite was a red Porsche 928. On August 12, 1982, Sanchez was driving the Porsche at a high rate of speed along the highway between Queretaro and his training camp at San Jose Iturbide, about one hundred sixty miles north of Mexico City. He was training for an upcoming title defense against Juan LaPorte at Madison Square Garden and people still wonder why the champion was out driving at 3:30 in the morning. Sanchez normally went to bed at 9:00 PM and was up at 6:30 AM to go running. Who knows? Some have hinted he may have sneaked out to visit a lady and was racing against the dawn, hoping to get back to camp before anyone noticed he was gone. If this was true, it would have been unusual

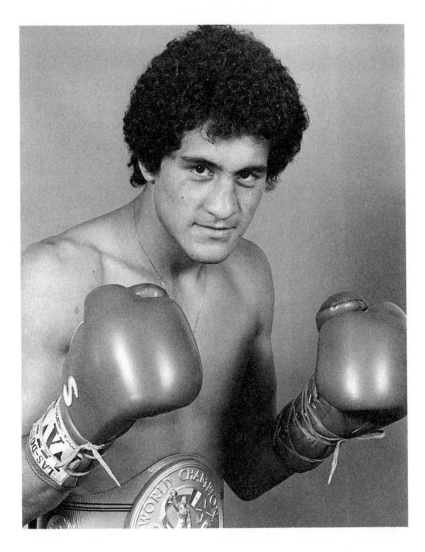

Mexican superstar Salvador Sanchez was still featherweight champion of the world when he met his premature death in 1982. (Photo courtesy of *The Ring* magazine)

behavior for Sanchez, who, in contrast to so many of Mexico's fistic stars, led a reasonably disciplined life on both sides of the ropes. Regardless of the reason for his nocturnal journey, his ultimate rendezvous was with death. Sanchez plowed his sports car into a heavily-loaded tractor-trailer, snuffing out the life of one of Mexico's most gifted champions. He was only twenty-three at the time and left behind a wife and two sons.

Among the first boxers to lose his life in an aviation accident was "Napoleon" Jack Dorval, a journeyman heavyweight whose plane went down over Pennsylvania in 1936. While only the most serious of boxing historians remember Dorval, it would be difficult to find a fan over fifty years of age who doesn't remember Marcel Cerdan, probably the finest fighting machine France has ever produced.

After stopping American Tony Zale in September 1948 to win the world middleweight title, Cerdan returned to France as the country's greatest sporting hero since Georges Carpentier. All of France basked in his glory. Even famed torch singer Edith Piaf found him irresistible, and despite the fact Marcel was married, the romance between the fighter and the *chanteuse* was the talk of two continents. But joy quickly turned to sorrow when Cerdan lost the championship to Jake LaMotta the following June. A rematch was scheduled for December 2, 1949, and the chunky Frenchman was confident he'd regain the crown.

"With all my strength, I want to get back that title that I so stupidly lost," he told friends. "For those who say I am washed-up I can say that despite my thirty-three years and one hundred ten fights, I feel myself at my peak."

Late the evening of October 26, Cerdan boarded an Air France Constellation in Paris for the trip back to New York. Just before the plane took off, he phoned his wife, Marinette, at their home in Casablanca (Piaf was already waiting for him in New York) and told her he would bring back the title. It was the last time she heard the sound of his voice.

In the early hours of the next morning, around 2:50 AM, the plane, in command of Capt. Jean de la Noue, dropped out of radio contact after sending the following message: "Having accomplished first part of trip normally, ready to land at 2:55 on Santa Maria Airdrome, Azores, weather being clear."

Eight hours later the wreckage was sighted near the summit of the 3,600-foot Algarvia Peak of Sao Miguel, ninety miles north of Santa Maria. All forty-eight people aboard were killed, including Cerdan and his manager, Jo Longman. French aviation officials were unsure how the plane strayed so far off course, but theorized that the pilot, confused by rain, fog and lowering clouds, had mistaken Sao Miguel for Santa Maria, an entirely different island.

The French were distraught. Cerdan's untimely death excluded all other topics of conversation in the cafes of Paris. In Casablanca, a large crowd gathered outside the cafe Cerdan owned there and placed wreaths of flowers around the entrance. Even in the United States, where Cerdan's magnetic personality and boxing prowess has earned him thousands of admirers, his death was deeply mourned. At a fight card held at Madison Square Garden the day after his demise, announcer Johnny Addie called the crowd to its feet while the bell tolled ten. Following Cerdan's "final count," Garden organist Gladys Goodding played a stirring rendition of "La Marseillaise." There was hardly a dry eye in the house.

Undoubtedly the most famous boxer to die in a plane crash was the "Brockton Blockbuster," Rocky Marciano. When Marciano hung up his gloves in April of 1956, he'd earned approximately $4 million with his fists and was firmly established as one of the most popular heavyweight champions of all time. His undefeated record of forty-nine consecutive victories (forty-three via knockout) set a division-record that still stands.

Retirement did not offer the best of times for Marciano. While he hosted a syndicated television program featuring old fight films, endorsed products and appeared in small parts on TV and in movies, his finances floundered. In 1959, he trained secretly for a

French hero Marcel Cerdan (third from top) boards an Air France plane for a flight to New York, where he hoped to regain the world middleweight title from Jake LaMotta. Several hours later the plane crashed, killing all 48 people aboard. It was in October, 1949. (Photo courtesy of *The Ring* magazine)

A pot-bellied Muhammad Ali (left) and a toupee-topped Rocky Marciano receive last minute instructions from producer-director Murry Woroner prior to their choreographed computer fight. (Photo courtesy of Big Fight, Inc.)

month while mulling over the possibility of a comeback, but eventually decided against it. Perhaps the memory of other champions such as Joe Louis, Jersey Joe Walcott and Archie Moore, all of whom lost to Rocky when well past their prime, kept him in retirement. But whatever the reason, he wisely lived up to his promise never to come back. The lone exception was several years later when "The Rock" was lured back into the ring for a computerized rematch against Muhammed Ali.

Both Marciano and Ali, who had temporarily lost his boxing license because of his refusal to be inducted into the Armed Forces, were strapped for cash. The choreographed bout was a degrading exercise, an insult to two of boxing's most revered champions. While Rocky appeared relatively trim compared to the grossly overweight Ali, he wore a tacky toupee that made him look like a middle-aged used-car salesman. Several different outcomes were filmed. The one distributed in the United States featured Marciano winning by a thirteenth-round knockout in a wildly exaggerated punchout, complete with globs of fake blood. The farce was eerily similar to a series of Hollywood potboilers produced many years later, starring Sylvester Stallone as a character ironically known as "Rocky."

On August 31, 1969, the day before his forty-sixth birthday, Marciano boarded a single-engine Cessna 172 for a flight from Chicago to Des Moines, Iowa, where a party was going to be held in his honor. About thirty miles east of Des Moines, pilot Glenn Belz, a building contractor, radioed the Des Moines air traffic controller that he was going to land at Newton. It was the last communication anyone had with the three men aboard. At around 10:00 PM, the aircraft crashed into a wooded area about two miles southeast of Newton Airport. All passengers were killed. If there was a silver lining to Marciano's premature death, it was the fact it happened before his travesty with Ali was released to the general public. If Rocky had still been around, he'd have probably died of embarrassment.

People in boxing have to cultivate a gallows sense of humor. It's one of the ways they survive. "I'm not afraid to die," wrote humorist Woody Allen. "I just don't want to be there when it happens." Of course, death is one joke we all get in the end. It's just a question of when.

It's unlikely, Rudell Stitch was thinking about death on the afternoon of June 5, 1960. He was a welterweight contender of considerable merit, having beaten the likes of Isaac Logart, Ralph Dupas, Holly Mims and Yama Bahama. He was just twenty-seven years old, fresh from a victory over Stan Harrington in Honolulu, and had every right to assume good things were in store. In fact he had everything to live for. But death blind-sided Stitch like a cheap shot after the bell.

He was strolling along the banks of the Ohio River near his home in Louisville, Kentucky, on that particular afternoon when he heard the desperate screams of a man floundering helplessly in the river. Showing the same bravery that had carried him through thirty-four professional fights, Stitch dove into the water and swam towards the drowning man. Exactly what went wrong is lost amidst the mud and silt that lines the bottom of the Ohio River. But Rudell Stitch never fought again. He drowned that sunny afternoon, died trying to save the life of a man he didn't even know. What made the tragedy so ironic was the fact Stitch had successfully rescued another man from the same river the previous year. Everybody said Rudell Stitch was a hero, but world champion was the only title he ever aspired to.

The watery death of former world bantamweight champion Joe Lynch on August 1, 1965, wasn't nearly as romantic as Stitch's. In fact, it remains somewhat of a mystery. Though officially ruled an "accidental drowning," there were suspicious circumstances surrounding Lynch's demise.

Tall and rangy for his weight, Lynch was much stronger than his skinny frame indicated. He'd built up considerable muscle working for his father, who ran a moving business, and following a very brief amateur career, turned pro in 1915. This was a golden age for bantamweights in the United States, and Lynch was a main event

Former two-time bantamweight champion Joe Lynch, who drowned in New York's Sheepshead Bay under mysterious circumstances. (Photo courtesy of *The Ring* magazine)

boxer from the very start. He won the world 118-pound title from Pete Herman, December 22, 1920, via a fifteen-round decision at Madison Square Garden. Herman regained the belt the next year, but soon lost it to Johnny Buff. Then it was Lynch's turn again. He stopped Buff in fourteen rounds, July 10, 1922, winning the crown a second time. Lynch held onto the title until 1924, when he lost it for good to Abe Goldstein. Lynch retired in 1926 (with more than one hundred and fifty pro bouts to his credit) and settled down with his wife, Anna, on a small farm in Rockland County, New York, he'd purchased with his ring earnings. Life was good for the ex-champ and he served for several years as the community's postmaster.

When his parents died, Lynch inherited valuable real estate in New York City and made regular visits to his old hometown every month to collect rents. It was while on one of these trips the old fighter met his puzzling death. He disappeared while visiting his brother-in-law, Francis Breen, in Brooklyn. Lynch was still alive when they hauled him out of Sheepshead Bay the next day, but made no statement and died en route to the hospital. Was it really an accident? Or was Lynch, age sixty-six, robbed of his rent money and thrown in the bay? Of course we'll never know the answer. The truth lies buried with Joe Lynch.

While the drowning deaths of Stitch and Lynch ranged from heroic to baffling, the passing of Albert "Chalky" Wright was downright pathetic. Born in Durango, Mexico, in 1912, Wright came up the hard way, engaging in over one hundred and forty professional bouts before getting a shot at world featherweight champion Joey Archibald. His father had deserted his mother when "Chalky" was just a boy, and Wright had to scuffle for a living: picking oranges, shining shoes and working on W.P.A. projects. Boxing was a blessed relief. So when his big chance finally arrived, Wright took full advantage of the opportunity and knocked out Archibald at Griffith Stadium in Washington, D.C., September 11, 1941.

Wright's victory was popular with both the press and the fans. He'd campaigned hard and long, winning not only the majority of

CHALKY
WRIGHT

Former world featherweight champion Chalky Wright as he looked in his prime. Wright's tragic death in 1957 remains one of boxing's most pathetic exits. (Photo courtesy of *The Ring* magazine)

his fights, but many friends along the way. Before his title bout, telegrams of encouragement poured in from around the world, including one from Henry Armstrong, who had relinquished the featherweight title several years before: "Win back the title I was forced to give up," Armstrong wired. "You can do it." Wright was so overcome with joy after starching Archibald, he broke down and cried in the dressing room. The new champ might have been a tough customer in the ring, but outside the ropes he was a sensitive, likeable fellow; the kind of guy who never let hardship and disappointment get him down.

Wright only managed to hang onto the title for a little over a year before losing it to Willlie Pep in November of 1942. Pep gave him a return match in 1944, but Wright had passed his peak and Pep outpointed him again. He fought on until 1949, when he retired at age thirty-six following a knockout loss to Ernie Hunick. For a while, he managed a stable of boxers with Eddie Stanley, but gradually faded away from the boxing scene. The last few years of his life, Wright worked at a bakery in Los Angeles.

In August of 1957, Wright had an argument with his wife, Jennie, and went to stay with his mother at her apartment at 8200 South Main Street. Later that week, on August 12, his mother went out shopping and left the forty-five-year-old former world champion at home alone. When Mrs. Clara E. Wright returned, she found her son dead. He had apparently slipped in the bathtub and drowned while unconscious from a head injury.

On occasion, death can be the final link in a chain of coincidence joining two lives. Mention of many fighter's names immediately brings to mind the name of another. It's kind of like the old word-association game. Someone says "Muhammed Ali" and you instantly think of "Joe Frazier." How about "Willie Pep" and "Sandy Sadler"? Then there are the guys who were good, but never really made it. Guys like "Charley Burley" and "Jimmy Bivins." And let's not forget "Zora Folley" and "Eddie Machen."

Machen and Folley were two of the best heavyweights around during the late 1950s and early 1960s. Though never wildly popular with the paying public, Folley and Machen were always respected as the fine craftsmen they were. Both featured cautious, standup boxing and a substantial punch; cuties with a kick, so to speak. How good were they? Suffice to say, both were astutely avoided by heavyweight champion Floyd Patterson. But it wasn't just their remarkably similar careers that welded Folley and Machen together. They were also united in death.

While their lives had many parallels, they were two totally different kinds of men. Folley, born May 27, 1932, joined the Army at age sixteen and served during the Korean conflict. He won the All-Army heavyweight title and Inter-Service crown twice. But his military career wasn't all gyms and tournaments. He also suffered severe frostbite on his feet when his platoon spent weeks in bitter cold and deep snow without shelter. In fact, by the time the Army flew Folley to Tokyo for treatment, he was in danger of developing gangrene. After convalescing, he returned home to Chandler, Arizona, only to discover his house had burned to the ground while he was away. It was a classic hard luck story: The wounded veteran comes bravely marching home, only to find out fate has shafted him. Broke and desperate for funds to rebuild his home, Folley turned to the only marketable skill he had—boxing.

Machen's early life took a vastly different path. In simplistic terms, he was the unruly one, the evil twin. Born less than two months after Folley, he fell among bad company as a kid and was convicted of armed robbery in 1952. He wasn't exactly Sonny Liston, but young Machen was no Gandhi either. He served three years in prison, where he learned how to box. It wasn't Korea, and Eddie didn't win any gold medals, but by the time he was paroled, he was just as ready for the pros as Folley was when he came out of the Army.

Folley was a kind man, gentle, beloved by all who knew him and generally at peace with the world. Though never wealthy, Zora once forked over $6 thousand to pay for a buddy's kidney surgery. The columnists on every Arizona newspaper wrote warm, sentimental tributes when he died. Some said it was his lack of a "killer instinct" that prevented him from becoming champion. They might have been right. Machen, on the other hand, was deeply troubled. He suffered fits of depression for most of his adult life and was admitted to Napa State Hospital in 1963 after threatening suicide.

Yet despite their contradictory personalities, they fought so many of the same opponents, it's hard not to think of Machen and Folley as a pair. They both beat the likes of Doug Jones, Mike DeJohn, Alex Miteff, Wayne Bethea and Roger Rischer. Machen knocked out Brian London, while Folley lost to the lumbering Englishman on points. Folley managed a draw with Karl Mildenberger, but the German southpaw decisioned Machen. They both lost to Sonny Liston and Ernie Terrell. The career comparisons are endless.

Machen and Folley also fought each other twice. Their first meeting in 1958 resulted in a twelve-round draw described by one critic as the "dullest bout involving top fighters ever staged in the Cow Palace." Even though their counterpunching styles inevitably guaranteed a stinker, they fought a rematch a year and a half later. Folley won the decision the second time around, but both men had better nights against aggressive opponents whose walk-in style complimented their defensive wizardry. Folley's best performance was probably his two-round knockout over Henry Cooper in London in 1961 and his points victories over George Chuvalo, Oscar Bonevena and Bob Foster. Machen was probably at his finest flattening Nino Valdes in 1956 and losing a close decision to Liston in 1960.

Folley was finally rewarded for his many years of dedicated service to the sport with a world title match against Muhammed Ali at Madison Square Garden in March of 1967. It was common knowledge that Ali was fond of Folley and wanted to give him a nice payday before his career was over. The great champion carried Zora for a few rounds and then dispatched him in the seventh with

Zora Folley (left) drives a left into the ribs of Eddie Machen during their
10-round draw, April 9, 1958, at the San Francisco Cow Palace. Machen
and Folley shared similar careers and similiar deaths. (Photo courtesy of
The Ring magazine)

clinical precision, making sure the old fellow didn't get hurt too
badly in the process. There was no such retirement benefit for
Machen. The closest he got to a title shot was in 1965 when he
challenged Terrell for the phony WBA version of the crown, losing
by decision over fifteen rounds.

After the Ali fight, Folley stayed active until he was un-
ceremoniously dispatched by Mac Foster, who knocked down old
Zora six times in the first round. After that, Folley wisely decided
enough was enough and retired in September of 1970. Machen
enjoyed one last moment in the limelight when he upset up-and-
coming Jerry Quarry in 1966. But five months later, future
heavyweight king Joe Frazier stopped Machen in the tenth round of
a bitterly contested brawl, effectively ending any hope Eddie may
have still harbored of winning the championship. Two losing fights
later, he also hung up his gloves for good.

If the careers of Machen and Folley were practically mirror
images, then their deaths were twin reflections of the frustration
and disappointment they shared. Neither man won the prize he
coveted so dearly. Neither man died peacefully in his sleep.
Machen's exit was almost predictable, but Folley's demise came as a
shock to those who knew him as a boxer and as a man.

The early minutes of July 8, 1972, found Folley visiting his good
friend Artis Broom at the Sands Motel in Tucson. Also present was
Broom's wife, Dorothy, and a young woman from Mesa named Ann
Young. They were having a few drinks by the pool and seemed to be
enjoying themselves. What Folley, the first black member of the
Chandler City Council and a married man with nine children, was
doing there is problematical. He was working as a salesman for the
truck division of Rudolph Chevrolet in Phoenix at the time, and
probably just wanted a little relaxation. Whatever the reason, he
would have been better off at home in bed with his wife, Joella.

Apparently, Folley and Broom were having fun, trying to see who
could throw the other into the swimming pool. Despite a warning
from a motel employee that the pool was closed, the men continued

to horse around. A little after midnight, tragedy struck. According to Sgt. Lyle Murphy of the Tucson Police Department, while the two men scuffled playfully, Folley slipped and fell, striking his head by the side of the pool.

A clerk at the motel said one of the women came running into the office and told him Folley had been badly hurt. "I found him with a large lump on the forehead, a hole in the top of his head, and another wound on the back of his head," reported the clerk. The stricken ex-boxer was rushed to Puma County Hospital and pronounced dead at 1:00 AM.

Just over a month later, it was Machen's turn to join the great majority. Things hadn't gone as well for him after boxing as they had for Folley. There was no appointment to the city council, no cushy job selling trucks and shaking hands with the yokels. He filed a bankruptcy petition the year before he retired and worked as a longshoreman the last few years of his life. In 1968, he was arrested following an altercation with a cop. His mental health also continued to deteriorate, and Machen was back under psychiatric care when the end came.

On the morning of August 8, 1972, the body of Eddie Machen was found in the parking lot of the apartment house where he lived. The San Francisco coroner's office said he either fell or jumped from his second-floor apartment. He had a history of sleepwalking and police further speculated that Machen may have taken sleeping pills before going to bed and that he sleepwalked to his death. A trail of blood was found leading from the spot of the fall to a car, indicating Machen had crawled about seven feet before he died. Still a fighter at heart, Eddie had obviously tried to beat the count. But the cement he landed on hit harder than Frazier or Liston. There was a gaping, one-inch hole at the corner of his right eye and abrasions over his body. The official cause of death was ruled as shock and loss of blood from a ruptured liver.

Maybe Machen was ready and wanted to go? But Folley was obviously still full of life. In the end it didn't matter what either of them wanted. The Cosmic Clown hit them both in the face with a concrete pie. It was the final indignity in the lives of two men destined to be remembered—if remembered at all—as a couple of guys who were good, but not quite good enough.

10

The Killer Instinct

There were times Carlos Monzon wanted to do more than just beat his opponents. Sometimes he wanted to kill them.

"When I fought the first time with Nino Benvenuti in Rome, he tried to be funny with me," said Monzon. "At the weigh-in, he touched my ass. I looked at him and thought, 'Tonight I will kill you.' Well, that night I put everything in my hands. When the referee stopped the fight, he was correct. That night I would have killed Benvenuti."

On another night, eighteen years later, there was no referee to check Monzon's ruthless instincts. According to the unanimous decision handed down by a three-judge tribunal, Monzon is guilty of murdering his lover Alicia Muniz. Today, the former middleweight champion of the world sits rotting in a small-town jail in Argentina, his freedom gone, his name forever dishonored. In his time, Monzon had tasted life's most intoxicating pleasures; fame, money, the love of beautiful women, the adulation of the masses. Now he has nothing, nothing except memories and regrets.

175

Sure, Monzon had always been a tough guy, but savagely beating a woman and then throwing her off a second-story balcony is depraved. How did it happen? How did a man, once considered among the finest middleweights of all time, sink so low? To understand what happened to Carlos Monzon, one must look beyond the boxing ring, back to his humble origins in San Javier, a small village in Argentina's rice country. As a child, he moved to Santa Fe, a city of a quarter of a million inhabitants on the banks of the Parana River. You see, Monzon's fall from grace began a long time before he killed the mother of his youngest son. That was just the explosive climax. The fuse was lit the day he was born.

Monzon grew up among poverty and violence. Like many of Argentina's economically deprived lower class, he is of Indian heritage, a member of an oppressed minority. As a boy, Carlos sold newspapers, shined shoes and delivered milk, anything to help his family of twelve brothers and sisters. As a teenager, he began to train in a tiny, dirt-floor gym in Santa Fe, and soon attracted attention with his raw ability. Monzon was tall and mean, a volatile mixture of anger and pride, hungry for a better life and willing to do just about anything to get it.

In February of 1963, Monzon had his first professional fight, in the small town of Rafaela, knocking out Ramon Montenegro in the second round. It was far from the big time. Purses are meager for a young boxer fighting in provincial Argentina, and despite the fact the bronze warrior was considered a decent prospect, life was a continual struggle. He fought eleven times that year, losing only to Antonio Aguilar in his Buenos Aires debut. In his last bout of '63, Monzon broke his right hand knocking out Rene Sosa in Parana. Short of funds and unable to fight, he grew frustrated and restless. Trouble was inevitable. It came one afternoon when Monzon, a rabid fan of the Union soccer club, instigated a riot at a game. He wasn't in jail long, but it was the first of numerous incidents when Monzon's volcanic temper landed him in serious difficulty.

Urgently in need of a payday, the unruly trouble maker returned to the ring in January of 1964, knocking out Roberto "Azucar"

Carabajal, another up-and-comer. It was a good win, but his hand, which had never healed properly, was reinjured. This time Monzon had no alternative but to stop boxing and give his hand a chance to mend. He wouldn't box again until June.

Of course, this didn't stop him from making unscheduled appearances, just to keep in fighting trim. He was soon back behind bars following a punchout on a public bus. To make matters worse, he was also pimping a string of girls. Monzon was getting out of hand, and the police told his manager Amilcar Brusa it would be a good idea if Carlos left town for a while. A cooling off period was in order, and definitely better than a lengthy stretch in the slammer. Brusa agreed and sent his protegeé to Brazil, where he suffered a humiliating defeat at the hands of Felipe Cambeiro in Rio de Janeiro. Cambeiro knocked Monzon down three times, but couldn't keep him down. Nobody ever did.

After his brief exile, Monzon returned to Argentina and launched a lengthy campaign that eventually took him to the championship of the world. It was no magic carpet ride. For the next seven years, he fought practically every month, winning both the Argentine and South American middleweight titles. While he appeared to campaign in the provinces, Monzon also appeared regularly at Luna Park, Argentina's equivalent of Madison Square Garden. His career was helped immensely by Juan Carlos "Tito" Lectoure, the Luna Park promoter and the most powerful man in Argentine boxing. Though Monzon was a well-kept secret outside of South America, Lectoure rectified the situation by importing opponents from the United States to boost Carlos' international recognition.

Monzon slowly developed into a magnificent fighter. He was tough, resilient, difficult to hit, with the kind of punch that sent men spinning dizzily to the canvas. Awkward and somewhat stiff of movement, he was, nevertheless, a skillful boxer who knew how to take full advantage of his imposing reach. A shrewd tactician, he understood when to lay back and when to open up. He was seldom flashy or flamboyant—just extremely effective. While statistics alone rarely give an accurate picture of a boxer's worth, it is a true measure of Monzon's greatness that he never lost a fight after October 1964. Especially when you consider he fought until 1977.

With the help of Lectoure's influence, Monzon finally secured a title shot. He'd had to leave South America for the first time in his life, but that was fine with him. As long as the world champion was in the other corner, he could care less where they fought. If ever a fighter was primed for the moment, it was Monzon the evening of November 7, 1970. Somebody was going to get hurt, and it wasn't going to be him.

Italy's Nino Benvenuti had ruled the middleweight division since 1968, when he emerged from a three-bout series with Emile Griffith as the undisputed champion. Handsome and dashing, he looked more like a tennis player than a boxer. Benvenuti certainly had talent, but his pampered, playboy image didn't go down too well with hardcore American audiences. They also resented the way European referees seemed to bend the rules in his favor. But the Italians loved him and so did the jet set. Frank Sinatra thought he was swell. And besides, who'd ever heard of this guy from Argentina?

It didn't matter whether or not Benvenuti took Monzon for granted. Benvenuti didn't have a chance anyway. He had grown soft, spoiled by his indulgent life-style. Underestimating his determined challenger was another big mistake. He failed to see that hungry-wolf look in his opponent's eyes until it was too late. Then there was the incident at the weigh-in. Benvenuti should have realized the exotic-looking man from Santa Fe was in no mood to joke around. From the moment the opening bell rang, it was all one-way traffic. Referee Rudolf Durst finally rescued a severely battered Benvenuti two minutes into the twelfth round. Monzon was champion of the world.

"When I became champion I was twenty-eight," he remembered many years later. "I was not a boy. It was a big change for me because I started to get big money. I could buy the biggest car. I learned to take care of my clothes. To become middleweight champion of the world is very important in any part of the globe, including my country. I know Argentinians were proud of me."

The new champion became an international figure practically overnight, defending the title both home and abroad. Though they would have preferred one of their own, American fans found him much more to their liking than his predecessor. He also quickly replaced Benvenuti in the hearts of Europe's idle rich, fighting in Rome, Monte Carlo and Copenhagen, with frequent appearances in Paris. Monzon became friends with French movie star Alain Delon, and began traveling in social circles far different than those he had inhabited during his early back-alley days in Argentina. Ruggedly handsome, Monzon had a regal look about him and carried himself well. Always immaculately tailored in expensive suits, he wore his hair long in the fashion of the day. He could have passed for a Latin rock star.

Monzon was at ease with his newfound wealth and celebrity status, equally at home hobnobbing with starlets on the Riviera as he was swapping sweat with his sparring partners in the gym. In Argentina, he was a national hero, even though some members of the country's aristocracy looked down their noses, vaguely unhappy that a man of such humble beginnings was attracting so much attention. Though Monzon's earlier indiscretions had been all but forgotten, many of the changes were superficial. A violent man still lurked beneath the veneer of civilization. His past was not about to relinquish its grip without a struggle.

By the beginning of 1973, Monzon had just about purged the middleweight division of viable challengers. He'd already made six successful defenses and was voted Fighter of the Year '72 by both *The Ring* and the Boxing Writers Association of America. He was at the peak of his powers. On the surface it seemed life couldn't be better. But trouble was brewing on the domestic front.

Monzon had been married to Beatriz Garcia since his early years as a boxer. A strong woman with a fiery temper, she was loyal to Carlos, despite the fact he'd always been a flagrant philanderer.

Former middleweight champion Carlos Monzon as he appeared during his championship days. Monzon was elected to the Boxing Hall of Fame in 1983, five years before he was arrested for murder. (Photo courtesy of Peltz Boxing Promotions)

Carlos Monzon and Alicia Muniz. He was convicted of killing her approximately three years after this photograph was taken in Buenos Aires. (Photo courtesy of *The Ring* magazine)

Beatriz was almost as tough as her husband and fought hard to keep her man. Not unexpectedly, their love-hate relationship was a constant battle ground. Matters came to a head around the end of February 1973. Though the exact bone of contention was over-shadowed by ensuing events, one thing is certain: Monzon wound up with two .22 caliber bullets lodged in his body.

According to the "official" story, it was all just an "accident." Monzon told police he'd been cleaning a pistol and dropped it, causing the weapon to discharge. The fact he'd been hit twice certainly makes this version difficult to swallow. The "unofficial" account sounded much more plausible. Supposedly, Beatriz flipped out during an argument and went after her husband with murder in her eyes, brandishing a revolver. She reportedly slipped and fell during the chase, clogging the gun barrel with mud. This stroke of luck probably saved Monzon's life. Beatriz allegedly squeezed off four shots, but the mud altered the direction of the bullets, and only two hit the target. One shell lodged in Monzon's right arm, the other in his right shoulder blade.

Ever the macho man, Monzon stayed out of sight for a couple of days and said nothing about his injuries. Finally, Brusa went looking for him and discovered what had happened. The wound in Monzon's arm was in danger of developing gangrene and his manager insisted he seek medical attention. The fighter was taken to San Miguel hospital where Dr. Nicolas Normando Rondon removed the bullet from his arm. The other bullet was left in his shoulder, where it still reamins, a permanent token of Beatriz's passion. While they were eventually divorced, it is interesting to note that many years later, during Monzon's murder trial, Beatriz was one of the few people from his past who came forth and stood by him.

Monzon's star continued to shine through the 1970s. He fought the best and beat them all. Jose Naploes, Bennie Briscoe, Jean-Claude Bouttier, Denny Moyer, Tony Licta, Tony Mundine, Gratien Tonna, Griffith, and others... all fell short in bids to wrest away the belt. If the middleweight king had a physical weakness, it was his brittle hands, which plagued him throughout his career and probably prevented him from scoring more knockouts than he did the last few years of his career. Between bouts he lived in the fast lane, attending parties, driving a Mercedes, always the center of attention. He met Argentine actress Susana Gimenez in 1974 and embarked on the great romance of his life. They made a glamorous couple, and Monzon even took time off from boxing to appear in several movies with her. The money was rolling in and they indulged in a luxurius lifestyle. Monzon and Gimenez lived in the most exclusive section of Buenos Aires and became creatures of the night, spending more and more time in nightclubs, sipping champagne, going to bed at dawn. Yet none of these excesses seemed to effect his boxing career. In the ring, Monzon could do no wrong.

In his only bout of 1976, Monzon retained the title with a unanimous fifteen-round decision over Colombian Rodrigo Valez in Monte Carlo. Though there was little doubt the champion deserved the close decision, he was beginning to show the first signs of age. Valdez was a talented, vicious-hitting fighter and they were rematched the following summer. Once again the fight took place in Monte Carlo, but this time, it was a far more demanding encounter. Valdez dropped Monzon with a right hand in the second round and cut his nose before the Argentine strongman regained control and punched out a convincing points win. After the fight, wire services carried a photograph of the bruised champion lying on his hotel room bed, wearing just a pair of bikini briefs and his championship belt. The sultry Gimenez was hovering nearby, practicing her Florence Nightingale routine.

"I had been inactive for a year," said Monzon of his second match with Valdez. "I was making movies and living as a playboy. Well, I still defeated him, I put into the ring all my energy, all my hate. When the bout ended and I looked at myself in the mirror, I said to myself, 'Monzon was never floored and never cut. He must be remembered as a great champion.' So I quit."

Monzon seemed set for life. The purse for his last fight alone was $500 thousand. It was a pleasant change to see such an outstanding champion go out on a victorious note, a refreshing respite from the usual horror story of a broken-down champion hanging on all the way to Palookaville. He'd held the crown for six years, nine months, and made an unprecedented fourteen successful defenses; two division records which could very well remain intact indefinitely. But like so many great fighters, the retired boxer never really found his niche outside the ring.

Soon after he quit boxing, Gimenez predictably faded from the picture. With little to occupy his time, Monzon tried a variety of business enterprises but met with no success. He blew $200 thousand importing Korean television sets to Argentina, and also lost a bundle on a clothing store. He was aimless, drifting from one ill-conceived venture to another. In 1981, he was incarcerated again, this time for having an illegal gun in his home. Though Monzon claimed the weapon to be just a collector's item, he spent twenty-eight days in the Santa Fe jail. The lone bright spot in his life was a new love, Alicia Muniz.

They met at Buenos Aires' Ezeina Airport in 1979, while waiting for a flight to France. Muniz was a dancer and Monzon was smitten. A romance blossomed, but the ex-champion was moody and difficult to deal with. He had begun to drink heavily after his retirement and there were also rumors of cocaine use. They separated a year later, but reconciled when Alicia became pregnant with Monzon's baby. Maximiliano Roque was born on December 28, 1981, and his father was elated. "This will be a new beginning for me," he told the press. But Monzon was still Monzon. The birth of his son and the relationship with Muniz didn't really change him. He spent his afternoons playing cards in the "La Cuyantina" barroom, and associated with a number of shady characters, including a man named Alberto Olmedo, who was reputedly connected to the cocaine business.

The stormy relationship between the dancer and the ex-boxer bounced back and forth, alternating between periods of estrangement and emotional reunions. It was the age-old story; they couldn't live with each other, and they couldn't live without each other.

"Yes, it is true. Sometimes Alicia left home," admitted Monzon. "But she always returned."

But during the last few months of her life, Muniz went to live with Monzon's parents, while he stayed in their apartment. Despite this arrangement, their love was not entirely dead. It was not unusual for them to spend a romantic weekend together. And on February 13, 1988, Muniz went to Mar del Plata to meet Monzon for just such a tryst. She had planned to spend one day there with him and Maximiliano, and then take the boy back to Buenos Aires with her on Monday. Monzon had booked a room for her at the Rivoli Hotel, but she decided to stay with him at a house on 1567 Pedro Zanni Street. The house had been rented by their mutual friend, television actor Adrian Martel.

Mar del Plata, about fifty minutes by air from Buenos Aires, is a popular resort, Agentina's equivalent of Atlantic City. But like Atlantic City, Mar del Plata also has a high crime rate and a flourishing drug trade. It is considered an exciting, but dangerous place to spend a vacation. About a month before Muniz's death, Monzon's buddy Olmedo, who was also friends with the aforementioned "Facha" Martel, died under confusing circumstances when he fell (or was pushed) from the eleventh floor of a building in Mar del Plata. Though nothing was proved, rumors circulated that cocaine had played a role in his plunge.

"We made love that Saturday afternoon," testified Monzon at his trial, recalling the weekend of Muniz' death. "And then we decided to take in a little fun and went out."

They spent some time at the Mar del Plata casino and then, in the early hours of February 14, went to the Club Penarol. After drinking some champagne with friends, they decided to return to the house on Pedro Zanni Street. Cabdriver Nestor Celso Tonnini remembered driving them home around 5:00 AM.

"They seemed to be in love the whole trip, kissing each other and talking," reported Tonnini.

What happened after Carlos and Alicia arrived is strictly a matter of who you want to believe. Several versions were given at Monzon's trial, but none of the witnesses were entirely credible. Monzon's testimony is revealing up to a point, but his memory of the final struggle before Muniz's death is conveniently hazy and leaves a crucial gap in the story.

"When we arrived, everything was okay," Monzon said. "Maximiliano was sleeping. We started to argue when Alicia asked me for money. I asked her to live with me again. 'You don't need to work for $10 again,' I said. The argument continued. I took a can of beer, a cigarette, and left the room. She was semi-nude. She came to me. I was outside near the balcony. She pushed me and the cigarette burned my breast. She started to run, and I followed her. I don't remember very well, but I suppose I took her by the neck with my hand. She was very near the balcony . . . and I can't remember what happened. It was just as if we were in a fog. I can only remember trying to catch her with my left arm. I can't say what happened. I woke up on the ground (below the balcony), with Alicia near me. I started to shout, asking for help."

Monzon tried to wake the caretaker, Carlos Guazzone, but he was sound asleep with his companion Maria Mercedes Vignole. Monzon then took a jar and smashed a glass door, rousing Guazzone, who phoned for help. Guazzone assisted Monzon, who had injured his left arm, into the street in front of the house, where the ex-fighter waited until a doctor arrived a few minutes later. Monzon said nothing about Muniz, and the doctor put him in an ambulance and left, apparently unaware anyone else had been hurt. The first policeman to arrive at the scene, Jorge Pereyra, found Alicia, face down in a pool of blood, her head caved in. Clad only in a pair of underpants, she was lying directly underneath the second story balcony, near the swimming pool.

Monzon steadfastly maintained Muniz's death had been an accident, but laboratory tests on her body aroused suspicion of foul play. There was evidence she had suffered tremendous manual pressure to her neck, and investigators wondered why she hadn't tried to break her fall with her arms or hands. There was also a lot of blood discovered inside the house. Monzon's tale just didn't fit the facts. He was placed in Batan jail and indicted for murder. The case was front page news throughout Argentina. Tabloids couldn't get enough of the sensational case and published lurid photographs of Muniz's body and funeral. Radio stations all over the country broadcast daily reports of the trial.

Two alleged eyewitnesses to the crime testified at Monzon's trial, both of them men of suspect character. In fact, it would be hard to come up with a more disreputable pair. These guys were pitiful.

Rafael Crisanto Baez claimed to be an ex-boxer, and while no record of his career could be found, his gnarled face indicated he was probably telling the truth about his former occupation—if about nothing else. Born October 26, 1931, in San Andres de Giles, he said he hated Monzon because the former champion had snubbed him once, many years before. Baez, a suicidal, former mental patient, had been in prison for sexually abusing his eight-year-old grandchild. When one of Monzon's lawyers, Señor De Le Canale, confronted Baez about the rape, he refused to answer. Officially, Baez was supposed to be outside the death house when he saw what occurred. But sources close to the case tell a different story: Baez had been *inside* the house stealing when Muniz died. According to the "off the record" version, the police needed a witness and made a deal with Baez. Supposedly, they accepted his story of being *outside* the house in exchange for his testimony. Despite the fact that he changed elements of his story several times, Baez stuck to his guns on several important details that would have been difficult to invent. In the long run, he may have been a more credible witness than one might assume, judging by his sordid personal history.

Baez said he saw a tall man on the balcony with a semi-nude girl... "and the blonde, she was running away from him, but he trapped her. He connected with a one-two combination and the girl fell. Then the man went into the house. He returned, and took the girl around the neck. She tried to defend herself like a little cat, using both hands. He picked her up and let her fall to the ground. She made a noise like a lot of glass breaking."

The other so-called witness was Alfredo Arturo Moyano, who told the court a different story than Baez. It almost seemed he was there just to counterbalance Baez, sort of an opposing "expert witness."

"Yes, they were arguing," testified Moyano. "Monzon took her by the neck and sat the girl on the balcony (railing), and at that moment they both fell at the same time."

While Moyano's version seemed to verify the defendant's claim that it had been an accident, his testimony was not completely believable, to say the least. He lived in Tucuman, a province almost a thousand miles away from Mar del Plata, and would normally have no reason to be in the neighborhood. Moyano produced a bus ticket from Tucuman to Mar del Plata in an effort to back up his story. He said he was visiting a girl he'd met at a dance, and had just taken her home when he heard shouting coming from the house at 1567 Pedro Zanni Street. He could not, however, remember the girl's name or where she lived. When one of the judges asked him why he'd saved a bus ticket for over a month, Moyano said, "I like to take care of bus tickets." It is impossible to know which man, if either, was telling the truth. Both have since been prosecuted for giving false testimony.

Following the conflicting accounts of Moyano and Baez, it was the medical experts' turn to testify. They made a tremendous mess of their technical speeches, but all agreed on one point: by the time Alicia Muniz fell to the ground, she was already unconscious. "The dead talk," declared Muniz's family. "The body of Alicia will talk." They were right. It was the medical and circumstancial evidence more than anything else that convicted Monzon. Nobody was neutral, everybody in Argentina had an opinion. On the chilly Monday morning of July 3, 1989, a three-judge panel—Jorge Issachs, Carlos Gustavo Pizarro and Alicia Ramon Fondeville— found Monzon guilty and sentenced him to eleven years in prison.

Theoretically, only Monzon knows what really happened on that fateful Sunday morning. But gossip persists that there is more to the tragedy than was revealed in court. Once again, cocaine is mentioned as a factor in the deadly equation. It has been suggested Carlos had consumed large quantities of the narcotic during the evening in question. It has also been rumored the house was used to store drugs, and that someone, allegedly Martel, "cleaned" the house before the police arrived. Others have taken the hypothesis one step further, speculating Martel may actually have been present when Muniz was killed. The similarity between the deaths of Olmedo and Muniz is also intriguing. Nevertheless, speculation and "off-the-record" allegations seldom lead to indictments. No charges have been brought against Martel, a man described as a second-rate actor with a first-rate level of living.

Following his conviction, Monzon was taken back to Batan jail to serve his sentence. But he did not stay long. At the time, there were about thirty prisoners suffering from AIDS housed with the general inmate population. They cut themselves with razor blades and glass, then rioted. The guards were afraid of infection and did nothing to stop the rampage. The other prisoners, including Monzon, signed a petition demanding that the AIDS-infected prisoners be sequestered, and overall prison conditions be improved. As a result, Monzon was moved to Junin, a city very close to his native province of Santa Fe. In October 1989, there was a massive escape from the Junin jail. First reports indicated Monzon was among the fugitives, but it was not true. He had arrived at Junin a few days before the breakout in a totally drunken state. For that reason, Monzon was placed in isolation and was in no position to join the approximately thirty-five inmates who fled.

Where Monzon's life will take him from here remains to be seen. He once rose from the bottom rung of Argentina's socioeconomic ladder to achieve great fame and fortune. But the anger and primitive aggression which carried him to the top of the boxing world also contributed to his eventual downfall. Even Monzon admitted as much when he lamented, "Me and my bad temper are the ones responsible for this. Yes, me and my bad temper." Perhaps Argentine journalist Carlos Irusta put it best when he wrote: "Monzon learned how to fight in the ring like the tremendous, unforgettable champion he was. He simply never learned, as most common men do, how to fight life's common battles."

It hurts when our heroes let us down, but shed no tears for the fallen champion. With time off for good behavior, Monzon could be paroled as early as 1995. He will have another chance. Alicia Muniz will not.

11

Tarnished Idol

The high-powered bullet entered the right nostril, ripped through the brain, exploded out the back of the skull, smashed through the window and finally came to rest on the sidewalk across the street. A few minutes later, a man and woman were seen leaving the house. They left behind thirty-eight cellophane packets of heroin on the dining room table and the body of boxer Tyrone Everett in the upstairs bedroom.

Six days later, Everett's girl friend, Carolyn McKendrick, surrendered to the Philadelphia police and was charged with his murder. The man seen leaving the scene of the crime with her, admitted homosexual and drug pusher Tyrone Price, soon became the chief witness for the prosecution. The story of sex and drugs that unfolded during the trial were to forever sully the memory of Everett, a gifted boxer who only six months earlier had been robbed of the WBC super featherweight title in one of the most scandalous decisions in boxing history.

Everett's career as a boxer was nothing short of spectacular. One of five brothers raised by their mother, Doris Everett, in South Philadelphia, he turned pro in September 1971 and was instantly recognized as a special talent. A mercury-quick southpaw, he developed a darting style that made him practically impossible to hit. Everett would prance around his opponents, jump inside long enough to land a crisp punch, and then vanish before a retaliatory blow could be launched. While his style often made for boring, one-sided fights, it is doubtful he lost more than a dozen rounds in a total of thirty-seven professional bouts. The only fight he ever lost was probably fixed.

Though Everett's less-than-macho methods alienated many of Philadelphia's old guard and blue-collar fans, he more than made up for it at the box office by attracting an entirely different element to his fights. They were generally a younger crowd, dressed in superfly threads and sporting top-heavy Afros. Everett had a big following among the 20th and Carpenter Street gang, a particularly fierce collection of inner-city kids who waged a successful street war against the Black Mafia for control of drug traffic in the neighborhood where Everett was raised. He also drew a large contingency of women, who were entranced by his pretty green eyes, swaggering ways and well-earned reputation as a lady-killer. Going to see Everett fight became the "in" thing to do, and thousands flocked to see the tiny dancing master every time he was on the bill.

Everett was, in many ways, a contradiction. He was polite, soft-spoken, and during his early success, almost timid among strangers. But as Tyrone's star rose, he began to expose the other side of his personality; the conceited, arrogant side. There was also an undeniable streak of cruelty, most blatantly expressed in the utter contempt in which he held most of his opponents. A perfect example was his bout with Korean Hyun Chi Kim in July 1975, at the Spectrum. Despite an inflated ranking, Kim was a limited fighter, vastly inferior to the Philadelphian. Everett administered a lopsided beating, but did it from a safe distance until the Korean was exhausted and demoralized. Once he realized his opponent was a sitting duck, the distasteful side of Everett's makeup asserted itself.

"Everett displayed his perverted sense of class last night by needlessly taunting a beaten, half-blind, bewildered opponent who might have jumped out of the ring if his handlers hadn't thrown the towel into it," wrote Jack McKinney in the Philadelphia *Daily News*.

" 'I'm mean, man, mean,' growled Everett, dramatizing his claim with grotesque facial contortions as he popped right hooks against the closed left eye of Hyun Chi Kim, an overrated and undermotivated Korean who didn't understand what Everett was saying, anyway.

"So, after twenty-seven wins, Tyrone Everett still leaves a lot of people with the distinct impression that he is a front runner whose courage is directly related to his recognition of his opponent's ineptness."

Had Everett been an ordinary boxer, both he and his tasteless hot-dogging would have been quickly forgotten. What made him so infuriating to the purist was the fact he was blessed with enormous talent. Among the most frustrated was J. Russell Peltz, the Spectrum's youthful Director of Boxing who agonized over Everett's indiscretions while gleefully counting the gate receipts. They developed an intriguing love-hate relationship that was still unresolved at the time of Everett's death. While they openly feuded, and at one point only communicated through Everett's manager, Frank Gelb, they shared more than a common business interest.

"My wife, Linda, thinks Tyrone was always trying to win my affection and acceptance. And that I would never give it to him," said Peltz. "Maybe she was right. In my opinion, Everett never realized just how good he really was. If he had gone all out, he would have knocked out practically every guy he fought."

Regardless of their personal difficulties, Peltz worked hard, along with Gelb, to secure Everett the title shot he had earned by beating practically every contender in the 130-pound division. At the time, the WBC title was held by Alfredo Escalera, a charismatic performer known for his toothy grin and proclivity for bringing a boa constrictor into the ring. The swashbuckling Puerto Rican was

Tyrone Everett, the brilliant Philadelphia dancing master who was shot to death in 1977 while still a leading contender for the world title. (Photo courtesy of Peltz Boxing Promotions)

Police and reporters gather outside the house in South Philadelphia where Tyrone Everett was murdered. The boxer's new Cadillac is seen parked in front.

no slouch, but by 1976, Everett was practically unbeatable. After considerable wrangling and postponement, the match between Everett and Escalera was made for November 30 at the Spectrum.

The promotion was a blockbuster and drew a record-breaking crowd of over 16,000. For the first twelve rounds, Everett fought his normal cautious fight, outboxing Escalera at every turn and scoring with snappy counters. Then, in the thirteenth round, a freakish accident tore open a wicked cut on Everett's forehead. Escalera's front teeth smacked into the Philadelphian's brow, severing a vessel and causing blood to spurt in an alarming manner. Everett responded magnificently, tearing into his adversary with more ferocity than he'd ever shown before. It was a revelation, especially to those who had questioned Everett's courage in the past. In what might have been his finest moment in the ring, he blinked away the gore, bit down on his mouthpiece and went for the gusto.

Ace cutman Eddie Aliano managed to hold Everett's ripped skin together for the last three rounds, but the blood-spattered boxer abandoned his aggressive attitude and reverted back to his usual hit-and-run tactics. Though it was the prudent thing to do and typical of Everett's fighting philosophy, it was also a decision which probably cost him the title. And maybe a whole lot more.

"Escalera's people told me later that if Everett had come forward the last few rounds, he would have won. Escalera was so tired he would have never lasted if Tyrone hadn't started dancing again," claimed Peltz.

At the sound of the final bell, the crowd, sure the local favorite was the new champion, erupted in a joyous celebration. Jubilation soon turned to anxiety as the tabulation of the official score cards was abnormally slow; often a sign that things aren't exactly kosher. When ring announcer Ed Derian finally read the split decision verdict in favor of Escalera, there was first a stunned silence. It was as if the people couldn't believe what they had just heard. Then they got angry—real angry. With the crowd teetering on the brink of violence, Pennsylvania boxing commissioner Howard McCall grabbed the microphone and told the snarling mob he was suspending the decision pending an investigation. This was pure baloney, and McCall knew it. Nevertheless, he desperately wanted to avert a riot. The ploy worked and the crowd gradually grumbled its way out into the night, convinced Everett had been shafted, but hopeful justice would eventually prevail. It didn't.

There was no investigation and the outrageous decision for Escalera stood. The most shocking aspect of the sordid affair, however, was the fact the pivotal vote for Escalera was cast by Philadelphia judge Lou Tress. It was a given that Puerto Rican judge Ismael Fernandez would vote for Escalera regardless of what transpired between the ropes, and he did by a 146-143 margin. Mexican referee Ray Solis, the only so-called neutral official, scored the bout 148-146 for Everett. But when Tress cast the deciding 145-143 vote for the defending champion, practically everybody was flabbergasted. Though Everett's camp had neither sought nor expected any favors from the sad-eyed man in a baggy grey suit, it was assumed Tress, as a Philadelphian, would at least render a verdict representative of the action inside the ring.

"I remember standing in the ring before they announced the decision," said Gelb, who is still haunted by nightmares about the infamous decision and its aftermath. "I peeked at the score cards and then looked around for Tress. He had already left his seat and was on his way out of the arena."

Tress died of cancer not long afterwards, but is remembered as a villainous character by practically everyone who saw the Escalera-Everett travesty. Rumors persisted that his pencil was guided by factors other than the normal criteria for judging a professional boxing match. According to gossip that circulated after the fight, the only way Everett was going to win on Tress's score card was if he knocked Escalera down for the count of ten. Though no charges were ever lodged, many boxing insiders nodded toward "Honest" Bill Daly as the culprit who had allegedly made the "arrangements" for Everett's downfall. Daly, who has also since passed away, was an elderly scalawag left over from the days when convicted felons Frankie Carbo and Blinky Palermo ruled much of boxing. He had

The alleged "fixed" fight between Tyrone Everett (right) and Alfredo Escalera, November 30, 1976, at the Philadelphia Spectrum. Everett handed Escalera a boxing lesson but lost a controversial decision many insiders believed was rigged in favor of the Puerto Rican champion. (Photo courtesy of Peltz Boxing Promotions)

retired to Puerto Rico a few years before Everett's challenge and was reputed to have a financial interest in Escalera. Surprisingly, considering "Squire Bill's" unsavory reputation, not an eyebrow was raised in Everett's camp when the old boy flew into Philly a few days before the fight. Adding more fuel was the fact Tress had a brother who worked at a race track in Puerto Rico.

"After the weigh-in I was sitting around in my hotel room relaxing before it was time to go to the fight," recalled Gelb. "There was a knock at the door and a well-known fight character came in. Let's just call him my 'mystery guest.' He said, 'Are you okay, Frank?' I told him yes and then he said, 'Are you sure you're okay?' I didn't know what he was talking about. But a few days after the fight, it hit me. I put two and two together and another piece of the puzzle fit into place. The guy was an old buddy of "Honest" Bill Daly's. Maybe if I'd taken the hint we could have worked out some sort of deal. Who the hell knows?"

The controversial loss to Escalera was a bitter setback to Everett, but he was young, and everyone assumed he would get another chance. The defeat certainly didn't deflate his ego, or take the sting out of his tongue. Peltz remembered when Everett showed up at the Spectrum not long after the debacle to view a videotape of the bout.

"He sat staring at the screen with a blank face for the longest time. He didn't say a word," recalled the promoter. "Then around the fifth or sixth round, he got Escalera so off balance, Alfredo's face was in his crotch. 'Look at that,' Everett squealed. 'I made him suck my dick.'"

It was Everett's sex organ that ultimately led him to an early grave. A father of four illegitimate children by the time he died at age twenty-four, some said he considered himself God's gift to women. And there were plenty of pretty young girls who agreed with his assessment.

"He treated me nice," a tearful Sherry Arthur told reporters after learning of her ex-boyfriend's murder. "After he won $10 thousand at the Spectrum, he bought me a living room set and bedroom set and a TV and a glass table. I know he was dating a lot of people, but I never seen any. Women flock around men like that anyway. A lot of people were jealous. You know, they said, he's not so great. But I know he loved me. I'll bet my life on it, and I used to love him, too."

Not all of Everett's lady friends shared Ms. Arthur's admirable opinion.

At her trial, Carolyn McKendrick painted a vastly different picture of the handsome young boxer. She maintained she'd shot him in self-defense and produced hospital records in an attempt to prove past abuse at Everett's hands. According to McKendrick, Everett beat her so frequently the incidents were too numerous to count. She said the punishment grew progressively worse as her lover's ring opponents gradually got tougher and tougher.

"He (Everett) punched her in the jaw. Her mouth was bleeding," testified Cynthia Laverne Dill of a beating the boxer allegedly gave McKendrick outside an after-hours club the summer before his death.

Robbin Evonne Craddock, a close friend of McKendrick, told the court about another alleged altercation between the boxer and his lover. Craddock said she was visiting McKendricks when a heated argument erupted.

"I went down to see if I could stop it, and when I got there she was holding his arm," said Craddock, who was upstairs when the sparks began to fly. "He jerked his hand back and hit her with his fist. She fell to the couch, but Everett jumped on her and continued to strike her. That's when she threatened him."

According to Craddock's testsimony, when Everett refused to leave the house, McKendrick picked up a glass ashtray and threw it at him. The boxer instinctively blocked the missile with his arm the same way he had thousands of punches, and then knocked her to the ground just as if she was one of his ring opponents.

Everett was "getting ready to kick her, when he spotted the broken glass from the ashtray, and picked up a piece," stated Craddock.

"I'm going to hurt you where you prize the most, your face," Everett threatened, clutching a chunk of broken glass.

"He jabbed at her," said the witness. "But I pulled him away."

The action was almost as hot-and-heavy in Judge Robert A. Latrone's courtroom. Neither the prosecution nor the defense pulled many punches. Both went for the knockout from the opening bell.

"I'm going to level with you," said McKendrick's attorney Stephen H. Serota at the beginning of her trial. "Carolyn McKendrick shot Tyrone Everett. Make no bones about it. The question is, did she have a good reason?"

With minor exceptions, both McKendrick and the prosecution's star witness, Tyrone (Terry) Price, gave the same account of Everett's death. As was his habit, the boxer slept at McKendrick's house at 2710 Federal Street the night before he was shot. Early the next morning, McKendrick departed to help her sister get her car repaired. Everett was left alone in the house with Price, a transvestite who appeared in court dressed as a woman. About twenty minutes later, McKendrick returned unexpectedly and discovered her bed in disarray and Everett sweating and flustered. Though Price claimed he never had sexual relations with the victim, McKendrick formed the opinion that her boyfriend and Price had engaged in a sexual encounter in her absence. She confronted Everett and demanded to know what had transpired while she'd been gone.

"She kept asking (Everett) who was in that room. He kept laughing," testified Price.

As the quarrel escalated, Everett "came at Carolyn with his fists up and I jumped into the middle of it," continued Price. "He didn't hit her. He kept telling her he was going to tell her (who had been in the bedroom)."

"I'm not going to take another beating from you," McKendrick allegedly told her lover as she picked up a .30 caliber Ruger Blackhawk from the bedroom bureau.

"That's no plaything," Everett said, startled, but still laughing.

McKendrick testified that when Everett raised his hands and moved towards her, she felt threatened. "I fired the gun and turned and ran. I thought he was still coming after me. As far as I could tell he was still moving forward. I didn't know I hit him."

In his closing argument. Serota asked the jury, "Was it reasonable for her to have done what she did? Aren't they (Everett's fists) weapons?" He went on to describe his client as a "love slave" fearful of another beating.

Prosecutor Roger King countered by calling the defendant a "love queen" who had murdered Everett in cold blood because she had been spurned in favor of a transvestite.

"Twenty-four years went up in smoke (that) comes out of the muzzle of a seven-inch gun. Was this act justified? I submit no," said King while asking the jury to bring back a verdict of first-degree murder.

After deliberating just two and one half hours, the jury of eight men and four women found McKendrick guilty of third-degree murder. The twenty-three-year-old woman was led away in handcuffs to begin serving her sentence. Serota was positive his client would have walked if the victim had not been a local celebrity. He filed an appeal on her behalf which was eventually denied. Carolyn spent exactly five years in prison and was then released.

Despite the outcome of the trial, many questions remain: Was Everett dealing drugs? Was he bisexual? Was Carolyn McKendrick really the one who pulled the trigger?

Price, who changed his story repeatedly during the course of intense questioning by police and district attorney's office, testified he had sold heroin for both the boxer and McKendrick.

"Tyrone would never do any drugs himself," insisted Tyrone's brother Mike Everett, who was also a world-class boxer. "I know my brother and he couldn't have fought the way he did and take drugs. But he was probably fronting people money to buy drugs. Once you start making a little money, you get a little greedy and look for ways to invest it and make some more. That's what Carolyn was into. That's the kind of life we were leading back then."

If Tyrone was investing part of his boxing purses in drugs, it couldn't have been a very profitable enterprise. According to reports published at the time of his death, Everett's 1976 yellow Cadillac Coupe de Ville was being repossessed and his telephone being disconnected.

Price also testified that although he had never been sexually intimate with Everett, at least four homosexual acquaintances had told him they'd had sex with the former number-one contender. It is an innuendo many of Everett's family and friends passionately deny.

"Tyrone was a ladies' man," said his mother, Doris Everett. "Those rumors were impossible."

"We don't believe all that junk," said neighbor Al Grushman, who was interviewed by the *Philadelphia Daily News* while the McKendrick trial was in progress. "He didn't need to mess with any fags. He had too many women. Even at his funeral, he must have left fifteen girls crying on a corner."

"I'm not a judge and jury, but you find a lot of stuff on the streets," Everett's trainer Jimmy Arthur told writer Bob Ingram many years after the tragedy.

The question of whether or not McKendrick actually shot Everett is just as titilating as the boxer's sexual propensities, if not more so. McKendrick wasn't exactly following in Mother Teresa's footsteps at the time of Everett's murder. She was on probation for two convictions on firearms and narcotics violations, as well as another bust for receiving stolen property.

"Carolyn was a very classy lady," said Serota. "But she came from people who were the scum of the earth."

Throughout her relationship with Everett, Caroline was married to Ricardo McKendrick, an authentic tough guy who was sentenced to prison in 1974 for distribution of heroin. Ricardo had been released shortly before Everett was killed and was rumored to have taken out a contract on the boxer's life. On June 4, 1977, nine days after the shooting, the *Philadelphia Tribune* carried an article by staff reporter Len Lear casting serious doubt on the State's case.

"Carolyn McKendrick, who has been charged by police with the slaying of boxer Tyrone Everett, is 'going to take a fall to protect the real killer,' reliable sources told the *Tribune*."

"Not true, just street talk," insisted Serota many years after McKendrick had already been released. "The details of the way it was told, by both Price and Carolyn McKendrick, are too involved. She knew too much. In my opinion, her story fit all the physical evidence too well to be bullshit. You want to know what I think happened? Well, I'll tell you: She came home and Everett was balling a fag. She got bent out of shape and told Everett to get the hell out of the house. She was incensed. He came at her and threatened her. He obviously could have hurt her. You could call it a lovers' spat, I guess. But at that point, I think she just wanted to end the relationship."

In an 1989 interview published in *PhillySport* magazine, both Tryone's mother and his brother, Eddie, said they still doubted Carolyn was the shooter. They also hinted Ricardo McKendrick may have been part of the deadly equation. If they're right, it is unlikely he was the trigger man. Boxing trainer George James— who had no reason to lie—claimed he was standing on the corner near the death house talking to Ricardo at the time Everett laughed his last laugh.

"It couldn't have been Rickie," James insisted. "He was with me when we both heard the shot."

"I know Rickie didn't have nothing to do with it," agreed Mike Everett. "I don't know why they dragged that boy's name into it. I don't think he had that much animosity about her and Tyrone. Carolyn did it because of jealosy or whatever went on behind closed doors."

The truth about what really happened to Everett is obscured by time and the conflicting accounts of those involved. But the stories persist. One anecdote still heard on the mean streets of Philadelphia tells how a hired gunman was so impressed by Everett's standing in the black community, he refused to go through with the contract and returned his client's money. Could the contract possibly have passed to Caroline?

Years after his brutally abrupt exit, the controversy surrounding the life and death of Tyrone Everett continues. Opinion on both his career and character are as divided as the score cards which robbed him of the super featherweight championship. In the final analysis, all we really know for sure is that a life was tragically wasted.

It has been suggested that things might have turned out differently if Everett had received a square deal in the Escalera fight. As world champion, Tyrone might have been able to shake the streets from his soul. Perhaps he'd still be alive today if he'd thrown caution to the wind and tried to win the championship by a knockout. Most observers believe such a result was well within his capabilities. But Everett knew boxing was a dangerous game and always played it safe inside the ring. Too bad he failed to follow the same code in the bedroom.

12

Down,
but Not Out

T he New Jersey State Penitentiary in Rahway is a grim looking place at the best of times. It sits just a few miles off the Jersey Turnpike, amidst the industrial sprawl and working-class neighborhoods that clog the southwestern approach to New York City. It's an aging, mustard colored citadel, topped by a grimy glass dome that looks like it hasn't been washed since Calvin Coolidge lived in the White House. It's the place New Jersey warehouses some of its most anti-social citizens, the end of the line for men who've run out of chances, often the proverbial last stop on the road to oblivion.

The old prison looked particularly foreboding on a rainy morning in November of 1989. The wind had stripped most of the leaves from the trees, and the bare branches scratched at the sky in a way that made the day seem even gloomier. Rahway isn't one of those country club prisons where crooked politicians and white-collar criminals idle away the hours playing shuffle board and canasta. Rahway is where hard men do hard time. A visitor has to get past five locked and heavily-guarded doors to reach the convicts inside its walls. There's good reason for such tight security. Nobody is there for stealing hub caps. Most of these men have committed violent crimes, ugly crimes. Some of them will never walk the streets again.

Deep within the prison, a small man stood waiting in a large room, empty except for a table in one corner. He was wearing a black polo shirt, black dungarees and high top sneakers. The clothes were clean, the sneakers new, his haircut recent. He looked familiar, but somehow different. It had been seven years since his visitor had seen him, and the circumstances were vastly different then. At their previous encounter, the man in black had been dressed in boxing trunks and celebrating his twenty-second straight win as a professional fighter. It was supposed to be his ticket to the big time, the victory that would earn him a shot at the world title. But things didn't turn out that way. On New Year's Day 1983, less than two months after his nationally televised knockout over Carlos Herrera, Tony Ayala was arrested for sexual assault. Except for a brief spell prior to his conviction, he's been behind bars ever since.

The used to call him "El Torito," the little bull. The name fit. Ayala would hurl his chunky body at his opponents like a cornered animal, slashing and hooking until the other boxer looked like a matador trampled in the dust. He didn't seem satisfied to just beat his opponents; it was if he wanted to humiliate them as well. Sometimes Ayala kept punching away after the referee had stopped the fight, apparently unable to control the passions that fueled his fury. On one occasion he spat at a prostrate adversary before strutting back to his corner, contemptuous even in victory. Yes, Ayala was mean, but more than that, he was good. Damn good. Only three of his twenty-two victims were around to hear the final bell, and they probably wish they hadn't. The experts said he couldn't be beaten. They said nobody could stop him from becoming a champion. But they were wrong. Ayala fought the only man who could beat him every day. He was the guy looking back at him when he combed his hair in the bathroom mirror. It didn't matter how many fights he won. Deep down inside, Ayala always felt like a loser.

"I was vicious, but my anger in the ring had nothing to do with my personal problems," claimed Ayala. "My anger came from an intense dislike for defeat. I knew it was a very real thing that could happen, but I wasn't going to accept it until it was thrust upon me. I would do anything I could to win a fight. I didn't care about the price I would have to pay. I didn't care if I had to get cut over both eyes. I didn't care if I had a bloody nose. I didn't care if I got my teeth knocked out. I just wanted to win. And if I was going to lose, they were going to have to knock me out. I wasn't going to stay on my stool and I wasn't going to stay with my butt on the canvas.

"That kind of determination came from my dad. He is a very honorable man. He lives by the creed that it is better to die on your feet than to live on your knees. It goes back to Emiliano Zapata, the Mexican revolutionary, and it became my attitude as far as living my life goes."

It was hard to believe the man standing in that barren room at Rahway was the same one who had clawed his way to the top of the boxing heap, the same man who'd been convicted of raping a former schoolteacher at knifepoint. Time and a lean prison diet had melted the layer of baby fat that once covered his powerful physique and gave his face a cherubic appearance. The look in his dark brown eyes had changed, too. They no longer flashed with anger. Instead, they radiated a quiet strength, the kind of strength that sometimes comes when a man has looked into his soul and discovered somebody is home after all. That's what Tony Ayala, Jr, would have you believe, anyway.

"I'm a born-again Christian, now," said Ayala. "I've always believed in Christ, but wasn't much of a churchgoer. But now I've had an experience. I can't describe it. There was no light, no voice or anything. Just something inside me happened. It put everything in perspective. It gave me a great sense of peace. I understand the reason for my incarceration, the reason behind it. Everything that happens, happens for a reason. It changed my attitude. In the past I thought if you did something bad and got away with it—fine. My attitude now is that you are held accountable to God. As men we have a responsibility. I believe there is more to life than just what happens on earth. We were created to do more than just make money."

For the first twenty years of his life, it seemed Ayala had been created to do just two things: fight and get into trouble. The third son of Tony and Pauline Ayala, he was born and raised in San Antonio, Texas, a product of a poor, working-class family. His father, a proud, domineering, ex-Marine with a love of boxing, ruled his brood with an iron fist. Nobody questioned Papa Ayala's total authority. He taught his sons to box, taught them well—some say too well. He dreamed of raising a world champion and the gym became the boys' second home as soon as they were old enough to learn how to hook off the jab. While all the Ayala brothers eventually fought professionally, they all fell short of their seemingly unlimited potential.

Mike, the oldest, got a shot at featherweight champion Danny "Little Red" Lopez while Tony, Jr., was still an amateur. It was a sensational fight, *The Ring* magazine's "Fight of the Year" in 1979. But Mike was strung out on heroin and blew a once-in-a-lifetime opportunity, losing a fight he might very well have won otherwise. Brother Sammy, a well-regarded junior welterweight, also failed to live up to his promise, abusing drugs and wrecking cars when he should have been punching the bag and getting his beauty rest. When Tony, Jr., began to follow in his brother's unruly footsteps, a lot of people pointed a finger at Papa Ayala. They said he was obsessed with raising a champion, that he pushed his sons too hard, had given them a warped set of values. It is a point of view Tony, Jr., is quick to dispute.

"We were all rebellious. We never listened to our father's advice outside the gym," Ayala said. "If we had, all three of us would have been world champions and multimillionaires. We were young and wanted to do things our way. What my dad wanted us to do was boring. He wanted us to stay home, be good. But what we wanted to do was more fun. It's a lot of fun doing wrong. It's a lot of fun getting high. I started drinking and doing drugs when I was about twelve.... heroin, cocaine, pills. I kept it hidden for a long time. Not even my dad knew about it until it became very evident. And even then, because he loved me, when I told him I wasn't doing nothing, he excepted my word. But I was doing drugs all the time except for ten days, maybe two weeks, before a fight.

"My dad worked three jobs at one point to feed us. When my mother had a nervous breakdown, my father took care of us. He would drop off my two elder brothers at school at 6:00 in the morning, drop me off at the center, go to work, and then come back and pick me up again. He would cook. He would do the laundry. That's why it hurts me and angers me when people keep criticizing my dad for my mistakes."

Is Ayala being overly protective? What about all the stories of physical and mental abuse, the endless browbeatings and constant pressure to live up to Papa Ayala's demanding standards? If nothing else, his methods certainly seemed extreme. Surely, these things played a role in the way his sons rebelled.

"My dad has a way of doing thinigs, a la Vince Lombardi," recallyed Ayala. "My dad is very strong, an ex-Marine. There was an incident in the gym when I was young people misinterpreted. He hit me with a jump rope and people said I was being abused. But there was a meaning behind what he did. My dad was preparing me for life, not just to box, not for just the next fight. He was teaching me how to put aside pain. How to ignore physical illness in order to reach your goal. If it wasn't for my dad's training, I wouldn't have made it in prison."

Maybe Ayala has reached a new understanding of what his father was trying to achieve, but there was a time when Tony, Jr., was just as anxious to pass the buck as other people were to make excuses for him. It was much easier to pretend everything was someone else's fault.

"For much of my life I was very much in denial as to who was responsible for what," confessed Ayala. "It was very hard for me to accept responsibility for screwing up my life. Being in denial, man, is like you want to blame everyone else. It was my dad's fault...It was boxing's fault...I didn't have a childhood...My mother beat me when I was a boy. The excuses never end. But I've been a convict for seven years and I've come to learn a lot about myself. No one else puts you where you're at. It's you alone and no one else.

"Boxing didn't hurt me. Boxing gave me something, opened a world to me I would never have seen if I wasn't a boxer. I'm fairly intelligent. I could have stayed in school, but I used boxing as an excuse to quit. I dropped out of school because I was a lazy bastard. I passed ninth grade and just never went back to school. Of course, the excuse was that I was going to prepare myself for the 1980 Olympics. It was a crock. Even when I was still going, I wasn't going to learn. I went to school drunk, hung out and tried to meet girls. The truth is, if it wasn't for boxing, I'd probably be dead by now. In fact, I'm pretty sure I'd be dead, either from a drug overdose or car accident. Or I would have blown my brains out. I almost did it once back home in San Antonio."

The fact Tony, Jr., was a very disturbed young man became evident in 1978 when he was accused of attempted rape in San Antonio. He was allowed to plead guilty to reduced charges of aggravated assault and placed on ten years probation after paying the woman's family $20 thousand. Though all the signs of serious trouble brewing were obvious, they were pushed aside by the enthusiasm surrounding Ayala boxing prowess. He turned pro under the management of Lou Duva and Shelly Finkel in June of 1980, and was quickly hailed a future champion. Duva, the bulldog-like patriarch of a family-run boxing business, became something of a second father to Ayala. They made quite a team. Duva, renown for his histrionics, was almost as aggressive as his father. When WBA titleholder Davey Moore seemed reluctant to accept Ayala's challenge, Duva cut loose with one of his trademark tirades: "I don't know what it takes to get him (Moore) in the ring, but when we do, we'll knock him the hell out. And if we don't get a contract, you'll see one mad Mexican and one mad Italian." These days, the normally verbose Duva is reluctant to talk about his fallen fighter.

"That's a touchy subject," said Duva when asked to give his insights into Ayala's downfall. "I just don't want to be involved with it in any way. Sometimes you're so close to a situation. It's a case where he hurt everybody around him so much. I loved the guy too much. He could have been the greatest fighter in the world."

The mention of his former co-manager still strikes an emotional cord with Ayala. For the first time, he looked away, dropped his head and picked at his fingernails as he spoke.

"Lou Duva was like a dad to me. For a long time I've wanted to communicate with him. But I'm ashamed, and I don't know whether or not he'd reject me. I know I wasn't the best person out there. I hurt a lot of people. But I had some problems."

Those problems continued to haunt Ayala as he ripped his way through the junior middleweight division. He beat every man they put in front of him, but he couldn't conquer the terrible feelings inside, feelings that were pushing him closer and closer to the edge. They were more powerful than any punch, trickier than the craftiest boxer, the kind of enemy who refuses to stand up and fight face-to-face. Not even the love of his common-law wife, Lisa, could exorcise the demons gnawing away at Ayala like a cancer. In 1983, he was caught wandering intoxicated through a neighbor's house after entering through a window. He spent a brief spell at a substance abuse clinic in Orange, California, but the treatment didn't even begin to scratch the surface of his problems. "El Torito" was quickly back in the ring, taking out his frustrations in a brutal, but slightly more socially acceptable manner.

If Ayala was driven to achieve success between the ropes, he seemed equally determined to throw it all away outside the ring. On the surface he had it made. By the time his inner torment reached a boiling point, Ayala was earning over $100 thousand per fight and was assured a championship bout within months. All he had to do was behave himself. Unfortunately, that was the one thing beyond his reach. According to testimony given at his trial, Ayala broke into an apartment of a West Paterson, New Jersey, woman and terrorized her and her roommate. The blonde former math teacher told the court she had been tied up in her apartment in the early hours of New Year's Day and subjected to a brutal sexual assault by Ayala at knifepoint. Though Ayala claimed the attractive thirty-year-old victim had invited him into her apartment and asked him to tie her up and have sexual relations with her, the jury of six men and six women didn't buy his story. On April 13, 1983, Ayala was convicted of burglary, aggravated sexual assault, threat to kill, making terroristic threats, and possession of a knife. His $75 thousand bail was revoked and he was taken into custody.

"When I was sentenced, the judge held up a copy of a magazine with the headline 'Tony Ayala: Boxing's Bad Boy,'" remembered Ayala. Four years later, a New Jersey appeals court affirmed his conviction and left intact the trial judge's order that Ayala must serve a minimum of fifteen years of his thirty-year sentence before he could become eligible for parole.

Ayala has had plenty of time to think about what happened to him. For years he suppressed the truth, but with the help of an inmate therapy group, the sad story has finally surfaced. He's still not ready to expose the sordid details, but reading between the lines, it's not too difficult to figure out what happened.

"I didn't like being important. I didn't see nothing important about me," revealed Ayala. "With the exception of the last eight months, I've always felt I was a real piece of shit; undeserving of success, undeserving of money, undeserving of a loving spouse, undeserving to live. An incident happened when I was a little kid. It messed up my way of thinking, my way of looking at life. It made me feel worthless, dirty, guilty. It confused me as far as my sexual makeup was concerned."

Not too surprisingly when one thinks about it, Ayala believes he recognizes parallels in the life of another boxer who has seen his own share of turmoil.

"Look at Mike Tyson. I see myself in him. I don't know where

Tony Ayala (left) on his way to a first round knockout victory of Jose Baquedano, September 16, 1981, at Las Vegas, Nevada. Ayala was undefeated in 22 pro bouts before going to prison. (Photo courtesy of *The Ring* magazine)

Former number-one contender Tony Ayala behind bars at Rahway in 1989. When Ayala was sentenced to thirty years for aggravated sexual assault in 1983, the judge stipulated he must serve a minimum of fifteen years before becoming eligible for parole. (Photo by Tom Casino)

he's headed, but I think Mike Tyson is confused. I think he's had a lot of similar things happen to him as happened to me in my childhood. He hasn't spoken about it. He hasn't admitted it. And that in itself is a problem, because there is going to come a time when he's going to have to be honest with himself. He's going to have to resolve some problems he's got within himself that are getting bigger and bigger. They don't go away on their own. They only go away when you seek an understanding and kick them out.

"This is the first time I've expressed this (publicly). It's been inside my heart, but I stopped doing interviews for five or six years. Randy Gordon [then a boxing writer, later the New York State Athletic Commissioner] wrote a story about me that was a lie. He made a request for an interview. And out of courtesy, because I knew Randy Gordon from the street, and because I thought I had a good relationship with the man, I called him. I said, 'Randy, I'm not giving any interviews. I just called you as a friend.' The next thing I know, there's a four or five page story telling about how he visited me in prison. I hadn't seen Randy Gordon since my last fight! It was a total crock of shit. It hurt me a great deal. I can deal with getting kicked when I'm down, but when you're kicked by someone you think is your friend, that's when you want to throw in the towel and say it's over."

But Papa Ayala didn't raise quitters. Tony, Jr., kept fighting, searching for answers, seeking redemption and hoping for forgiveness. If nothing else, he certainly learned all the right things to say.

"I'm the first to admit I've made mistakes. And I'm very sorry. If I could, by giving up my life, go back and change things, I would do it in a second," he asserted. "But I can't do that. I'm bound by my life, by the rules of life. I can't go back. So, should I just give up? Or should I take responsibility and change? Look into my life. Look into why I was the way I was. Am I mean? Am I evil? I've asked myself these questions for the past six years, and I've come to realize that I'm a good person who made a bad mistake. No one is perfect, but knowing that doesn't mean I have to settle for my flaws. It's my responsibility to change as much as I can."

Ayala has attempted to continue his boxing career while incarcerated. Fellow Rahway inmate James Scott had been permitted to engage in several lucrative TV bouts while behind bars, but that was during a prior administration. Though Ayala has offered to donate his entire purse to charity, the current warden has been unreceptive to the idea of Ayala boxing in prison.

"I don't understand what it is exactly the State or society wants," said Ayala. "I can understand the punishment, but what do you do with a man after he's done his time? What is expected of him? Do they expect him to work as a dishwasher for the rest of his life? Someday I'll be out. They can hold me for another ten years, and that's a long time. But if you think about it, it's a short time compared to the rest of my life."

Ayala's case is still in the court system, pending one final appeal. It's highly unlikely, however, that his status will change. Most likely, he'll spend at least another ten years locked away in Rahway or some other similar hell hole. That will make him at least thirty-seven by the time he's free to pursue any kind of career. Surely, too old to box again.

"If Roberto Duran can do it at forty, I can do it at thirty-seven," Ayala said, a smile crossing his face and then quickly disappearing. "But I don't think I would dishonor the boxing public by doing that. You see Duran, Sugar Ray Leonard and George Foreman still fighting, but they're old horses. They're gone. They're past their prime, but they continue to make the fans pay to see them. I think the fans, the sport, deserves better than that.

"Boxing was great. I love boxing. I still fantasize about fighting again, redeeming myself and becoming the world champion. But life doesn't begin or end with boxing. I don't want to sound like a wacko, but everything has perspective now. I've just realized that boxing is nothing in comparison to life. And life is nothing in comparison to eternity with God."

A healthy dose of skepticism is mandatory. Ayala is hardly the first man to claim he found God while serving time. Born-again cons are practically an epidemic in all penal institutions. It's also easier to walk the straight-and-narrow when the alternatives—and temptations—are limited. One can't help but wonder if Ayala's resolve will be just as strong when he finally walks out the door a free man. It's a question Lt. Alan August of the New Jersey Department of Corrections claimed can only be answered after the fact.

"Tony has never been in any trouble since he's been in Rahway," said August, one of the originators of "Scared Straight," a program that takes juvenile offenders inside the prison in an attempt to frighten them into toeing the line. "But you can't predict what an inmate's behavior will be once he's back on the street and subjected to drugs, peer pressure and all the rest. Sometimes the guys you think most likely to make it are right back in here before you know it. But the opposite is also true. Sometimes there are guys you figure are sure to come back and you never see them again."

There is no doubt society needed to be protected from Ayala, or that he deserved to be punished. Not even Ayala would deny it. The larger question is one of redemption and forgiveness. Can a violent man change? Should he be given another chance?

"I would like people to take a second look at me. I'd like them to be objective," stressed Ayala. "Whether that's possible or not, it's okay. It's my responsibility to extend myself. Not everybody is going to be able to look beyond my mistakes. But I was basically a kid when these things happened. I'm man enough to stand on my own merits. If you want to judge me, judge me by what has happened since I've been incarcerated. Leave the past in the past."

Obviously, prison affects different men in different ways. The statistics tell us that the overwhelming majority are released unprepared for life on the outside, corrupted by their ordeal and bitter with the hand life has dealt them. Ayala is abundantly aware of the familiar syndrome, and is predictably determined to beat the odds. This time he's training to go the distance.

"It is important to me to remain human while I'm incarcerated, not to become a hateful animal. I don't want to let the experience of being incarcerated kill of the good part of me, make me resentful and unable to experience love. I would prefer death."

For Tony Ayala, Jr., the toughest fight is yet to come.

13

Another Kind of Punch Drunk

B oxing had always been the best part of Bruce Curry's helter-skelter life. It was the only thing that made him feel good about himself, perhaps his only touchstone with reality. When they told him he was washed-up and it was time to quit, Curry flipped out and tried to kill the one man who had helped him the most.

Curry was never a great boxer, but he put his heart and soul into every fight he ever had. He was the kind of fighter who took a punch for every dollar he earned, and win or lose, always gave the fans their money's worth. And for ten short months, he was WBC super lightweight champion of the world.

When his younger brother, Donald Curry, won the WBA welterweight title in February 1983, they became the first brothers in boxing history to hold world championships simultaneously.

"I first saw Bruce at the gym in Los Angeles sometime in 1976," remembered Jessie Reid, the man who trained and managed Curry throughout most of his professional career. "He'd only had about two pro fights at the time, but he looked so good, so quick. He had great determination, tremendous heart, and a really good feeling about himself. He thought he was going to be the greatest fighter of all time. And that's a good thing in a fighter. I was so impressed, I bought his contract for $1,200."

But the relationship wasn't strictly business. Reid took a paternal interest in the undisciplined kid from Fort Worth, and did everything he could to help Curry get his act together.

"In the beginning, it was like a marriage. He was a super-hard worker. The only problem I could see that was he wasn't very well educated. I tried to get him jobs at a couple of places; first in a gardening shop, helping landscapers. Then I tried to get him a job as a file clerk. But he couldn't get the hang of things."

Curry's problems went a lot deeper than his lack of education and inability to hold a job outside of boxing. Since his childhood in Fort Worth's predominately black south side, he'd shown signs of emotional instability. He was moody and erratic; happy one minute, fighting mad the next. Luckily, he found an outlet for his frustrations in boxing and enjoyed considerable success as an amateur, winning a number of Golden Gloves titles before turning pro in 1976 at the age of twenty. When Reid took over his contract, his career took off.

Curry won his first fourteen fights, including several in Japan, where his aggressive style made him such a favorite, he went by the name of Bruce Curry Fuji (after the Japanese network that televised his Oriental bouts). His modest professional success, however, wasn't enough to refocus his distorted view of life. Bruce's emotional problems continued to bubble just below the surface and it wasn't too long before he began to exhibit overt signs of mental illness.

"The weird stuff didn't really start until we'd been together about two years," recalled Reid. "But when it started, I was scared. I told my wife I thought the kid was having a lot of problems. Bruce had a very short fuse, and if someone said the wrong thing, he might blow his top. He just didn't seem to understand basic things. Like, if

Bruce Curry discusses strategy with trainer Jessie Reid prior to training session. Several years later, when Reid told Curry it was time to retire, the boxer flipped out and tried to kill his mentor. (Photo courtesy of *The Ring* magazine)

someone put their high beams on him on the freeway, Bruce would think they were following him. I got him an apartment, but they kicked him out because he played his radio loud at night and threw a TV set through a door—crazy things like that."

Reid took his troubled boxer to a therapist, who diagnosed Curry as borderline schizophrenic.

Reid's next step was to inform the California Athletic Commission of the boxer's mental condition. It was hard to know what to do. But as long as Curry kept winning, the commission felt it would be doing more harm than good by yanking his license. To make matters worse, the bad vibes that had shadowed him most of his life were about to follow him into the ring.

Practically everybody who saw Curry's 1978 bout with Wilfred Benitez at Madison Square Garden agreed Bruce was screwed out of the decision. Benitez was the "house fighter," the Garden's latest golden boy, a phenomenal talent who would eventually win three world titles. Curry was supposed to be just another notch on his fistic resume. Of course, nobody bothered to explain the script to Bruce, and he went out and fought with all the passion at his command. He poured every ounce of pent-up frustration into the fight and handed Benitez what should have been his first professional defeat. But when the judge's score cards were added up, Benitez got the verdict and Curry got the shaft.

The raw deal he received in the Benitez fight acerbated Curry's problems and reinforced his paranoid fantasies. He was positive Reid had set him up. His irrational fears didn't end there. He ripped through his purse money like it was toilet paper and then accused the bank of stealing his money. Curry was obviously headed for a full-scale mental breakdown, and no one was more aware of that fact than Reid.

"It got to a point where I couldn't handle it anymore," confessed Reid." I was tired of the headaches. I figured he might be better off if he went back to Texas to be around his family. I told him I would send for him when he had a fight scheduled."

Even though Curry continued to win most of his bouts, he also suffered several devastating defeats, including a knockout loss to Thomas Hearns. Reid was quick to admit he'd made a mistake putting Bruce in with the murderous-punching "Hit Man," but the bummer career move was the least of Curry's problems. Returning home to Fort Worth was also a disaster. According to Reid, Curry's relationship with his family wasn't exactly the stabilizing factor he'd hoped it would be.

"It was hard to know what to think. Bruce always changed his opinions about everything. First, he'd tell you his mother loved him and his brother would do anything for him. Next thing you know, he'd say they all hated him. You just didn't know what was the truth. But I know he wasn't really close with Donald. It wasn't so much that Donald didn't like Bruce. Bruce was jealous of Donald because he was brighter and got all the attention."

Eventually, Reid came to realize Bruce's family was only adding to his misery; a fairly common occurrence in boxing, especially when the smell of money is in the air.

"Whenever he'd have a fight, his family would come around and want to know where his paycheck was. It was really a bad situation," maintained Reid. "In the end, his mother took a lot of his money out of the bank, and a couple of weeks later, she threw him out of the house. That made Bruce mad at the world. He was so angry he was ready to fight King Kong."

Though Curry continued to earn decent money, Reid desperately wanted to escape the private hell in which he'd been caught up. He didn't have the heart to sell Bruce's contract, so he finally gave it to Billy Baxter, a professional gambler from Las Vegas who dabbled in managing prize fighters.

"I warned Billy I wasn't doing him any favors," insisted Reid. "But Billy was interested in signing Donald Curry and figured he'd have a better chance if he was already working with Bruce. Well, about five months later, Billy called me up and said he needed my help. Bruce had already gone through quite a bit of Billy's money and wrecked a car he'd bought his fighter. Billy told me, 'The kid won't train for anyone else. He won't fight for anyone else. He wants you.'"

Reid, strapped for cash at the time, reluctantly agreed to move to Vegas for a year and see what he could do to help Baxter. It proved a bittersweet decision. From a boxing point of view, Reid worked wonders with the unpredictable fighter. Reunited with his old trainer. Curry put together a winning streak, and with the help of the influential Baxter, maneuvered himself into position to fight Leroy Haley for the WBC super lightweight title. Haley was not the most dominating of champions, and in May of 1983, Curry outpointed him to win the belt. Unfortunately, achieving his lifelong desire failed to curb Curry's bizarre behavior.

"He was always doing something crazy," recollected Reid. "For some reason, he was afraid someone was going to attack him, and one day the cops picked him up carrying a baseball bat. He also stole a watch from Wonderland just because he liked it, even though he had plenty of money. Then there was the time he went out to the UNLV stadium and climbed up to the top of the basketball court and started yelling he was Spiderman. He never did anything to do any bodily harm to anybody, just crazy things. I told Billy I thought we should get a doctor because Bruce needed something to calm him down. But Billy said it would be bad publicity for a world champion, and thought it would be better if I handled him, just keep things quiet."

Keeping things quiet gave Curry the opportunity to make two successful defenses of his title, but when he absorbed a vicious beating at the hands of Billy Costello in January 1984, he lost more than the championship. He also lost what was left of his self-control. Reid's worst fear soon became a reality.

"I told Billy, 'If something happens to this kid's career, he's coming after me because I'm the closest person to him.' And that's what happened," said Reid. "When Billy told him to quit boxing, it hurt Bruce's feelings. He kind of went into a shell for a couple of days and then came by the gym to talk to me. It was the first time since the Costello fight I'd really had to come to the point with him and tell him how I felt.

"I told him, 'Bruce, I think you should get away from everybody, go off by yourself and review the tapes (of the Costello fight). Look at it and you'll see that you're not the same fighter anymore. You've been a champion. You've had a lot of fun with the sport. I think it's time for you to quit before you get hurt.'"

As one might expect, this was not what Curry wanted to hear. He rejected Reid's advice and informed his trainer he'd be back in two days to show him he could still fight. Over the next forty-eight hours, Curry's emotions slowly simmered to the boiling point. His whole world had been suddenly taken away from him and he wasn't about to surrender without a fight. Reid was more than just a trainer and former manager. He was a father figure who had rejected him. As Bruce had never known his natural father, this was a particularly stunning blow. To Curry's warped way of thinking, there was only one solution to his dilemma: he would beat up Reid, thus proving he could still fight. Then, he rationalized, his old mentor would be forced to take him back again.

Exactly two days after his previous conversation with Reid, Curry arrived at the Golden Glove Gym in Las Vegas and proclaimed he was going to "kick Jessie's ass." Nobody bothered to warn Reid. Not only was he one of the few white men in a mostly black gym, he'd come from California and taken work away from other trainers. There were some who relished the idea of seeing him taken down a peg. After announcing his intentions, Curry parked his car out of sight, at the side of the gym, and waited for Reid to appear. It was a day the burly ex-Marine will never forget.

"When I got to the gym, I saw this car peel around the corner and come shooting right at me," said Reid. "I was scared to death, but I tried not to show it. When Bruce got of the car, he had his hands wrapped and a pair of those baseball batting gloves, with the fingers cut out, pulled over the bandages. It looked like he was wearing brass knuckles.

"He came walking over and said, 'You know, Jess, you and me have to get it on.' I tried to reason with him. I said, 'Bruce, I'm a forty-something-year-old man. What's it going to prove if you whip me? You're not getting paid for this. It's crazy.'"

Curry didn't want to hear it. It was too late to turn back.

"No, if I beat you, you're going to want to train me again," replied Curry. And then he snapped.

"The next thing I knew, he let out this karate-like yell and started throwing punches," said Reid. "What really surprised me, when it was all over and I thought about it, was that he didn't hit me with anything. It was like he really didn't want to hit me, just prove that he could still fight. But I didn't realize that at the time. All I could see was punches wrapping around me, hitting my arms and banging around my body. Finally, I grabbed him and put him on the ground. I told him to stop this crazy stuff. He started yelling, 'Keith...Keith, help me.' I'd never heard of Keith before, but later on I found out he was Bruce's half-brother."

According to Reid, Keith jumped out of the car with a Bowie knife in his hand and started to run toward Curry. Fortunately, another of Reid's boxers, who had come outside the gym to watch the altercation, tripped the knife-wielding Keith and knocked him to the ground—just like in the movies. His quick action allowed Reid to give his undivided attention to Bruce, who had once again begun swinging.

"By then I'd had enough," stated Reid. "I told him, 'Bruce, you've been asking for it for a long time. If you want it, come and get it.' He came running in and I hit him with an overhand right in the forehead. He went down with his head split wide open. He'd been cut in the Costello fight and it hadn't had a chance to heal properly. After that, I thought it was over and started to walk away."

Before Reid could reach the gym, Curry jumped up again and said, "I've got a gun."

"It was like a nightmare," Reid said. "My whole body was trembling. I went into the building and locked the door. The next thing I knew, Bruce had gone around to the back door where the doorknob was missing and poked a gun through the hole.

"Dennis Fikes was in the ring shadow boxing and saw the barrel of the pistol. He yelled "gun" and went flying out of the ring. I shot up against the wall behind a piece of iron. Then I heard a gunshot. It echoed through the building and sort of sounded like a starting pistol. But I looked over and there was a bullet hole about a yard away from where I was standing, chest high."

A few seconds later, the sound of squealing tires was heard as Curry and his half-brother raced away. Reid pressed charges, but told the police he wasn't interested in seeing Curry in jail.

"At that point he'd reached the edge of the cliff and needed medical help," said Reid. "He needed someone who could understand the really deep problems he was having."

A Nevada judge agreed with Reid and committed Curry to a mental hospital in Reno, where he spent the next nine months. Reid was worried when he heard Bruce was going to be released, fearful there would be a recurrence of the previous violence. Thankfully, his misgivings proved groundless. Medication had knocked the fight out of Curry more effectively than any ring opponent. He emerged from the hospital, a forlorn, but apparently harmless man, his anger and delusions suppressed by a daily dose of pharmaceuticals.

Several years later, Curry attempted a comeback. By then, however, all of his skills had deserted him and he soon fell by the wayside. Reid sees him periodically at the Broadway Gym in Los Angeles. There are no hard feelings between them and they always greet each other with a hug. Reid has gone on to have his share of success with other fighters, but for Bruce all that is left are his dreams. He still clings to the hope he'll one day box again and is always full of stories about how various promoters are trying to lure him into making another comeback.

"Of course, it's all in the mind," said Reid, a note of sadness in his voice. "Every now and then, Bruce will phone promoters and try to sell himself. He's done it thirty or forty times since he got out of the hospital. But nobody is interested. You know, I always respected how hard he tried. He fought every fight the best he could. He deserved better than he got from the leeches and rats of this world."

Bruce Curry was far from the first man to use boxing as an emotional safety valve. It's one of the sport's unspoken contributions to society, a way of harnessing abnormal behavior and turning it into an athletic asset. The most famous case was that of Joe Louis, the immortal "Brown Bomber."

While practically everybody with even a passing knowledge of boxing knew about Louis' epic struggle with the Internal Revenue Service, only his family and closest associates were aware of the former heavyweight champion's psychiatric problems. All that changed May 1, 1970, when officers of the Denver sheriff's office arrived at Louis' home at 2675 Monaco Parkway with an order from Judge David Brofman of the probate court. In part, the judge's order directed that Louis be "delivered to the Colorado Psychiatric Hospital, Forthwith."

Confronted by the sheriff's deputies and other officers of the court, a distraught Louis told them he would not leave unless he was first permitted to call the White House. Acutely aware the rumpled old man they had come to escort was a living icon, the officers acquiesced.

"I know Nixon, I want the President to know what you are doing to me," said Louis, according to Barney Nagler, who wrote a detailed account of the incident in his book, *Brown Bomber*.

When the operator told the old champ he could not talk directly to Nixon and would have to settle for a White House aide, he changed his mind and decided to phone the *Denver Post* and the *Rocky Mountain News* instead.

"I want everybody to know what you're doing to me," declared Louis.

Within minutes, reporters and photographers flooded the house. Any hope of discreetly handling the news of the legendary boxer's

Former heavyweight champion Joe Louis as he appeared during the last years of his life. Former wrestler Count Billy Varga is seen on the "Brown Bomber's" left. (Photo courtesy of *The Ring* magazine)

embarrassing circumstances vanished. Later that day, practically every newspaper, TV and radio station in the free world spread the sad news: Joe Louis was mentally unbalanced.

After his attorney arrived, Louis allowed himself to be taken away quietly. Actually, whether he knew it or not, Louis had very little choice but to accompany the officers. He was under legal restraint, and, if push came to shove, he could have been taken by force.

Though Louis' son, Joseph Louis Barrow, Jr., signed the application, Joe's third wife, Martha, had been the person most instrumental in having Joe committed. Long concerned about her husband's rapidly deteriorating mental health, Martha had frequently urged Louis to seek help. But Joe didn't think he was sick and refused to even consider psychiatric treatment. Finally, Martha took matters into her own hands and petitioned the court to have Louis hospitalized.

Louis's inner turmoil began many years before he was forcibly institutionalized by the State of Colorado. The seeds of torment were probably planted during his deprived childhood in rural Alabama. Louis was only two years old when his father, Munroe Barrow, was sent to the Searcy State Hospital for the Insane in Mt. Vernon, where he spent the rest of his life. When Louis was twelve, he journeyed north with his mother and stepfather and settled in Detroit. It was there he eventually began his fabled boxing career.

Countless publications and film and television documentaries have told the rags-to-riches story of Louis' ascension to the heavyweight championship of the world. His legendary fighting prowess, endless income tax difficulties, and significant role in improving race relations are all part of the fabric of American culture. But not until the publication of Nagler's revealing biography did we learn the melancholy details of Louis's private purgatory.

"(Louis) believed that members of the Mafia were pursuing him, intent on destroying him with poison gas," wrote Nagler. "Wherever he went, he perceived them in his consciousness, and they provoked outbursts of suspicion and rage.

"Formerly he had worked out his inner hostilities in the ring. Outside the ring, he consumed himself in frivolity and made many mistakes, none of which he blamed on others. When, finally, he was overcome by bizarre aberrations, he was suddenly devoid of dignity, pride and determination. He externalized his fantasies, and this rendered him a pitiable figure."

One of the strange ways in which Louis's illness manifested itself was the ritual he performed before going to bed at night. Whenever he stayed in a hotel room with air conditioning, he would attempt to paste newspapers over the vents in an effort to keep the "poison gas" from filtering into his room. Later, as his delusions grew progressively worse, Louis began to erect flimsy, tent-like structures over the top of his bed made from sheets and pieces of furniture as an added precaution. Perhaps the most pitiful of these episodes came when poor Joe smeared mayonnaise all over the ceiling of his room in an effort to prevent gas from leaking through the cracks.

Louis also believed he was being followed by mysterious strangers, and would frequently change travel plans, abruptly switching airplanes and destinations. It was not unusual for him to drop out of sight for days at a time. He neglected his grooming and frequently vegetated in bed watching television. Adding to Martha's concerns was the rumor that Louis's paranoid delusions were aggravated by cocaine abuse. By the time his wife and son took legal steps to insure the aging boxer received the medical attention he needed, Louis was severely ill.

A few days after entering Colorado Psychiatric Hospital, Louis was transfered to the Veterans Administration Hospital at 1055 Clairmont Street in Denver. Dr. Martin, chief of the psychiatric ward, prescribed heavy doses of the tranquilizer Thorazine to be administered to Louis daily. The Colorado law which permitted Louis to be hospitalized against his will allowed for a patient to be held for a period of three months, with an additional three-month extension if it was deemed medically advisable. After the first three months, it was decided Louis should continue his treatment on an out-patient basis. Dr. Martin saw him twice a week and kept Joe on a steady diet of tranquilizers.

For a few months, Louis stuck to the schedule, but eventually rebelled against therapy, left Colorado and never came back. Later, Dr. Martin was to write the following about his famous patient: "Contact with close friends, relatives and a private physician revealed that he (Louis) had regressed to a point of emotional disturbance at least as severe, if not more so, as he had when he was first admitted to my care."

Louis spent the last decade of his life living in Las Vegas, working as a glorified meeter-and-greeter at Caesars Palace. While some people's sensibilities were offended because such a legendary fighter was obliged to earn his living in this manner, Louis, despite his continued paranoid delusions, was relatively happy. He had money in his pockets and was still the center of attention and adulation. A few years before he died on April 12, 1981, Louis suffered a stroke, which effectively relegated his previous difficulties to secondary status. Toward the end, the once unbeatable fighting machine seemed barely aware of his surroundings and appeared in public propped in a wheelchair.

Following Louis' death, Caesars erected a larger-than-life statue to his memory in the elevator lobby of the casino. Louis appears in a classic fighting stance, starring blankly out upon the gaming tables and slot machines. The boxer's body is as finely chiseled as he was in his prime, but his face is that of a middle-aged man; the way Joe looked during his final, losing bout against Rocky Marciano. There is something oddly out of kilter about the statue and its placement. The overall effect creates an unintentional commentary on the darkness and despair which haunted the man known as the "Brown Bomber," a permanent reminder of the internal anguish which often stokes the fires of greatness.

14 _____

Goodbye, Gypsy Joe

Gypsy Joe Harris died at age forty-four and we'll never see his likes again. It's hard to explain to someone who never saw him fight. There are no reference points. But in or out of the ring, Gypsy Joe was unique, a once-in-a-lifetime phenomenon.

To begin with, the brilliant little boxer from North Philadelphia looked more like a gnome than a fighter. Even in his early twenties he had the appearance of a little old man. But when he flashed his snagged-tooth smile, which was almost all the time, his mischievous face lit up like a six-year-old kid's at a birthday party.

He had an irrepressible, cartoon quality about him. If Gypsy Joe couldn't make you laugh, it was time to check your pulse.

Gypsy (nobody from Philly called him Harris) had charisma before the word became fashionable. A born showman, he would prance into the ring with bells tied to his boxing boots, dressed in ring attire that made him look like a court jester. Sartorially, he was decades ahead of his time.

But what made Gypsy Joe so special wasn't his extravagant mode of dress or flamboyant personality. It was what he did after the bell rang.

Blessed with blazing speed, Gypsy was a constant blur of contorted motion. He would bend and twist his agile body into amazing positions, throwing punches from every conceivable angle. His style was an intoxicating blend of street swagger, classical boxing and improvisational genius.

Gypsy Joe's repertoire of tricks seemed endless.

One of his favorite ploys was to stand with his back against the corner post, one hand grasping the top rope, the other dangling at his side. From this position, he would invite his opponents to hit his seemingly unguarded chin. But it was a sucker's game.

No matter how fast and furious the punches came in his direction, Gypsy would duck and dodge out of harm's way. Then, with unbelievable skill, he would lash out with stinging counters and skip away, leaving his bewildered adversary seething.

Another of his crowd-pleasing antics was a variation of the old Jersey Joe Walcott walk-away. Suddenly, often in the middle of a bristling exchange, Gypsy would pivot and nonchalantly stroll away from the action. Then, before his puzzled foe had a chance to recover his bearings, Gypsy would attack from another direction.

Everything Gypsy Joe did in the ring was unorthodox; every feint wildly exaggerated, each combination flashier than the last. Some people, confused by his bizarre methods, made the mistake of calling him a clown. But they were wrong. Gypsy Joe was an artist.

The secret to his highly individual style was simple: Gypsy was blind in one eye! He was forced to employ any means available to keep his good eye on his opponent. He not only overcame a practically insurmountable handicap, he turned it into an advantage. His weird style was a masterpiece of creativity, a monument to the little warrior's ingenuity and courage.

The tremendous excitement Gypsy generated made him a star while he was still boxing in the preliminaries. He turned pro in late 1964, and by the end of the following year was the hottest thing to hit Philadelphia boxing in some time.

The match that established Gypsy as a legitimate contender was his 1966 bout with local rival Stanley "Kitten" Hayward, who had earned the No. 1 spot in the welterweight rankings by outpointing Bennie Briscoe.

Hayward, a super smooth boxer-puncher, dropped Gypsy early in the bout with a left hook, but couldn't keep him down. Gypsy unloaded combination after combination, finally reducing "Kitten" to a bloody pulp. The fight was stopped in the seventh round to save the battered Hayward further abuse.

A little over a month later, Gypsy soundly outpointed Jose Stable to cement his standing as the leading contender for the welterweight title, then held by Texan Curtis Cokes.

Unable to obtain an immediate crack at Cokes's belt, Gypsy stopped crosstown rival Johnny Knight, and then accepted a non-title bout with Cokes, March 31, 1967.

It was the pixie-like Philadelphian's only appearance at Madison Square Garden and perhaps his finest hour. He completely dominated the classy champion, winning ten out of ten rounds. Just like everybody else Gypsy fought, Cokes was totally befuddled.

The victory over Cokes earned Gypsy a rare honor when he was selected as a *Sports Illustrated* cover subject. In fact, he was the first boxer to grace the cover of the prestigious magazine who was neither a heavyweight nor a world champion.

Despite his celebrity status and lofty standing in the boxing world, Gypsy remained completely undisciplined and carefree. He would disappear for days, driving trainer Willie Reddish crazy. Gypsy's idea of preparation was to show up at the gym three or four days before a match and engage in a few rounds of frenzied gym warfare with the toughest boxers available.

As unbelievable as it may seem, he could literally come off the street and beat the best in the world. But the one thing he couldn't beat was the scales. Regardless of how much money the Athletic Commission fined him for coming in overweight, Gypsy refused to train with any sort of regularity. By mid-1967, it was a struggle for him to make the junior-middleweight limit.

Gypsy Joe Harris executes behind-the-back shot to show his prowess at pool just before reporting for workout at Champs Gym in North Philly. Usually, the brilliant little ring wizard spent far more time in the pool hall than in the gym. (Photo courtesy of Peltz Boxing Promotions)

Even though Gypsy hadn't weighed 147 pounds in over a year, Texas promoters were anxious to stage a return match with Cokes for the title. They flew the Philly favorite to Dallas in May of '67 for a showcase fight against Benny Bowser. Gypsy delivered his usual rousing performance, getting off the deck to stop Bowser in the fourth round.

Though a date for the title fight with Cokes was set for the summer, the bout never took place. The promoters, who eventually ended up in jail for counterfeiting currency, had already stiffed Cokes once. They had staged his successful Dallas defense over Frenchman Francois Pavilla earlier in the year, but only paid the champion $15 thousand of his contracted purse of $30 thousand.

Strangely enough, Cokes actually weighed-in for the non-existent bout. But Gypsy, unable to approach the weight and suspicious of the promoters, never left Philadelphia. Later, it was discovered the shady characters putting on the fictitious fight had printed unnumbered tickets in an underhanded attempt to oversell the venue.

Undaunted, Gypsy continued on his merry course, laughing his way through life and drawing profitable crowds whenever he fought. He narrowly decisioned tough Puerto Rican Miguel Barretto in August, handily outpointed Bobby Cassidy in October, and then soundly thrashed Barretto in a December rematch. Sure he was wild and crazy. But what could you tell a man who owned a chartreuse suit and a mink bow tie?

Following a victory over Dick DiVeronica in February of 1968, Gypsy signed for a major match against Emile Griffith, who had recently lost the middleweight crown to Nino Benvenuti. From a financial point of view, the promotion was a blockbuster. The match lured almost 14,000 fans into the Spectrum, setting an indoor attendance record for a non-title fight that stood until Briscoe fought Marvin Hagler at the same venue ten years later.

The fight itself was a huge disappointment as far as Philadelphia fans were concerned. Griffith was in charge the entire way and handed Gypsy his first (and only) defeat in a twenty-five-bout career. For the first time in his life, the magician failed to pull a rabbit out of his hat.

"I think Griffith was just a little too big, a little too strong for Gypsy Joe that night," said Gil Clancy, Griffith's trainer. "Harris had the ability to be a champion. It was just the luck of the draw."

The saddest part of the whole evening—though nobody realized it at the time—was that Gypsy Joe would never fight again.

Later that year, Gypsy signed to fight Tex-Mex contender Manuel Gonzalez. Once again, things did not go as planned. The first time Gonzalez arrived in Philly, Gypsy was unable to make weight and the bout was postponed. A new date was set, but when Gypsy showed up for the pre-fight physical, the commission doctor suddenly *discovered* that the little wizard was blind in one eye. His boxing license was immediately revoked.

Once his disability was revealed, Gypsy came clean. He said he'd been injured in a street fight over a bag of candy when he was a kid. He claimed the other boy hit him with a brick.

According to the fighter, he'd fooled the commission doctors for years by memorizing the eye chart. While this is possible, another story soon surfaced; a far more sinister one.

Gym gossip whispered that powerful members of the Philadelphia boxing community had known all along about Gypsy's infirmity, and had chosen to ignore it because he was such a big money-maker. But after cashing in big on the Griffith fight, they grew weary of Gypsy's unreliable ways. It was decided his services would be terminated.

Whichever story is true, it was a poor reflection on the Pennsylvania Athletic Commission. It either allowed a half-blind boxer to fight professionally for four years, or regularly administered eye examinations of a totally superficial nature.

Several years after being banned, Gypsy Joe hired a lawyer and attempted to have his license reinstated. There was much local sentiment in favor of allowing him to box. But as luck would have it, one member of the commission also just happened to be sightless in one eye.

At the climax of the hearing, the commissioner dramatically popped out his glass eyeball and showed it to the gathering. After that, Gypsy didn't stand a chance. Once again, the ruling went against him. In a way, the commission also signed his death warrant.

Without boxing, Gypsy was lost. He was an artist without a canvas, a tortured soul set adrift in a sea of indifference. For a number of years, he attempted to drown his sorrows in drugs and alcohol. He became a pitiful sight, rheumy-eyed and bloated, a grotesque caricature of the man who once performed miracles in the boxing ring.

In the mid-1970s, Gypsy checked into a hospital and kicked the drug habit that was slowly, but surely, killing him. However, even after he beat his deadly habit, Gypsy's lot did not improve.

He never really found his place in life after boxing and eventually was reduced to living on government handouts. Yet despite his dismal circumstances, Gypsy retained his cheerful disposition, always jolly and ready to make people laugh.

Bad luck continued to haunt Gypsy, and in 1988 he suffered the first of four heart attacks. Then, on February 10, 1990, he was admitted to Temple University Hospital for what doctors described as a "weak and flabby heart." He lingered until March 6, when he died at 3:25 PM. But in a way, he'd really died a long time ago, back on the day they told him he couldn't box anymore.

At his memorial service, Gypsy's ex-wife Gladys reminisced about how her former husband always used to say he hoped it rained on the days he fought. When she asked why, Gypsy told her he figured that if it rained, it meant God was blessing him and that he would win.

There was light rain the day they buried Gypsy Joe Harris. Maybe they gave him back his boxing license when he reached the pearly gates?

15

The Ulitmate Sacrifice

J asper J. Golden awoke to a lovely autumn sunrise the morning of September 13, 1842. Normally, he would have instantly stripped the covers from his bed and quickly dressed himself, eager to begin his busy schedule. But this particular day, Golden lingered a few extra minutes beneath the sheets, hesitant to face the world. His reluctance was short lived. Golden knew what he had to do, and was damned well going to do it. After all, who could question the absolute correctness of his mission? Prize fights were both illegal and a moral outrage. He'd put a stop to this sinful business—or at least give it his best effort.

Golden was a respected citizen of Dobbs Ferry, a small town about twenty-five miles up the Hudson River from New York City. He worked as a teacher for the Hastings school district and also served as a local magistrate. Rumors had reached his ear concerning the strong possibility his tiny community would be the site of a bare-knuckles prizefight. Golden considered himself a man of high moral standards and was steadfastly opposed to such barbaric spectacles and thoroughly disgusted by the unruly mob who patronized them. As far as he was concerned, prize fighting was no better than dog fights or badger-baiting. In fact, they were worse. Instead of wild animals tearing each other to shreds, pugilists were men made in God's image. It was a shameful, dehumanizing enterprise, populated by the dregs of society.

It was Golden's fervent hope that the dozen steamboats carrying the fighters and their followers would sail on past Dobbs Ferry and dock elsewhere, as far out of his jurisdiction as possible. While he knew this was probably wishful thinking, Golden decided to conduct classes as usual. There was no point in adding to the day's transgressions by neglecting the children's lessons. But before lunchtime, Golden received the news he'd been dreading: A wretched horde of almost two thousand miscreants had arrived. Some of them were already erecting a ring on a small plateau overlooking the Hudson Valley, just a short distance from his schoolhouse.

Puffed with righteous indignation and armed with a desist-and-disperse order, Golden intrepidly marched to the battle grounds and confronted Yankee Sullivan, the noted pugilist and saloon keeper. Sullivan was not scheduled to fight that day, but was the best-known personality present and had served as a quasi-matchmaker for the proposed encounter between Christopher Lilly and Thomas McCoy. Golden stated his business and Sullivan politely gave him permission to read his decree to the assembly.

Golden glanced around at the unruly gathering, later described by Justice Charles R. Ruggles as a collection of "gamblers, bullies, pickpockets and thieves; the idle, disorderly and dissolute." The schoolteacher said a silent prayer, took a deep breath and proceeded. His declaration was greeted with jeers and derogatory jibes. Cries of "Kick him out," and "Heave him in the river," rendered his little speech practically inaudible. When he was finished, Golden stepped aside, satisfied he had done his best. But the plucky schoolmaster decided to stay and watch the fight. Who knows? He might be later called upon to give testimony against the shameful exhibition he was about to witness. Anyway, that's the justification he gave himself for lingering at the site. A more honest appraisal of his motives might also have included a smidgen of curiosity.

Lilly and McCoy were relatively small men, both weighed less than one hundred-forty pounds. The contest was held under the rules of the London prize ring, which meant a round ended when a man was either thrown or knocked to the ground. The boxers were then given a thirty-second rest period before they were required to continue. McCoy, a dues-paying member of the body-punching school of attack, got off to a good start, and was the betting favorite after fourteen rounds. Of course, the trouble with attacking the body is that one leaves oneself open to punches to the head. Following another fifteen rounds of fighting, it became apparent that Lilly's hard blows to the head were gradually reducing McCoy to a bloody pulp.

Though each man connected with heavy punches, McCoy's ultimate defeat was inevitable. According to a report carried in the September 17, 1842, issue of the *Spirit of the Times,* by the seventieth round "McCoy was now indeed a most unseemly object: both eyes were black—the left one nearly closed, and indeed that whole cheek presented a shocking appearance. His very forehead was black and blue; his lips were swollen to an incredible size, and the blood streamed profusely down his chest."

What had begun as a prize fight had turned into a sickening slaughter, and even the hard-bitten crowd gathered at Dobbs Ferry had seen enough. Many in attendance shouted for the fight to be stopped, and Sullivan, who worked Lilly's corner, asked McCoy's seconds to concede and save their man's life. McCoy refused to surrender. "Nurse me...nurse me and I'll whip him yet," he reportedly begged his handlers at the conclusion of the one hundred eighteenth round. McCoy fought one more round and then collapsed and died on the spot. A coroner's inquest determined he'd drowned in his own blood, the result of his wounds draining into his lungs. McCoy's death was the first recorded fatality in American boxing.

The Battle of Hastings, as the infamous Lilly-McCoy bout became known, caused a major scandal. In order to avoid prosecution, Lilly fled to Canada and from there to England. A Westchester County grand jury indicted eighteen accessories, including Sullivan, who, along with George Kensett (one of McCoy's cornermen) and John McCleester (who seconded Lilly), were convicted of fourth-degree manslaughter. As organizer of the match, Sullivan received the stiffest punishment and was sentenced to two years in Ossining prison. However, Sullivan had numerous political connections and was given a governor's pardon after serving just a few months.

It took boxing in the United States around five years to recover from the Lilly-McCoy tragedy. The few bouts that took place during that time were held in the notorious gambling town of Natchez, Mississippi. But by the mid-1850s boxing once again began to flourish throughout the country. Like most boxing fatalities, McCoy's death proved little more than an interruption.

Though exact records have not been kept, according to computations made by *The Ring Record Book & Boxing Encyclopedia* and *The Guiness Book of Boxing Records & Facts,* there have been approximately five hundred ring deaths since the adoption of the Queensbury Rules in 1884. How many occurred prior to that is anyone's guess. But it's safe to assume the percentage of fatalities must have been far greater under the London Prize Ring and old Broughton rules. In fact, until Jack Broughton killed George Stevenson in a match held at Tottenham Court, London, England, April 24, 1741, there were no written rules at all. Broughton, hoping to limit further tragedies, wrote boxing's first crude code of conduct in 1743. His labors also earned him the title of the Father of Boxing.

While occasional fatalities due to the physical hardships of fist fighting are inevitable, refinement of the rules and upgrading of medical and safety standards have drastically lowered the risk of traumatic injury. A greater peril, by far, is the insidious threat of chronic, latent brain damage, known as *pugilistica dementia* or the punch-drunk syndrome. Usually, this debilitating disease doesn't catch up with its victim until several years after the boxer has retired from the ring. Therefore, it is largely ignored by the general public and those who wish to ban pugilism. Instead, the attention of both fans and reformers is usually focused on the more spectacular, if far less frequent, occurrence of death resulting from injuries sustained in the ring.

It has only been in light of fairly recent advances in neuroscience that the true hazards of boxing have been completely understood. While one punch can theoretically kill a man, ring history has shown us that death between the ropes is frequently the result of the accumulative effect of a series of beatings—or even an outside accident—prior to the bout in which the fatality actually occurred. An obvious case in point was the death of heavyweight Ernie Schaaf, who died four days after being knocked out by Primo Carnera, February 10, 1933, at Madison Square Garden.

Some ring historians trace Schaaf's death to a winning bout he had with "Two-Ton" Tony Galento the previous June. Galento, a beer-bellied slugger who specialized in illegal tactics and a powerful left hook, lost the decision, but not before leaving his calling card. He roughed up Schaaf in the clinches, chopping away at the back of his opponent's neck with thumping rabbit punches. The numbing experience left Schaaf in such a weakened state, he was unable to leave his dressing room for several hours after the fight.

Schaaf endured another punishing outing against future heavyweight champion Max Baer, August 31, 1932. After holding his own over the first eight rounds, Schaaf was savagely pummeled by Baer and knocked down with just two seconds remaining in the tenth and final round. The battered loser was carried from the ring on a stretcher and forced to remain in Chicago Stadium for four hours before he was ambulatory.

Earlier beatings were not the only medical factor contributing to Schaaf's eventual death following the Carnera bout. Less than a

Former heavyweight contender Ernie Schaaf, who died after his 1933 bout with Primo Carnera at Madison Square Garden. (Photo courtesy of *The Ring* magazine)

month before entering the ring against the 6'5½", 264-pound Italian known as the "Ambling Alp," Schaaf spent a week in a Boston hospital suffering from a severe case of influenza. Clearly weakened by his illness and the punishment absorbed in previous fights, Schaaf "dropped as if felled by a blackjack" in the thirteenth round after taking a left hand punch to the head unanimously described as nothing more than a "tap." As the stricken fighter was rushed from the ring, cries of "fake" echoed throughout the Garden. The blow which had put him down was so light that most of the crowd thought Schaaf had "gone in the tank." In actuality, the twenty-four-year-old boxer had sustained an intercranial hemorrhage, and despite a three-and-one-half hour operation to relieve the pressure on his brain, he died at 4:10 the morning of February 14.

The death of welterweight Jimmy Doyle in 1947 following a knockout loss to Sugar Ray Robinson has been the topic of much interest over the years, mainly because Robinson had a premonition of disaster. According to Robinson, the night before the fight, he dreamed about killing an opponent in the ring. The vivid nightmare and its subsequent realization so unnerved the welterweight champion that he seriously considered quitting the ring. There was, however, nothing supernatural about Doyle's death. He had no business being in the ring with Robinson in the first place.

Fifteen months prior to his fatal encounter with Robinson at the Cleveland Arena, Doyle was near death from a concussion suffered in the same ring at the hand of middleweight Artie Levine. According to postmortem testimony given by the fighter's brother, Edward Delaney, Doyle was a "changed man" after the head injuries suffered in the Levine bout. Delaney told the coroner that before the Levine fight, his twenty-two-year-old brother had been very active, a great dancer and always "sparring around" the house. Afterwards, the boxer would sit for hours reading a book, was always quiet and insisted he would never again enter the ring.

Nevertheless, following a nine month hiatus, Doyle returned to boxing and somehow secured a title fight against Robinson, who was rapidly approaching the physical peak of his fantastic career.

According to published reports of the match, Doyle was completely outclassed and "never landed a single damaging blow on the champion." James P. Dawson, who covered the fight for *The New York Times,* wrote, "Only for his courage under fire could Doyle be credited. For the doughty little Californian, though buffeted about a sea of blows against a champion who is a master boxer and a paralyzing puncher as well, never stopped coming."

In the eighth round, Robinson delivered a short left hook to the jaw and Doyle dropped in his tracks, striking his head against the ring floor with "resounding thud" as he fell. The injured boxer never regained consciousness and died seventeen hours later after an operation failed to save him. Like Schaaf against Carnera, Doyle was badly damaged goods by the time he entered the ring for the last time. Another eerie coincidence was the fact that he had also banged his head against a ring support in the Levine fight. Far from being exceptions to the rule, these two famous ring tragedies are textbook examples of the most frequent cause of boxing fatalities.

Following the advent of the relatively civilized Queensbury Rules, and before the years when television became the main medium for bringing boxing to its audience, there was seldom a hue and cry to abolish boxing on the grounds it was inherently dangerous. Periodic attempts to ban the sport usually stemmed from charges of corruption, or, as in the case of England during the Regency Period, because the authorities feared large gatherings of the proletariat for any reason. Now that practically every major boxing match, and a multitude of lesser contests, are available to hundreds of millions of viewers via television, the public's sensibility toward boxing's sporadically lethal consequences has been heightened. There's nothing like watching a man get beat to death on the tube to hammer home the point that boxing can be detrimental to its participant's health.

Two televised ring fatalities stand out as examples of the electronic media's tremendous influence on the welfare of the sport and its practitioners. The first of these two landmark fatalities was the ill-fated third bout between Emile Griffith and Benny "Kid"

The legendary Sugar Ray Robinson dreamed he killed a man in the ring. Tragically, his nightmare came true when Jimmy Doyle died as a result of injuries suffered in his welterweight title fight with Robinson in 1947. (Photo courtesy of Peltz Boxing Promotions)

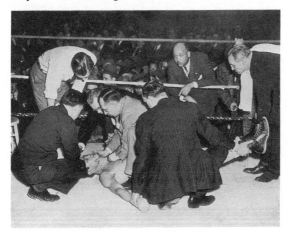

Jimmy Doyle is examined by Dr. Arthur F. Hagedorn after suffering a brain concussion in a bout with Artie Levine, March 12, 1946. A little over a year later Doyle died as a result of another severe beating, this time at the hands of Sugar Ray Robinson. (Photo courtesy of *The Ring* magazine)

Paret, March 24, 1962, at Madison Square Garden. This was a genuine grudge match. Paret had lost the title to Griffith and then regained it via a controversial decision. The bad blood between the pair was exacerbated at the weigh-in when Paret, a former $4-a-day sugar cane cutter from Cuba, called Griffith a "marecon" (Hispanic street slang for "faggot"). Griffth rose to the bait and angrily promised to show Paret who the real man was when they met in the ring that evening.

The bout was fiercely intense from the start. Griffith generally held the upper hand, but Paret remained dangerous throughout and floored his challenger with a sneak right hand in the sixth round. Saved by the bell, Griffith recovered quickly and rallied back. In the twelfth, he pinned Paret in a corner and proceeded to administer one of the most barbarous beatings ever seen in the boxing ring. Unable to fall because his body was trapped against the ropes, Paret was ravaged by dozens of clean blows, his head knocked back and forth in the manner of a speed bag mounted on a swivel. Referee Ruby Goldstein finally intervened and restrained Griffith, who was so caught up in his deadly assault, he seemed temporarily deranged. Paret was rushed to Roosevelt Hospital where he underwent a three-hour operation on his brain. Doctors gave him less than a thousand-to-one chance of recovery.

Paret lingered nine days in a coma before finally developing pneumonia and dying April 3, 1962. The ensuing uproar came close to killing boxing as surely as boxing killed Paret. The bout had been part of ABC's "Gillette Fight of the Week" series and was witnessed by millions of viewers across the United States. Goldstein, considered one of boxing's top referees, was widely criticized for not stopping the fight earlier, and though absolved of any wrong by the New York State Athletic Commission, he never worked another bout. Griffith, an exceptional fighter and a warm, carefree man outside the ring, fought on successfully for many years. But he never again went all-out for a knockout, preferring instead to win the majority of his bouts on points.

Cornermen rush to the aid of Benny "Kid" Paret at the conclusion of his notorious bout with Emile Griffith, March 24, 1962. Paret lapsed into a coma and died ten days later. (Photo courtesy of Peltz Boxing Promotions)

The Paret tragedy placed boxing and its numerous faults under intense public scrutiny. Politicians who had never seen a boxing match suddenly presented themselves as experts. Calls to abolish the sport ran rampant for months. Those genuinely concerned, as well as those who hoped to use the scandal as a political football, all jumped on the anti-boxing bandwagon. It was hard to find a public figure who was not screaming for reform or outright abrogation. State Republican leaders in Albany launched a legislative investigation financed by a $25 thousand appropriation of public funds. A bill in the Massachusetts House to ban boxing was filed even before Paret succumbed to his injuries. (It was narrowly defeated by a vote of 49-40.) Three thousand miles to the west, California Governor Edmund G. Brown attacked professional boxing, calling it a "dirty, rotten, brutalizing" sport. Even the Vatican got in on the act when a radio broadcast by a group of Catholic moralists branded boxing "condemnable by its very nature, aims and methods." The statement went on to deplore the "harsh, merciless law of business" and the "fanaticism" of the crowds at professional cards.

But the most damaging blow to boxing came from the medium that had helped create the monster—television. With sponsors running scared under the harsh light of nationwide criticism, executives didn't need much of an excuse for dropping boxing from their regular schedule of programs. When, less than a year later, featherweight champion Davey Moore died as the result of injuries suffered in a bout against Ultiminio "Sugar" Ramos, television quickly turned to other forms of vicarious thrills to lure its viewers. It was not until the emergence of Muhammad Ali as a mega-attraction several years later that boxing began to recover from the effects of the twin disasters of Paret and Moore.

Television's dalliance with boxing had again flowered into a torrid romance by 1982, when the next catastrophe rocked the sport. Lightweight Ray "Boom Boom" Mancini was, for the most part, a media creation. Technically and physically limited, he nevertheless captured the hearts of America (white America, at any rate) with his choirboy looks and sentimental story of wanting to win the title for his father, a former contender whose own opportunity had been derailed by World War II.

Mancini was tailor-made for television consumption, carefully groomed and maneuvered into a title shot. When his dream came unglued against multi-talented Alexis Arguello, Mancini's course was rerouted along an easier path to glory. Matched against Art Frias for a bogus version of the championship, Mancini finally ascended to the throne. It didn't matter that his kingdom was built on a foundation of sand. His TV ratings were excellent.

Mancini's second defense came against Duk-Koo Kim, a Korean virtually unknown in the United States, but designated as the World Boxing Association's No. 1 contender nonetheless. Before the fight, Kim reportedly wrote "Kill or be killed" on the lampshade in his Las Vegas hotel room. It proved to a prophetic slogan. The bout was a savage, seesaw punchfest, with Mancini ultimately prevailing by knockout in the fourteenth round. The final right hand to Kim's head sent him careening to the canvas and into a coma. Though brain dead from virtually that moment on, Kim was kept alive for four days with aid of artificial life-support systems until his mother arrived from Korea. And after Nevada District Judge Paul Goldman ruled Kim legally dead, the twenty-three-year-old boxer was disconnected from the machines that kept his heart and lungs pumping and allowed to die.

As was the case in the Griffith-Paret calamity, the lethal beating Kim absorbed was witnessed by millions of horrified television viewers. It was the largest audience to ever see a ring fatality and the long-term consequences of the sad event continue to haunt boxing. For while there was no serious attempt to abolish boxing following Kim's death, the sport's power structure scrambled to make cosmetic changes in an effort to spruce-up its image. Many positive reforms (in the areas of stricter pre-fight physicals and tighter commission control over matchmaking) were already in place, but various governing bodies, particularly the World Boxing Council,

Duk-Koo Kim (left) takes a right hook from Ray "Boom Boom" Mancini during their tragic bout in 1982. Korean Kim died as a result of the beating he absorbed during their match for the WBA middleweight title. (Photo courtesy of *The Ring* magazine)

still felt the need to tinker with some of boxing's time-honored traditions. So along with regulations that genuinely made boxing safer, the sport was encumbered with so much excess baggage, the structure began to collapse beneath its weight.

The most radical rule change prompted by the Kim tragedy was the truncation of world championship bouts from fifteen to twelve rounds. Proponents of this departure from tradition claimed shorter-length bouts would curtail injuries caused by fatigue. Not surprisingly, these shortsighted reformers put the cart in front of the horse. The problem was not fatigue. In the case of Mancini and Kim, the real problem can be traced back to the proliferation of the very groups who wish to regulate the sport.

As of the last decade of the 20th century, there were no less than four worldwide organizations competing for a slice of boxing's multimillion dollar pie. Each governing body touted its own list of champions and challengers in an ever-growing selection of weight divisions. By 1990, there were frequently four different men of the same weight classification calling themselves "world champion." This absurd situation has so cheapened the meaning of "world champion," the phrase has practically become a contradiction in terms. After all, there is only *one* world! Mancini and Kim were not true champion-caliber boxers, and should not have been subjected to boxing's ultimate test of fifteen rounds.

The greed that has finally overtaken boxing was there all along, but until the 1970s, it was held in check to some degree by logistical limitations. When most of boxing's revenue was derived from live gate receipts, it was necessary to maintain a modicum of legitimacy regarding championship matches. However, when closed-circuit and pay-per-view television sent boxing revenues through the roof, all semblance of respect for the sport's heritage was conveniently forgotten. Promoters, eager to satisfy television's voracious appetite for title fights, worked hand-in-hand with the governing bodies to create surplus weight divisions, meaningless titles and phony champions. Consequently, for every forward step taken in terms of ring safety, a backward step has been taken in terms of integrity.

While the risk to the boxer has been significantly reduced (though far from eliminated), boxing itself is in greater peril than ever. It is only a matter of time before consumers tire of second-rate performers battling for watered-down championships. If boxing remains in the hands of those presently at the administrative helm, the ultimate sacrifice will not be that of the boxer laying down his life at the altar of his art, but the sacrifice of boxing itself. Should this come to pass, Jasper Golden would probably think it poetic justice.

For the Record

In some respects, statistics mean less in boxing than most other sports. While the old saying "you're only as good as your last fight" isn't entirely true, it accurately sums up boxing's preoccupation with a fighter's most recent performance. Take, for instance, the case of Mike Tyson. He was regarded as almost superhuman until knocked out by James "Buster" Douglas. Now, like all who came before him, he is considered eminently human. Regardless of what Tyson accomplishes in the future, his aura of invincibility is gone forever.

Another important factor to remember when studying a boxer's win-loss record is the quality of opposition. A dozen wins over third-raters frequently proves far less than a close loss to a talented adversary. In other words, quality of opposition is much more significant than quantity. Young Stribling, for example, had over five times as many bouts as Sonny Liston, but even Stribling's most ardent admirers would be forced to admit Liston was the superior fighter.

Though many rank among boxing's all-time greats, those discussed in this book range from members of the Boxing Hall of Fame to run-of-the-mill club fighters. As this is not a record book, there is no attempt to give a fight-by-fight chronicle of any boxer. Instead, a brief synopsis of his career statistics is offered in an effort to give a clearer picture of his accomplishments. Unfortunately, records of bare-knuckle fighters who were not world champions are sketchy at best. Therefore, the records of Yankee Sullivan, Christopher Lilly and Thomas McCoy do not appear.

A few tips for readers unfamiliar with boxing records: we have made no distinction between knockouts and technical knockouts; all bouts stopped inside the scheduled distance are listed as knockouts. The numerous "no decision" bouts that appear on the records of many of the old-time boxers refer to fights which took place in jurisdictions where it was, at that particular time, against the law to render a verdict.

TONY AYALA: Fought professionally from 1980 until 1982 ... engaged in 22 bouts, won 22 ... scored 19 knockouts.

OSCAR BONAVENA (OSCAR NATALIO BONAVENA): Fought from 1964 until 1976 ... engaged in 67 bouts, won 57, lost nine ... boxed one draw ... scored 39 knockouts and was knocked out once ... unsuccessfully challenged Joe Frazier for world heavyweight title, December 10, 1968, losing via 15-round decision.

MARCEL CERDAN: Fought professionally from 1934 until 1949 ... engaged in 109 bouts, won 105, lost four ... scored 60 knockouts and was knocked out once ... won world middleweight title, September 21, 1948, with 12-round knockout over Tony Zale ... lost title to Jake LaMotta, June 16, 1949, via 10-round knockout ... elected to *The Ring* Boxing Hall of Fame, 1962.

BRUCE CURRY: Fought professionally from 1976 until 1986 ... engaged in 43 bouts, won 34, lost nine ... scored 17 knockouts and was knocked out five times ... won WBC super lightweight title, May 20, 1983, with 12-round decision over Leroy Haley ... made two successful defenses ... lost title to Bill Costello, January 29, 1984, via 10-round knockout.

AL "BUMMY" DAVIS (ABRAHAM DAVIDOFF): Fought professionally from 1937 until 1945 ... engaged in 79 bouts, won 65, lost 10 ... boxed four draws ... scored 46 knockouts and was knocked out three times ... never fought for a world title.

FRANK DE PAULA: Fought professionally from 1962 until 1969 ... engaged in 30 bouts, won 20, lost seven ... boxed three draws ... scored 15 knockouts and was knocked out twice ... unsuccessfully challenged Bob Foster for world light heavyweight title, January 22, 1969, losing via second-round knockout.

GUS DORAZIO (GUSTAVE VINCOLATO): Fought professionally from 1937 until 1946 ... engaged in 83 bouts, won 58, lost 23 ... boxed two draws ... scored 10 knockouts and was knocked out eight times ... unsuccessfully challenged Joe Louis for world heavyweight title, February 17, 1941, losing via second-round knockout.

JIMMY DOYLE: Fought professionally from 1941 until 1947 ... engaged in 52 bouts, won 42, lost seven ... boxed three draws ... scored 14 knockouts and was knocked out twice ... unsuccessfully challenged Sugar Ray Robinson for world welterweight championship, June 24, 1947.

TYRONE EVERETT: Fought professionally from 1971 until 1977 ... engaged in 37 bouts, won 36, lost one ... scored 20 knockouts and was never knocked out ... unsuccessfully challenged Alfredo Escalera for WBC junior lightweight title, Nov. 30, 1976, losing via 15-round decision.

TIGER FLOWERS (THEODORE FLOWERS): Fought professionally from 1918 until 1927 ... engaged in 156 bouts, won 115, lost 13 ... boxed six draws, 21 "no decisions" and one "no contest" ... scored 54 knockouts and was knocked out nine times ... won world middleweight title, February 26, 1926, with a 15-round decision over Harry Greb ... made one successful defense ... lost title to Mickey Walker, via 10-round decision, December 3, 1926 ... elected to *The Ring* Hall of Fame, 1971.

ZORA FOLLEY: Fought professionally from 1953 until 1970 ... engaged in 96 bouts, won 79, lost 11 ... boxed six draws ... scored

44 knockouts and was knocked out seven times . . . unsuccessfully challenged Muhammad Ali for world heavyweight title, March 22, 1967, losing via seven-round knockout.

VICTOR GALINDEZ: Fought professionally from 1969 until 1980 . . . engaged in 70 bouts, won 55, lost nine . . . boxed four draws and two "no contests" . . . scored 34 knockouts and was knocked out twice . . . won vacant WBA light heavyweight title, December 7, 1974, with 13-round knockout over Len Hutchins . . . made nine successful defenses . . . lost title, September 15, 1978, to Mike Rossman via 13-round knockout . . . regained title, April 14, 1979, with ten-round knockout over Rossman . . . lost title, November 30, 1979, to Marvin Johnson via 11-round knockout.

HARRY GREB (EDWARD HENRY GREB): Fought professionally from 1913 until 1926 . . . engaged to 299 bouts, won 106, lost eight . . . boxed three draws and 182 "no decisions" . . . scored 49 knockouts and was knocked out twice . . . won world middleweight title, August 31, 1923, with 15-round decision over Johnny Wilson . . . made six successful defenses . . . lost title, February 12, 1926, to Tiger Flowers via 15-round decision . . . elected to *The Ring* Boxing Hall of Fame, 1971.

EMILE GRIFFITH (EMILE ALPHONES GRIFFITH): Fought professionally from 1958 until 1977 . . . engaged in 112 bouts, won 85, lost 24 . . . boxed two draws and one "no contest" . . . scored 23 knockouts and was knocked out twice . . . won world welterweight title, April 1, 1961, with 13-round knockout over Benny "Kid" Paret . . . made one successful defense . . . lost title to Paret, September 30, 1961, via 15-round decision . . . regained title with 12-round knockout over Paret, March 24, 1962 . . . made two successful defenses . . . lost title to Luis Rodriguez, March 21, 1963, via 15-round decision . . . regained title with 15-round decision over Rodriguez, June 8, 1963 . . . made four successful defenses and then relinquished welterweight title to campaign as middleweight . . . won world middleweight title, April 25, 1966, with 15-round decision over Dick Tiger made two successful defenses . . . lost title to Nino

Benvenuti, April 17, 1967, via 15-round decision ... regained title September 29, 1967, with 15-round decision over Benvenuti ... lost to Benvenuti, March 4, 1968, via 15-round decision ... selected *The Ring's* Fighter of the year, 1964 ... elected to *The Ring* Hall of Fame, 1981.

GYPSY JOE HARRIS: Fought professionally from 1964 until 1968 ... engaged in 25 bouts, won 24, lost one ... scored eight knockouts and was never knocked out.

JACK JOHNSON (ARTHUR JOHN JOHNSON): Fought professionally from 1879 until 1928 ... engaged in 107 bouts, won 70, lost ten ... boxed 11 draws and 16 "no decisions" ... scored 40 knockouts and was knocked out six times ... won world heavyweight title, December 26, 1908, with 14-round knockout over Tommy Burns ... made six successful defenses ... lost title to Jess Willard, April 5, 1915, via 26-round knockout ... elected to *The Ring* Boxing Hall of Fame, 1954.

STANLEY KETCHEL (STANISLAUS KIECAL): Fought professionally from 1904 until 1910 ... engaged in 64 bouts, won 52, lost four ... boxed four draws and four "no decisions" ... scored 49 knockouts and was knocked out twice ... won vacant world middleweight title, May 9, 1908, with 20-round KO over Jack "Twin" Sullivan ... lost title, September 7, 1908, to Billy Papke via 12-round KO ... regained world championship, November 26, 1908, with 11-round knockout over Papke ... held title until his death, October 15, 1910 ... elected to *The Ring* Boxing Hall of Fame, 1954.

DUK-KOO KIM: Fought professionally from 1978 until 1982 ... engaged in 20 bouts, won 17, lost two ... boxed one draw ... scored eight knockouts and was knocked out once ... unsuccessfully challenged Ray Mancini for WBA lightweight title, November 13, 1982, losing via 14-round knockout.

SONNY LISTON (CHARLES LISTON): Fought professionaly from 1953 until 1970 ... engaged in 54 bouts, won 50, lost four ... scored 39 knockouts and was knocked out three times ... won world heavyweight title, September 25, 1962, with one-round knockout over Floyd Patterson ... made one successful defense ... lost title to Cassius Clay, February 25, 1964, via seventh-round knockout.

JOE LOUIS (JOSEPH LOUIS BARROW): Fought professionally from 1934 until 1951 ... engaged in 66 bouts, won 63, lost three ... scored 49 knockouts and was knocked out twice ... won world heavyweight title, June 22, 1937, with eight-round knockout over James J. Braddock ... made 25 successful defenses (a division record) ... announced retirement, March 1, 1949, while still champion ... made comeback in 1950 and lost 15-round decision to Ezzard Charles, September 27, 1950, in unsuccessful attempt to regain title ... selected as *The Ring's* Fighter of the Year 1936, '38, '39, and '41 ... elected to *The Ring* Boxing Hall of Fame, 1954.

JOE LYNCH: Fought professionally from 1915 until 1926 ... engaged in 133 bouts, won 42, lost 13 ... boxed 15 draws and 63 "no decisions" ... scored 29 knockouts and was never knocked out ... won world bantamweight title, December 22, 1920, with 15-round decision over Pete Herman ... lost title to Herman, July 25, 1921, via 15-round decision ... regained, July 10, 1922, with 14-round knockout over Johnny Buff ... lost title to Abe Goldstein, March 21, 1924, via 15-round decision.

CHARLES "KID" McCOY (NORMAN SELBY): Boxed professionally from 1891 until 1916 ... engaged in 109 bouts, won 86, lost seven ... boxed seven draws, seven "no decisions" and three "no contests" ... scored 64 knockouts and was knocked out four times ... won vacant world middleweight title, December 17, 1897, with 15-round knockout over Dan Creedon ... relinquished title to fight as light heavyweight and heavyweight ... elected to *The Ring* Boxing Hall of Fame, 1957.

EDDIE MACHEN: Fought professionally from 1955 until 1967 ... engaged in 64 bouts, won 50, lost 11 ... boxed three draws ... scored 27 knockouts and was knocked out three times ... unsuccessfully challenged for WBA heavyweight title, March 5, 1965, losing to Ernie Terrell via 15-round decision.

RAY MANCINI (RAYMOND MICHAEL MANCINI): Fought professionally from 1979 until 1988 . . . engaged in 33 bouts, won 29, lost four . . . scored 23 knockouts . . . won WBA light weight title, May 8, 1982, with one-round knockout over Art Frias . . . made four successful defenses . . . lost title to Livingstone Bramble, June 1, 1984, via 14-round knockout.

ROCKY MARCIANO (ROCCO FRANCIS MARCHEGIANO): Fought professionally from 1947 until 1955 . . . engaged in 49 bouts, won 49 . . . scored 43 knockouts . . . won heavyweight title, September 23, 1952, with a 13-round knockout over Jersey Joe Walcott . . . made six successful defenses and retired undefeated . . . selected *The Ring's* Fighter of the Year in 1952, '54, '55 and '56 . . . elected to *The Ring* Boxing Hall of Fame, 1959.

ROBERTO MEDINA (JUAN E. GARCIA): Fought professionally from 1985 until 1987 . . . engaged in 18 bouts, won 13, lost four . . . boxed one draw . . . scored nine knockouts and was knocked out once.

FREDDIE MILLS: Fought professionally from 1936 until 1950 . . . engaged in 97 bouts, won 74, lost 17 . . . boxed six draws . . . scored 52 knockouts and was knocked out six times . . . won world light heavyweight title, July 26, 1948, with 15 round decision over Gus Lesnevich . . . lost title, January 24, 1950, via 10-round knockout to Joey Maxim.

CARLOS MONZON: Fought professionally from 1963 until 1977 . . . engaged in 101 bouts, won 89, lost three . . . boxed eight draws and one "no contest" . . . scored 61 knockouts and was never knocked out . . . won world middleweight title, November 7, 1970, with 12-round knockout over Nino Benvenuti . . . made 14 successful defenses (a division record) . . . was still champion upon retirement . . . *The Ring's* Fighter of the Year, 1972 . . . elected to *The Ring* Boxing Hall of Fame, 1983.

DAVEY MOORE: Fought professionally from from 1980 until 1986 . . . engaged in 23 bouts, won 18, lost five . . . scored 14 knockouts and was knocked out three times . . . won WBA junior middleweight title, February 2, 1982, with sixth-round knockout over Tadashi Mihara . . . made three successful defenses . . . lost title to Roberto Duran, June 16, 1983, via eight-round knockout.

MASAO OHBA: Fought professionally from 1966 until 1973 . . . engaged in 38 bouts, won 35, lost two . . . boxed one draw . . . scored 15 knockouts and was never knocked out . . . won WBA flyweight title, October 22, 1970, with 13-round knockout over Berkrerk Chartvanchai . . . made five successful defenses and was still champion when he died.

BENNY "KID" PARET (BERNARDO PARET): Fought professionally from 1955 until 1962 . . . engaged in 50 bouts, won 35, lost 12 . . . boxed three draws . . . scored 10 knockouts and was knocked out four times . . . won world welterweight title, March 27, 1960, with 15-round decision over Don Jordan . . . made one successful defense . . . lost title to Emile Griffth, April 1, 1961, via 13-round knockout . . . regained title, September 30, 1961, with 15-round decision over Griffith . . . lost title to Griffith, March 24, 1962, via 12-round knockout.

HENRY "HEN" PEARCE: Fought professionally from 1803 until 1805 . . . engaged in seven bouts, winning all seven by knockout . . . won bare-knuckle heavyweight title, August 12, 1803, with 15-round knockout over Joe Berks . . . made five successful defenses . . . retired in 1806 due to ill health while still champion.

SUGAR RAY ROBINSON (WALKER SMITH, JR.): Fought professionally from 1940 until 1965 . . . engaged in 202 bouts, won 175, lost 19 . . . boxed six draws and two "no contests" . . . scored 110 knockouts and was knocked out once . . . won vacant world welterweight title, December 20, 1946, with 15-round decision over Tommy Bell . . . made four successful defenses and then relinquished title to campaign as a middleweight . . . won world middleweight title, February 14, 1951, with 13-round knockout over Jake LaMotta . . . lost title to Randy Turpin, July 10, 1951, via 15-round decision . . . regained title, September 12, 1952, with 10-round knockout over Turpin . . . made two successful defenses and retired still champion on December 18, 1952 ... returned to the ring, January 5, 1955 ... regained world middleweight title, December 9, 1955, with two-round knockout over Carl "Bobo" Olson ... made one successful defense ... lost title to Gene Fullmer, January 2, 1957, via 15-round decision ... regained title, May 1, 1957, with five-round knockout over Fullmer ... lost title to Carmen Basilio, September 23, 1957, via 15-round decision ... regained title, March 25, 1958, with 15-round decision over Basilio ... lost title to Paul Pender, January 22, 1960, via 15-round decision ... selected *The Ring's* Fighter of the Year, 1942 and 1951 ... elected to *The Ring* Boxing Hall of Fame, 1967.

SALVADOR SANCHEZ: Fought professionally from 1975 until 1982 ... engaged in 46 bouts, won 44, lost one ... boxed one draw ... scored 32 knockouts and was never knocked out ... won WBA featherweight title, February 2, 1980, with 13-round knockout over Danny Lopez ... made nine successful defenses and was still champion when he died ... selected *The Ring's* Fighter of the Year, 1981.

DAVE SANDS (DAVID RITCHIE): Fought professionally from 1943 until 1952 ... engaged in 104 bouts, won 93, lost eight ... boxed one draw and two "no contests" ... scored 62 knockouts and was knocked out once.

BATTLING SIKI (LOUIS PHAL): Fought professionally from 1912 until 1925 ... engaged in 93 bouts, won 64, lost 18 ... boxed five draws, five "no decisions" and one "no contest" ... scored 35 knockouts and was knocked out three times ... won world light heavyweight title, September 24, 1922, with sixth-round knockout over Georges Carpentier ... lost title to Mike McTigue, March 17, 1923, via a 20-round decision.

RUDELL STITCH: Fought professionally from 1956 until 1960 ... engaged in 34 bouts, won 27, lost seven ... scored 13 knockouts and was never knocked out.

YOUNG STRIBLING (WILLIAM LAWRENCE STRIBLING): Fought professionally from 1921 until 1933 ... engaged in 286 bouts, won 222, lost 12 . . . boxed 14 draws, 36 "no decisions" and two "no contests" . . . scored 126 knockouts and was knocked out once . . . unsuccessfully challenged Paul Berlenbach for the world light heavyweight title, June 10, 1926, losing via 15-round decision . . . unsuccessfully challenged Max Schmelling for world heavyweight title, July 3, 1931, losing via 15-round knockout . . . elected to *The Ring* Boxing Hall of Fame, 1985.

ARNOLD TAYLOR: Fought professionally from 1967 until 1976 . . . engaged in 49 bouts, won 40, lost eight . . . boxed one draw . . . scored 17 knockouts and was knocked out three times . . . won world bantamweight title, November 3, 1973, with 14-round knockout over Romeo Anaya . . . lost title to Soo-Hwan Hong, July 3, 1974, via 15-round decision.

RANDY TURPIN (RANDOLPH ADOLPHUS TURPIN): Fought professionally from 1946 until 1964 . . . engaged in 75 bouts, won 66, lost eight . . . boxed one draw . . . scored 45 knockouts and was knocked out five times . . . won world middleweight title, July 10, 1951, with 15-round decision over Sugar Ray Robinson . . . lost title, September 12, 1951, to Robinson via 10-round knockout.

PANCHO VILLA (FRANCISCO GUILLEDO): Fought professionally from 1919 until 1925, engaged in 105 bouts, won 73, lost five . . . boxed four draws and 23 "no decisions" . . . scored 22 knockouts and was never knocked out . . . won world flyweight title, June 18, 1923, with a seventh-round KO over Jimmy Wilde . . . made four successful title defenses and was still champion when he died . . . elected to *The Ring,* Boxing Hall of Fame, 1961.

JOE WALCOTT: Fought professionally from 1890 until 1911 . . . engaged in 150 bouts, won 81, lost 24 . . . boxed 30 draws and 15 "no decisions" . . . scored 34 knockouts and was knocked out four times . . . won world welterweight title, December 15, 1901, with fifth-round knockout over Rube Ferns . . . made two successful defenses . . . lost title, April 29, 1904, to Dixie Kid via 20-round foul . . . elected to *The Ring* Boxing Hall of Fame, 1955.

Index